A
HISTORY
OF THE
POPES

A
HISTORY
OF THE
POPES

*From Peter
to the Present*

JOHN W. O'MALLEY, S.J.

A SHEED & WARD BOOK
ROWMAN & LITTLEFIELD PUBLISHERS, INC.
Lanham • Boulder • New York • Toronto • Plymouth, UK

A Sheed & Ward Book
Published by Rowman & Littlefield Publishers, Inc.
A wholly owned subsidiary of The Rowman & Littlefield Publishing Group, Inc.
4501 Forbes Boulevard, Suite 200, Lanham, Maryland 20706
www.rowmanlittlefield.com

Estover Road, Plymouth PL6 7PY, United Kingdom

British Library Cataloguing in Publication Information Available

Library of Congress Cataloging-in-Publication Data
O'Malley, John W.
  A history of the popes : from Peter to the present / John W. O'Malley.
    p. cm.
  Includes index.
  ISBN 978-1-58051-227-5 (cloth : alk. paper) — ISBN 978-1-58051-229-9
(electronic)
  1. Papacy—History. I. Title.
  BX955.3.O43 2010
  282.092'2—dc22   2009015746

FOR JEANNE RUESCH
WITH GRATITUDE AND AFFECTION

CONTENTS

PREFACE

This book originated in a series of thirty-six audio-lectures I recorded that were published in 2006 by Now You Know Media. My intention in reworking the lectures for the book has been to provide a history of the papacy that would make clear the basic story line in a way accessible to the general reader. Papal history stretches over a period of two thousand years, which means there are lots of players on a field where lots of complicated games were being played. It is easy to get lost and befuddled. The relationship of the popes to "the emperors," for instance, was so volatile and shifting over such a long stretch of time that sometimes it is hard even for professional historians to keep track of what was going on at any given point.

I have tried, therefore, to tell the story in as straightforward a way as possible, which means I have had to pass over much that I would have liked to include. My hope is that the leaner narrative will provide a recognizable path through complicated terrain and ensure readers can keep their bearings. I have, however, spiced the narrative with details that enliven it and at the same time illuminate the bigger issues. My further hope is that the book will spark interest in this fascinating institution and lead readers to pick up other works that treat aspects of it at greater length.

In that regard I recommend the "Bibliographical Essay" that concludes Eamon Duffy's admirable *Saints and Sinners: A History of the Popes* (third edition, Yale, 2006), a book similar to mine but more ample by far. For detailed bibliographies on the popes and every aspect of the institution (including such items as popes' animals and barbers), I recommend the three volumes for which I was the English language editor, Philippe Levillain's, *The Papacy: An Encyclopedia* (Routledge, 2002). To learn about individual popes a handy guide is still J. N. D. Kelly's *The Oxford Dictionary of the Popes* (Oxford, 1986). For more general background the volumes in The Penguin History of the Church, beginning with Henry Chadwick's *The Early Church* (revised edition, Penguin, 1993), are by first-rate scholars and of reasonable length. Even modest libraries will have all these works on their shelves.

Several people have made the production of this book possible, and to them I want to express my gratitude. Ross Miller, formerly senior editor at Rowman & Littlefield Publishers invited me to write the book, encouraged me through the process, and provided me with transcripts of my lectures for Now You Know Media. Sarah Stanton, who took over after Ross Miller, and Krista Sprecher, guided me through the final stages of publication. By reviewing my text with sharp eyes, James P. M. Walsh and Sara Singho saved me from many errors. Michael T. Bloom, chief executive officer of Now You Know Media invited me to undertake the lectures and kept up a gentle pressure until I finally agreed to do so. He then graciously granted permission for use of them by Rowman & Littlefield in producing this book. Although the text I ended up producing differs considerably from the original lectures, the basic outline and development of argument remain the same.

INTRODUCTION

This book is about the oldest living institution in the Western world, an institution that began some two thousand years ago but that is as vital today as perhaps ever in its history. The papacy, which traces its origins to Saint Peter, Jesus's chief disciple, is embodied today in Pope Benedict XVI. In between Peter and Benedict there have been some 265 individuals who claimed to be Peter's successors and whose claim is today generally recognized as legitimate. Some were saints; some were sinners. Pope Leo the Great and Pope Gregory the Great were men of heroic stature, but Pope John XII, who became pope at the age of eighteen, led such a debauched life that he was a scandal even in the debauched Roman society of the tenth century. There were, besides, many other individuals who claimed to be pope, but whose claims contemporaries or posterity rejected as invalid, the "anti-popes." They figure heavily in some parts of our story.

The popes differed among themselves in social class. Pope Callistus I was a former slave, and Pope Pius IX a noble. Pope Pius XII was from the Roman aristocracy, but his successor, Pope John XXIII, came from peasant stock. Popes have been Greek, Syrian, African, Spanish, French, German, Dutch, and of course Italian. There has been only one English pope, Hadrian IV, and only one Polish, John Paul

II. None has been Portuguese, Irish, Scandinavian, Slovak, Slovenian, Bohemian, Hungarian—or American. A fair number were not priests when they were elected. Pope Leo X, for instance, was a deacon, and Benedict VIII, Benedict IX, as well as others, were laymen. Popes were not always elected in Rome. As late as 1800 Pope Pius VII was elected in Venice.

If you are at all interested in either religion or history, you have to be interested in the papacy. Within our own lifetimes, popes have been front-page news. Pope John Paul II is sometimes spoken of as the Man of the Century. The popes were players in virtually all the great dramas of the Western world in the last two thousand years, and in those dramas they were often major protagonists. The history of the popes is not a history told in a sacristy.

In this book I tell the popes' story as a historian, not as a theologian, but by the very nature of the subject theology must at times enter it. Indeed, the whole edifice of the papacy is built upon a theological interpretation of what we may take as historical fact: Peter's preeminence among "the Twelve," Jesus's closest disciples, and his subsequent ministry and death in Rome. Peter was thus the first bishop of Rome and therefore the first pope. All the popes since then claim to be his successors and to have inherited his leadership role. I tell their story neither to justify nor challenge that theological claim, and I tell it neither to defend nor to condemn the popes and their actions. I tell it to make clear what happened and how the institution got to be the way it is.

We need to keep the story in perspective. The history of the popes is not a history of Catholicism, which is a much, much bigger reality. The popes are only a part of that history. We might easily confuse the two because, especially for the past hundred years, the papacy has played a larger role in Catholics' self-definition than ever before. This new preeminence is due to many factors, but among them the modern means of communication like radio, television, and now the Internet are especially important. In the year 1200, for instance, perhaps 2 percent of the population knew there was such an institution as the papacy or believed it had anything significant to do with their religion. How would they have known about it? The papacy was not mentioned in any creed, and it did not appear in any catechism until the sixteenth century. With Protestant rejection of it at that time came Catholic preoccupation with it, and both positions got relatively widely broadcast by the new invention of the printing press. Soon thereafter to be Catholic was to define oneself as a papist.

The history of the popes is not always pretty. The popes were human beings. Even the saints among them had their dark sides. While a few were reprehensible from almost every viewpoint, most of them strove to lead a good life according to their lights. But their weaknesses showed up glaringly because of the responsibilities they bore.

The popes as bishops of Rome faced a particular temptation almost from the earliest days. Devout Christians in and around the city made donations in land or goods to "Saint Peter," that is, to the Church of Rome. The bishops of Rome, though they would face hard times, tended to be wealthy, and this fact made the office attractive to the wrong people, who sometimes succeeded in obtaining the office. Moreover, the real estate held by Saint Peter eventually expanded into the Papal States. Of that vast territory that stretched almost from Naples north and east across the peninsula to Venice, the pope was monarch. As ruler of a state he was easily distracted from his religious duties and drawn into political schemes. That was a situation that prevailed from the eighth century until 1860–1870, when the Papal States were confiscated by Italian forces and incorporated into the new kingdom of Italy.

For most of the periods covered by this book, therefore, the popes had a notably different job description than popes of more recent times. Today popes appoint bishops. They did not always do that. They write encyclicals. That is a development of the past hundred and fifty years. The popes speak to huge crowds and travel the globe. That was not possible until the era of trains, planes, and automobiles.

Popes of earlier eras conceived their job differently. Among the major tasks they set themselves was to guard and protect the tombs of saints Peter and Paul against profanation; to make sure the great basilicas and other churches of Rome had dignified services; to provide for orphans, widows, and other needy persons in the city; to intervene to settle doctrinal disputes among bishops; to protect Rome and the surrounding territories from foreign enemies, which meant maintaining an army and navy; to rally Christian monarchs to lead crusades; to govern the city of Rome, to tend to its provisioning, and to enhance it with churches, fountains, and public buildings of various kinds; and to rule the Papal States—to be a monarch and the maker of monarchs.

The complications that arose from such tasks can make this book seem as if the papacy did nothing but career from one crisis to another. Readers must remind themselves, therefore, that the book skips over relatively long periods of "business as usual." Even those periods are interesting, and I pass them over with regret because business as usual was rarely perfectly usual. My hope is that the drastically pared down story I tell will be enough to whet the appetite to pursue the subject further and especially to delve into those eras slighted in this telling.

Four defining moments of papal history can serve as milestones in what sometimes seems like a zigzag course. The first is around the year 64, which is when Peter and Paul were martyred in Rome during the persecution by Nero. As mentioned, all the subsequent claims of the papacy to its preeminent place in the Christian church are based on the ministry and martyrdom of Peter in Rome. The second defining moment is the reign of the Emperor Constantine in the early fourth century. He did more than tolerate Christianity and, as the expression goes, let it emerge from the catacombs. He favored it. He encouraged its bishops to assume public and civic responsibilities, so that the church got woven into the fabric of the sociopolitical order of society. The third is in the eighth and ninth centuries when the Papal States began to form as a more or less definable unit and the popes emerged as its temporal ruler. The fourth is 1860–1870 when the States came to an end and Rome became the capital of Italy. With the Lateran agreements in 1929 between the Holy See and the Italian government, the papacy surrendered all claims to the States and to Rome, and the Italians recognized Vatican City as an independent, sovereign state.

In a history of the popes a few terms and titles come up frequently. "The emperor" is the Roman emperor Constantine and those who claimed to be his descendants, whether in Europe or in Constantinople, present-day Istanbul. The emperor was at the peak of the secular hierarchy and was different from a king. In the West in the Middle Ages and early modern period, he might also be a king in his own right, but as emperor he was at least theoretically the king of kings. The point to keep in mind is that especially for the early part of our story the popes dealt on the highest level with the emperor and sometimes with two emperors at once, one in the East and one in the West.

Even today the words Rome and the Vatican are sometimes used interchangeably. That is because until 1870 the popes, although they had several palaces in the city of Rome, lived most often in the so-called Apostolic Palace in the Vatican area of the city. Since 1870 that Vatican palace has been the popes' exclusive residence. From the earliest days the popes, although their cathedral was the basilica of Saint John Lateran, especially identified with the Vatican area because that is where Saint Peter was believed to have been buried after his martyrdom and over whose shrine Constantine built the magnificent basilica.

Among the cities of the ancient Roman world, Rome was unique in that it was the site of the preaching and death of *two* apostles—Peter and Paul. Rome's "double apostolicity" allowed it to refer to itself as apostolic not only because of Peter's leadership role among the disciples of Jesus but because the great Paul also came to Rome and died there. The bishopric of Rome became *the* "Apostolic See." See is the English equivalent of the Latin *sedes*, meaning chair but by extension meaning residence or dwelling place. Thus see is where bishops are located. Bishops, moreover, preached seated in a chair—a *sedes* or a *cathedra* (hence, cathedral). Among the sees, the Apostolic See was obviously the most prestigious.

Popes have borne a number of titles, the most fundamental of which is bishop of Rome. A man is pope because he is bishop of Rome, not vice versa. He occupies the Apostolic See, and therefore is pope. Today the pope is the only bishop who bears the title pope, though in the early centuries of the church the term was applied to all bishops. Pope is the English-language form of the Latin *papa*, which means simply father. Beginning in the fifth century in the West, about the time of Pope Leo the Great, the title pope became increasingly reserved to the bishop of Rome.

As suggested above, though popes gloried in the double apostolicity of their city, they identified themselves not with Paul but with Peter. Some popes seemed incapable of distinguishing themselves from

xvi   A History of the Popes

him, as if Peter and they were one mystical person. More commonly, however, they saw themselves as his agent in the world and referred to themselves as "the vicar of Peter," *vicarius Petri*. That title appears prominently in Leo the Great and was taken up by his successors for the next eight centuries. Only rarely did popes refer to themselves as vicars of Peter and Paul, as did Pope John VIII in the ninth century.

Instead of vicar of Peter, popes today present themselves as "vicars of Christ." Like pope, the term vicar of Christ in the early centuries was applied to all bishops because they had authority to govern the church and perform their functions in Christ's name, but it was also applied to priests and to secular rulers. As late as the eleventh century, for instance, Emperor Henry IV loudly proclaimed himself the vicar of Christ. By the next century, partly through the agency of Saint Bernard of Clairvaux, the title came to refer exclusively to the pope, and at the beginning of the thirteenth century Pope Innocent III officially adopted it to express an authority more far-reaching than that of other bishops. Subsequent popes gladly followed his example.

In the early Middle Ages popes sometimes referred to themselves as "patriarch of Rome" and later as "patriarch of the West," which in the nineteenth century entered the official lists of papal titles. It always had a somewhat vague meaning, however, and was dropped from the list in 2006. Papal documents today designate the pope as the Supreme Pontiff, *Summus Pontifex*. Like so many other papal titles, this one too once applied to all bishops. By the year 900, however, it appears in official papal documents to refer to the pope and within a few centuries it established itself as the title most frequently used in official documents to designate him.

The polar opposite of Supreme Pontiff is "Servant of the servants of God." The term is found as early as the fifth century, but, again, was not applied exclusively to the popes until the thirteenth century. It is the most beloved of all the papal titles, and the one that expresses Christ's message to Peter and the others at the Last Supper when he washed their feet and told them that they should do the same for others if they wanted to be his disciples. Because Vatican Council II, 1962–1965, laid great stress on the servant-quality of all leadership in the church, Pope Paul VI added the title to the official list.

PART

I

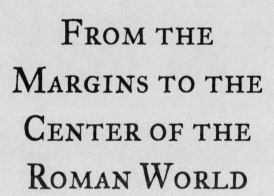

FROM THE MARGINS TO THE CENTER OF THE ROMAN WORLD

PETER: BISHOP OF ROME?

About a mile outside the ancient walls of the city of Rome is a small chapel on the Via Appia, the old Roman road. The name of the chapel is *Quo Vadis*, a Latin expression meaning Where are you going? The legend attached to the chapel was first recorded in the apocryphal Acts of Peter in the late second century. According to the legend Peter, fearing for his life in the year 64 during the persecution of Nero, fled Rome. As he raced down the Via Appia he met a man walking toward the city whom he recognized as the Lord. "Where are you going," Peter asked him. "To Rome, to be crucified again." With that Peter realized that his duty was to return to Rome and stay with his flock during this difficult time, which probably meant dying as a consequence. The legend has no foundation in fact, but it raises the crucial question: did Peter really come to Rome and suffer martyrdom there? I repeat: the whole subsequent history of the papacy depends on an affirmative answer to the question (see fig. 1.1).

The story of Peter and the papacy begins, however, not with Rome but with the New Testament. For Christians the New Testament is an inspired book, written under the guidance of the Holy Spirit as the fundamental and authentic testimony about the life and message of

Jesus. It is the touchstone of faith for the Christian church, to which the church must always have recourse and from which it can never deviate in its basic beliefs. For historians and biblical scholars, in contrast, the New Testament is a collection of documents written within a century of Jesus's death by different authors with different concerns and viewpoints. It consists of four historical narratives (the gospels), a narrative of the spread of Christian teaching in the first generation (the Acts of the Apostles), and a number of epistles, especially those by Paul, and an apocalyptic vision (the book of Revelation).

For our purposes two things are remarkable about that collection, even aside from its purportedly inspired character. The first is the sheer quantity of information those documents provide about Peter.

He is, next to Jesus himself and possibly Paul, the most fully documented of any New Testament character. Second, the sources are consistent in the picture they paint of him. What do we know? Named Simon Bar Jona, he was a fisherman like his brother Andrew. He had earlier been a disciple of John the Baptist. He lived in Capernaum on the shores of the Lake of Galilee with his wife and his mother-in-law. He was warm, loyal, impetuous, and a wonderful friend. At the Garden of Gethsemane he drew his sword in defense of Jesus and cut off the ear of a servant of the high priest.

He had a dark side. He was not as steadfast and brave as he imagined himself to be. At the Last Supper (Luke 22), Jesus said to him, "Simon, Simon, behold Satan demanded to have you, that he might sift you like wheat. But I have prayed for you that your faith may not fail, and when you have turned again, strengthen your brethren." To which Peter said, "Lord, I am ready to go with you to prison and to death." Then Jesus, "I tell you Peter, rock, the cock will not crow this day until you three times deny you know me." It turned out, as we well know, just as Jesus predicted. But we also know from the early chapters of the Acts of the Apostles that after Jesus's resurrection Peter became a fearless and steadfast preacher of the Good News.

Just as clear in the New Testament as his character is the preeminence Peter enjoyed among Jesus's inner circle, "the Twelve," and then later in the early church. According to Paul's Epistle to the Galatians, which is the earliest document in the New Testament to mention Peter,

1.1: Saint Peter, "*Quo vadis, Domine*?"

Carracci, Annibale (1560–1609). Christ appearing to Saint Peter on the Appian Way (Domine, Quo Vadis?), 1601–1602. Oil on wood, 77.4 x 56.3 cm. Bought, 1826 (NG9).National Gallery, London, Great Britain.

Paul went to him after his conversion on the road to Damascus to learn about the faith. Peter gave Paul a crash course in fifteen days. In chapter 2, however, Paul confronts and rebukes Peter when Peter tries to back down from his previous table fellowship with Gentiles. What is important here, however, is not that Paul withstood Peter to his face, but that Paul could vindicate his own authority by a backhanded recognition of Peter's—that even *Peter* backed down.

In the first twelve chapters of the Acts of the Apostles, Peter is the dominant figure. Leader of the church in Jerusalem, he presided at the election of the successor to Judas the traitor. He spoke for the church on Pentecost and worked miracles in Jesus's name. He was an apostle to the Jews but also to the Gentiles, as is clear from the story of his conversion of the Roman centurion Cornelius. Rescued from prison by an angel, he was without question the center and focus of the narrative of these chapters.

In three of the gospels Peter is the first of the Twelve to be called by Jesus. In the synoptic gospels—Matthew, Mark, and Luke—he is the first mentioned in every list of the Twelve, and he acted as their leader and spokesperson. Jesus chose him, along with Andrew and John, to witness his Transfiguration on Mount Tabor, and he took the same three to watch with him in the Garden of Gethsemane. In Mark's gospel after the resurrection the angels told the women to go tell "the disciples and Peter" about what they have seen. In John's gospel Peter is the first to enter the tomb.

Two passages, however, are particularly crucial. The first is from Matthew, chapter 16:

> He said to them, "But who do you say that I am?" Simon Peter replied, "You are the Christ, the Son of the living God." And Jesus answered, "Blessed are you Simon, Bar-Jona! For flesh and blood has not revealed this to you, but my father in heaven. And I tell you, you are Peter, and on this rock I will build my church, and the powers of death shall not prevail against it. I will give you the keys of the kingdom of heaven, and whatever you bind on earth shall be bound in heaven.

The meaning of the passage has been much disputed, especially since the Reformation. Some biblical experts argue, for instance, that the church is built not on Peter but on the confession of faith that Peter made, or even on Peter's faith itself. In other words, built on the belief in Jesus's special person and mission, which Peter happened to articulate. The consistent papal interpretation is that the church is built on Peter himself—and then on his successors through the ages. The passage is, in any case, extraordinary—no other disciple is singled out from the others in such a striking way in any of the four gospels.

The second passage is from the last chapter of John's gospel and is set on the shore of the Lake of Galilee after Jesus's resurrection:

> When they had finished breakfast, Jesus said to Simon Peter, "Simon, son of John, do you love me more than these?" He said to him, "Yes, Lord: you know that I love you." He said to him, "Feed my lambs." A second time he said to him, "Simon, son of John, do you love me?" He said to him, "Yes, Lord; you know that I love you." He said to him, "Feed my sheep." He said to him the third time, "Simon, son of John, do you love me?" Peter was grieved because he said to him a third time, "Do you love me?" And he said to him, "Lord, you know everything; you know that I love you." Jesus said to him, "Feed my sheep."

These two passages dramatize what all the other passages in the New Testament about Peter point to: his leadership role and his special relationship with Jesus. That much is clear. Two sets of questions crucial to the papacy, however, remain to be answered. First, was the leadership Peter exercised unique to him, so that it was not to be passed on to others in the church? Was it so identical with the person of Peter and with the situation of the first generation that it ended with him? Or, did Peter signify a pattern that was to persist after his death? Did Peter launch a trajectory that was to continue in the church until the end of time? The simple answer is that it is difficult to understand why the authors of the New Testament would have paid so much attention to Peter if his role in the church had no significance beyond his lifetime.

The second question: what happened to Peter? Despite his prominent role in the Acts of the Apostles up to chapter 12, he disappears
from the narrative after that, and Paul takes over. How did Peter end
his days? More specifically: did he go to Rome, assume a leadership
role in the Christian community there, and die a martyr's death under
the Emperor Nero?

To answer that question we need to look at a range of evidence,
because no one piece of it states in straightforward and unambiguous
language either that Peter ever went to Rome or that he died there.
Nonetheless, the evidence all points in that direction, and none contradicts it or points in another direction. The cumulative effect of this
circumstantial evidence is persuasive. Moreover, even before we look at
the evidence, we must remember that Rome was the communications
center of the empire. Anybody with a message to spread would do well
to go there, and Peter surely had a message to spread and a leadership
role that required him to spread it. It seems almost inconceivable that
for such a prominent figure in the New Testament the early community would have so soon after the event mistakenly remembered
him. The consensus today among scholars from every religious tradition (and from no religious tradition) is that, from a strictly historical
viewpoint, Peter almost certainly lived his last days in Rome and was
martyred and buried there.

The evidence is textual and archeological. The New Testament
provides a few clues. In the passage from the last chapter of John
quoted above, Jesus predicts a martyr's death for Peter. More important is the ending of the First Epistle of Peter which, even if it was not
written by Peter himself, was written under his inspiration. "By Sil-
vanus, a faithful brother as I regard him, I have written briefly to you,
exhorting and declaring that this is the true grace of God: stand fast in
it. She [your sister church] who is in Babylon, who is likewise chosen,
sends you greetings, and so does my son Mark." Babylon was a common designation for Rome among Christians, a cryptic name necessary
in time of persecution for a world power hostile to the Gospel. The
passage suggests, or even indicates, that Peter is in Rome at the time
the letter was written, which was probably about the year 63.

Sometime around the year 96 a letter, unsigned but written by a presbyter in Rome named Clement, was sent in the name of the Christian community in Rome to the community in Corinth. In one passage the author brings up Peter in a way that suggests both a special Roman relationship to him and direct information about what he suffered. "Let us set before our eyes the noble Apostle Peter, who by reason of wicked jealousy, not only once or twice but frequently endured suffering, and thus bearing his witness went to the glorious place that he narrated. By reason of rivalry and contention Paul showed how to win the prize for patient endurance."

The passage does not give us a two-plus-two-equals-four indication that Peter and Paul went to their deaths in Rome, but that is a reasonable inference from a document written just a generation after the events would have happened. About fifteen years after that, another leading figure in the early church, Ignatius, bishop of Antioch in present-day Syria, wrote a series of letters to different churches when he was on his way to Rome, where he was going to be put to death for his Christian faith. In his letter to the church in Rome, he said in one passage, "I do not command you as Peter and Paul did. They were apostles. I am a convict. They were at liberty. I am in chains." The passage might mean that Ignatius could not command the Romans as if he had the authority of Peter and Paul, but that interpretation seems less likely than that Peter and Paul in some way commanded or headed the Church of Rome.

Much further along in the second century Saint Irenaeus, bishop of Lyons, wrote that the church had been "founded and organized at Rome by the two glorious apostles, Peter and Paul." Irenaeus's writings were well known in his day, and no one, in the Mediterranean communities, which were jealous of any connection they might have had with the apostles, contested his assertion about the Roman church.

From the textual evidence, then, it is clear that by the end of the second century, at the latest, well informed Christians were convinced that Peter and Paul lived and died in Rome. Archeological evidence supports the textual. The most impressive instance of it comes from excavations under Saint Peter's basilica conducted in the middle of the twentieth century. As mentioned, Constantine built the original church, which was substantially finished by the year 330. He built it where he did because by that time it was taken for certain that that was where Peter either died or was buried or both. That church was torn down in the sixteenth century to make way for the church we know today. But the new church was built on exactly the same spot, and the new altar located precisely where the original altar had been. In the early sixteenth century, when work on the new church was just beginning, the architect Bramante wanted to change the orientation of the church and move the altar, but Pope Julius II would not hear of it because he was not going to touch the tomb. And by tomb he meant Peter's.

That was the sixteenth century. We need to fast-forward to 1939. Monsignor Ludwig Kaas, then the administrator of the basilica, asked Pope Pius XI's permission to clean up the area under the church called the Sacred Grottoes, which is where many of the papal tombs were located. The area was in disarray. For reasons still not clear, the pope denied permission but, curiously enough, that is precisely where he wanted to be buried.

When Pius died on February 10, 1939, Kaas went down into the Grotto area looking for a place to install the pope's tomb. In the process he ordered a marble plaque to be removed from the wall and, as it was being done, the wall behind it collapsed and exposed an ancient vault. What else was there, in this now exposed area? When the new pope, Pius XII, heard of what happened, he ordered a full-scale investigation of the area, which was carried out over a ten-year period, followed by further excavations begun in 1952. The excavations uncovered a number of ancient tombs and a cemetery dating no later than the second century. They also uncovered a red-wall complex into which was built a small edifice, called a *Tropaion* (tomb or cenotaph), and alongside the edifice the wall containing devotional inscriptions referring to Peter.

The results of the excavations were published. Controversy ensued about the way the excavations were conducted and about conclusions drawn from them. Nonetheless, two facts are certain and uncontested. First, in the area of the excavations right under the main altar there was a shrine dedicated to Peter, seemingly a burial place, and dating from about 150. At the time the shrine was built, Christians surely venerated the spot as sacred to Peter. Second, a century and a half later Constantine expended tremendous effort to build the church where he did. He had to desecrate a Roman cemetery and then move tons of dirt to level the area. Then he saw to it that the altar be located precisely over the spot where the little shrine was found.

Since all the evidence available, both textual and archeological, confirms the traditional belief about Peter and Paul in Rome and none contradicts it, the tradition can be accepted as true beyond reasonable doubt. Three questions, however, remain. First, did Peter and/or Paul found the Christian community in Rome? To that question the answer, despite what Irenaeus said, is a clear negative. The community was already in existence. Paul's Epistle to the Romans, surely written before he went there, is proof positive of the fact.

The next question: was Peter the first pope? The answer depends on the answer to the third question: was Peter the first bishop of Rome? And that answer is both yes and no. The earliest lists of popes begin not with Peter but with a man named Linus. The reason Peter's name does not appear is because he was an apostle, which was a super-category, much superior to pope or bishop.

But did he, apostle though he was, actually function as bishop, as the leader and supervisor of the church in Rome? The Christian community at Rome well into the second century operated as a collection of separate communities without any central structure. In that regard it was different from other cities at the time where, as in Antioch, Christians thought of themselves and acted as a single community over which a bishop presided. Rome was a constellation of house churches, independent of one another, each of which was loosely governed by an elder. The communities thus basically followed the pattern of the Jewish synagogues out of which they had developed. By the middle of the first century Rome had a large and prosperous Jewish community, with maybe as many as fifty thousand members, who worshiped in over a dozen synagogues.

If a bishop is an overseer who leads all the Christian communities within a city, then it seems Peter was not the bishop of Rome. But that is a narrow and unimaginative approach. Peter being Peter, who had eaten and drunk with Jesus and was a witness to his resurrection, surely must have exercised a leadership role in Rome that was greater than that of any single elder/presbyter. It is inconceivable that Peter, an apostle, came to Rome, the capital of the empire, and did not have a determining role in that community whenever decisions were made. If that is true, then it follows that Peter can, with qualification but justly, be called the first bishop of Rome. And if he is the first bishop of Rome, then he is the first pope.

AFTER PETER AND PAUL

The period between the death of Peter and the toleration of Christianity by the Emperor Constantine in 313 has often been represented as a time of the pure church, the church of the catacombs, the church of great simplicity, the church where all Christians lived flawless lives and were ready to die for their faith. No doubt, there is much to admire about the Christians of these early centuries, but they were human beings with faults, failings, and sometimes grave weaknesses.

What did the church of Rome look like fifty or seventy-five years after Peter? Fundamental to it during this period was the ongoing impact of its origin in the Jewish community. Christians soon began to separate from the synagogues but, as mentioned, they organized themselves into similarly discrete units. They met, as did Christians in other cities, in the homes of wealthier Christians, and there they held their religious services. As the communities grew they rented space in public edifices. Each of these house-churches or neighborhood communities had a leader or elder—a "presbyter," the synonym for elder. As late as the second century, a document called the *Shepherd of Hermas* spoke of the Church of Rome as having many rulers.

This raises a problem for those lists of popes that begin with Linus, Cletus, and Clement. The fact that Clement was responsible for the letter to the church of Corinth suggests that there was at least an informal hierarchy among the elders. There surely were occasions when the Christians in Rome wanted or needed to act as a group. Saint Paul's Epistle to the Romans shows that, despite the fact that they had no central organization, they looked upon themselves as a single church and were looked upon that way by others. Clement's letter comes from the whole church of Rome, not from a particular house-church.

Elsewhere in the church bishops emerged as leaders of the community, a pattern eventually followed by Rome. The Christian communities provided for poor relief, with special care for orphans and widows. This activity needed organization and supervision, not simply on a house-to-house basis but in a way effective for a whole urban reality. Moreover, the Christian churches began to experience bitter disagreements.

An early and particularly divisive issue was about when to celebrate the most important of the Christian anniversaries, the resurrection of Christ. The Christians of the eastern part of the Roman Empire tended to celebrate it to coincide with the Jewish Passover, no matter on what day of the week Passover fell, whereas the Romans, for instance, celebrated it every Sunday. As time went on the Romans began to celebrate it more solemnly once a year on the Sunday after Passover. This issue soon erupted into a rancorous argument among the churches, and each church needed somebody to speak for it.

Another problem requiring the same solution was the relationship between the Hebrew Scriptures, the Old Testament, and the more properly Christian documents, those of the New Testament. In the middle of the second century a Christian named Marcion rejected not only the entire Old Testament but even parts of the New. What documents deserved to be considered normative and therefore canonical? A further, more profound question was the relationship between Father, Son, and Spirit. A heresy known as Modalism sprang up that said that the distinction between Father and Son was purely nominal or only transitory, two "modes" of an identical reality. Then, a disciplinary question: what to do with apostates, those people who during persecution abandoned their faith by sacrificing to Roman gods and who afterward repented and wanted to be reconciled to the community. Clear leadership was required to deal with problems like these. No later than the middle of the second century, Rome like other cities had evolved into a pattern of a single leader for the community.

By that time the Church of Rome had also evolved from primarily Greek-speaking to Latin-speaking. The community then numbered at least fifteen thousand, probably many more. Within a century the number grew incrementally and more than doubled. By 300 it had tripled or quadrupled to become a sizable body that had made inroads into the highest levels of Roman society. The bishops were elected as elsewhere in the Christian world by the presbyters, now increasingly considered and called priests (*sacerdotes*), and they were then confirmed or approved in some fashion by other members of the local church. The process developed naturally, without legislation determining or governing it. This lack of clear procedures led to controversy and contention, which sometimes reached scandalous levels.

At first the bishops were married men with children. A number of the early popes were married, and a few of them in these early centuries were descended from previous popes. Pope Silverius (536–537), for instance, was the son of Pope Hormisdas (514–533). By the end of the second century, nonetheless, a consensus began to form that bishops could continue of course in their marriage but, once they were ordained bishop, were to live with their spouses as brother and sister—married, yes, but expected not to have marital relations with their wives. Indeed, around the year 305, the Synod of Elvira (near Granada) forbade not only bishops but also priests and deacons from such relations.

Meanwhile in Rome an ever sharper awareness developed that the Church of Rome was an apostolic church and that that fact gave it a special character. The Roman church, therefore, had special responsibilities regarding other churches. Correlatively, the other churches wanted to validate their decisions by being in communion with the Roman church and in concert with what the bishop of Rome thought best. In these first several centuries that concern to be in agreement with Rome was vague, unformulated, and did not everywhere prevail, but it is clear that a pattern was in the making very early. The pattern would, however, have a rough time fully establishing itself.

This is still "the church of the catacombs," not in the sense that Christians lived in them but in the metaphorical sense that even in the religiously tolerant atmosphere of the Roman Empire, Christians were persecuted. The problem the Romans had with Christians was their refusal to sacrifice to pagan gods and, more specifically, their refusal to sacrifice to the deified emperors. The Roman Empire, in which most of the population was illiterate, was held together and given a sense of cohesion through symbols and images. Busts and statues of the emperors were everywhere, and they represented a reality that went beyond their person. Not to sacrifice to them made Christians seem a danger to the state—made them, in our terms, unpatriotic, even subversive.

By the Middle Ages a tradition had grown up that all the popes from Peter until Constantine died as martyrs. Since the records are not always complete or reliable, it is often difficult to know just what happened to whom. Nonetheless, it is now certain that, while a few popes died as martyrs, the majority did not. Until the persecution of the Emperor Decius in the middle of the third century, the persecutions, even in the city of Rome, were intermittent, uncoordinated, and often local, which helps explain why popes escaped the death penalty.

This situation also meant that Christians as individuals (and also as communities) owned property. By no later than the third century, moreover, they had built and owned churches in which they could worship as they pleased, even though the property might be seized during a persecution and the community dispersed. The era of the house-church was definitively over. Christians in Rome were *not* living in catacombs because they had never lived in them and, despite romantic legends, did not use them even as places of refuge. The catacombs were simply their burial grounds in which, however, religious ceremonies were sometimes held.

Between Linus and Pope Miltiades, who was pope when Constantine issued his edict tolerating Christianity, the records list thirty-one popes—Linus, Cletus (or Anacletus), Clement, Evaristus, Alexander, Sixtus, Telesphorus, Hyginus, Pius, Anicetus, and so forth. Their names, the kind of functions they performed, and the dates of their election and death become ever more reliable as time moves on. By the time of Pius (about 142–155) and Anicetus (about 155–165) the records provide basically sound but minimal information, and from then on they get more ample. A good deal is known about the popes of the third century.

Pope Callixtus I (217–222), is hardly typical, but his pontificate provides a window into the church of Rome at the time and reveals some of its problems. Callixtus, born in Rome, was a slave of a high-placed Christian named Carpophorus. He served as Carpophorus's financial steward, which meant he was entrusted with large sums of money. Something went wrong—Callixtus was accused of embezzlement. To avoid prosecution he fled the city and tried to board a ship at Ostia. But he was caught, brought back to Rome, and put to work on a treadmill. Eventually released, he was arrested for causing a disturbance in a synagogue on a Sabbath. This time he was handed over to the prefect of the city, who had him flogged and exiled to the mines in Sardinia, where many other Christians were also enslaved on that notorious "island of death." He was probably about thirty years old at the time.

These events took place during the reign of Pope Victor (189–198), an African, the first Latin-speaking pope. Victor brought to his office an insistence on the strictest discipline for the clergy and was certainly the most forceful, even imperious, of the second-century popes. His attempts to get other churches to adopt the Roman calendar for the celebration of Easter were resisted and resented in Asia Minor, but they were probably primarily directed to dissidents within his own flock at Rome.

Victor is the first pope known to have had dealings with the imperial court. Marcia, the mistress of Emperor Commodus, was, it seems, a Christian. Through her the pope was able to arrange for the release of many of the Christians in Sardinia. Although Callixtus was not on the list of those to be released, he managed in this atmosphere of amnesty to obtain his freedom. He returned to Rome sometime around the year 190. He then began his clerical career and was soon ordained a deacon. Pope Zephyrinus, Victor's successor, appointed him administrator of the Christian cemetery on the Appian Way, probably the first cemetery the church legally owned. It contains the "crypt of the popes" where the remains of a number of third-century bishops of Rome were laid to rest. Today it is called the catacomb of Callixtus.

Callixtus's new position showed off his administrative skills, which resulted in an ever closer relationship with Zephyrinus. He quickly became a person to reckon with. Upon Zephyrinus's death he was in 217 elected by the Roman clergy to succeed him, but Hippolytus, a Roman presbyter, refused to accept Callixtus and had himself elected by a faction of the clergy inimical to Callixtus. Two popes! This is the first of many such papal schisms. Hippolytus goes down in history as the first anti-pope, a person who claims to be pope but whom contemporaries or later historians judge illegitimate.

Hippolytus accused Callixtus of many things. He said he was a Modalist—but at least while Callixtus was pope he spoke in orthodox fashion about the Father and Son, and he excommunicated Sabellius, the intellectual leader of the Modalists. Hippolytus saw Callixtus as somebody weakening Victor's strict policies and accused him of disciplinary laxity—Callixtus gave "full reign to human passions and said that he pardoned everyone's sins." More specifically, Hippolytus accused him of letting bishops stay in office even when they had committed some grievous fault or given scandal, of refusing to condemn clergy who married, and even of allowing into the episcopacy and priesthood men married two or three times.

These accusations came from a hostile source and must be judged accordingly. Hippolytus was a rigorist who could not tolerate the gentler approach that Callixtus took. Callixtus tried to reconcile to the church clergy that a harsh discipline had driven out, for which he should more likely be praised than excoriated. Despite his questionable early career, he conducted himself with dignity and effectiveness during his brief reign. He also is credited with setting an important precedent by permitting Christian women of noble birth to marry men of lower status, something that civil law disallowed. In so doing he staked a claim for the church in regulating matrimony.

Like all the popes of the first three centuries, Callixtus has been revered as a martyr but, since there was no persecution during his reign, he almost certainly was not one. According to one account he was seized by a lynch-mob during a local anti-Christian riot in the Trastevere section of Rome, which probably erupted because of resentment of Christian expansion in the neighborhood, and thrown to his death from a window. Although we do not know for sure how he died, we know where he was buried. His tomb was discovered in 1960 under the ruins of an ancient Christian oratory on the Via Aurelia and was positively identified.

Callixtus's pontificate is significant in that it shows how it was possible to rise from the lowest social status to the highest position in the Church of Rome. It reveals the internal dissensions within the Christian community and the different approaches to ecclesiastical discipline, which would continue to disturb the peace of the church. It presents us with the first papal schism, which Hippolytus would continue during the reign of the next two popes until his death in 235.

But Hippolytus's claim to fame rests on a better basis than leading a schism. He was a prolific and respected writer on doctrinal matters and was one of the most accomplished theologians of his day. Unfortunately, his moral and disciplinary rigor turned him into a divisive figure in a community that needed to stand united. In 1959 Pope John XXIII installed an ancient statue of him at the entrance to the Vatican Library. The statue of this man of great learning is the first thing visitors to the library lay their eyes on.

Pope Stephen I is a great contrast to Callixtus, though like him he had a short reign, 254–257. Stephen was a Roman aristocrat from the Julian family, at the very opposite end of the social scale from Callixtus. He is in that regard symptomatic of the increasingly heavy infiltration of Christianity into the higher levels of Roman society by the middle of the third century. An ancient source states that Pope Lucius "after fulfilling his ministry for slightly less than eight months . . . on his deathbed passed his functions to Stephen." The statement suggests the indeterminate way in which popes were chosen, though even with Lucius's designation Stephen probably required ratification by the clergy of the city. It also suggests that the transition was easy, without the contention that troubled Callixtus and his two successors. The political situation for Christians dramatically improved during Stephen's pontificate because the emperors Valerian and Gallienus put an end, temporarily, to the persecutions instigated by Decius and Trebonius Gallus.

Stephen is important because through his conflict with Saint Cyprian, the powerful bishop of Carthage in North Africa (near present-day Tunis), he reveals the growing influence, prestige, and claims of the bishop of Rome, and reveals as well the resistance Roman claims met. During the persecution of Decius many clergy and laity had "lapsed" and sacrificed to the gods. Among them were two bishops from the Iberian peninsula. Basilides of León and Martial of Mérida had sacrificed and thus saved themselves. Their flocks repudiated them. When the persecution ended the question arose as to their fate. Basilides appealed to Stephen for himself and Martial. The pope readmitted them not only to communion with the church but also to their sees. The Spanish churches then appealed to Cyprian, who convoked a meeting, a "synod," of North African bishops, which confirmed the deposition and excused Stephen's actions on the grounds that he had been deceived by the reports he had received.

How to deal with these *lapsi* became a huge and ongoing problem for the church in this period. Stephen had to face it again when bishop Marcian of Arles refused to reconcile them even on their deathbeds. Cyprian on this occasion pleaded with Stephen to assemble the Gallic episcopacy against Marcian and have them come up with a successor. Cyprian's letter was an implicit acknowledgment that Stephen had authority over other churches.

But the bishop of Carthage did not acknowledge any *carte blanche* authority of the bishop of Rome. The major conflict between these two powerful personalities erupted over the question of the validity of baptism administered by heretics or schismatics. Cyprian was adamant that it was not valid. He had on his side most of the churches of North Africa as well as those of Syria and Asia Minor, an impressive line up. Baptism could be conferred only within the church. This stance was simply a conclusion from Cyprian's broader principle, "outside the church, no salvation" (*extra ecclesiam nulla salus*), which would be invoked thousands upon thousands of times in subsequent centuries to justify or oppose a spectrum of theological opinions.

Stephen held the milder view that rebaptism was not necessary. He had on his side the tradition not only of the Roman church but also of the churches in Alexandria and Palestine. Stephen tried to impose the Roman tradition on the churches of Asia Minor and threatened to break communion with them if they resisted. Meanwhile, in 255 Cyprian wrote a treatise on the subject and then held two synods in Carthage, 255 and 256, that categorically affirmed his position. Without mentioning Stephen's name Cyprian obviously targeted him when he said that nobody sets himself up as a bishop over other bishops and tries to force his colleagues into obedience.

When Cyprian sent envoys to Stephen to justify his position, Stephen refused to see them or grant them hospitality, and treated them as heretics. This was a shocking breach of courtesy to a fellow bishop. The situation was explosive. Bishop Dionysius of Alexandria, who agreed with Stephen's position on baptism, wrote to him, however, and begged him to adopt a more conciliatory attitude. Stephen's enemies accused him of glorying in his position and of recklessly endangering the unity of the church. Bishop Firmilian of Cappadocia reacted strongly to Stephen's threats and reproached him for thinking his powers of excommunication were limitless.

It is difficult to imagine what might have happened if Stephen and Cyprian had lived even a little while longer. Stephen, though reputed to be a martyr, almost certainly died peacefully in Rome in 257. He was succeeded by the conciliatory Sixtus II. A year later Cyprian died a heroic martyr's death in a new persecution. With the deaths of the two protagonists, the tension was diffused. Eventually Stephen's position on baptism prevailed, was adopted even by the African churches by the beginning of the next century, and is the one followed today in mainline Christian churches. If Stephen is important for his strong stand on that issue, he is also important because it seems he was the first pope to find a basis for papal primacy over other churches in the passage from Matthew's gospel, "Thou art Peter, and upon this rock I will build my church."

CONSTANTINE:
THE THIRTEENTH APOSTLE

Constantine was not a pope but the Roman emperor from 312 until 337. Yet he was, with the exception of Saint Peter himself, more important for the papacy and for Christianity itself than any pope. Some people hailed the decree of Vatican Council II (1962–1965) on church-state relations as the "end of the Constantinian era," by which they meant the end of seventeen hundred years of certain patterns of church-state relationships that had their origins with the emperor. The assertion may be exaggerated, but it at least indicates that something momentous happened to the church with Constantine.

By the middle of the third century, the situation in the empire was not good. Plague often ravaged cities, and civil wars broke out intermittently. Over the course of a fifty-year period twenty-five different emperors sat on the throne. Only one of them died in his bed. On the vast and far-flung frontiers of the empire, the Romans were having to pull back. "Barbarians," members of Germanic and other tribes, had long ago drifted into the cities and infiltrated the army. The infiltration may not have been a bad thing in and of itself, but it was disturbing to many people and indicative of profound social change. Among the upper classes a sense of a fatal decline in discipline in public life and public office had taken hold.

Things took a turn very much for the better in 285 with the accession to the imperial throne of Diocletian, who held the office for twenty years. The very length of his reign indicates that he brought stability to the office, but he did much more, to the point of sometimes being considered the second founder of the Roman empire. He was a hard-bitten soldier of low birth, who rose from the ranks to be the commander of the imperial bodyguard and thence to become emperor

Diocletian reorganized imperial finances, restored discipline to the army, decentralized the bureaucracy of the empire and, most importantly, divided the administration of the empire into four parts. This four-part system collapsed after his death, but it threw light on a deep and long-standing cultural division between East and West and even contributed to it. The fact that Diocletian felt a division necessary indicates the empire's complexity, massive size, and the difficulty of holding it together.

Despite the fact that his wife and daughter were avowedly sympathetic to Christianity, he toward the very end of his reign, in 303, launched the fiercest ever imperial persecution of the church. Historians consider the persecution his worst mistake, the biggest blot on his record. Diocletian was an ardent lover of ancient Roman discipline and tradition. He moved from a policy of toleration to persecution because he became convinced Christians weakened the body politic. Since they would not sacrifice to the gods, they were subversive and could not be counted upon in a crisis.

There had of course been many persecutions before Diocletian's, but his was empire-wide and unrelenting. It is properly known as the Great Persecution. Large numbers of Christians were put to death. Imperial agents burned churches. They confiscated cemeteries and the private property of individual Christians, who were also deprived of all their rights, privileges, and honors. As the persecution intensified Christians, even Roman citizens, were arrested, tortured, burned, starved, and forced into gladiatorial contests for the amusement of onlookers. Clerics were forced, as a symbol of compliance, to hand over the books of Scripture to be burned or themselves to be executed. Although many Christians heroically held on to their faith, many defected under the pressure.

The persecution was especially severe in Rome, and the church there suffered grievously. Upon it, however, fell a particularly heavy blow: in May 303, Pope Marcellinus handed over copies of the Scripture and sacrificed to the idols. Elected in 296, he presided without incident over his church for seven years before the persecution broke out. Although the story of his defection has been challenged, the evidence for it is convincing. Reliable documents treated the story as an established fact even as they tried to present it favorably, especially by saying he immediately repented, recanted, and died a martyr. Although he was eventually venerated as a martyr, there is no reliable evidence for it. Because of the ongoing persecution and internal divisions, the church in Rome was not able to choose a successor to Marcellinus for at least three and a half years.

Diocletian retired in 305, the first emperor to do so voluntarily, and within a year or so the persecutions ended. Marcellus was then elected pope, probably because he held the church together during the difficulties of the previous years. He pursued a hard-line policy toward the lapsed, demanding from them long and difficult penances, which turned the majority opinion in the community against him. The resulting disorder, with bloody riots in the streets, was so great that Maxentius, the new emperor, had to intervene. The emperor banished the pope from the capital as a disturber of the peace. Marcellus died shortly afterward, in 308. His body was returned to the city for burial in the cemetery of Saint Priscilla, a private property not confiscated during Diocletian's persecution.

Who would have believed that within twenty years this despised sect, torn with internal divisions and crippled by the defection of its principal leader, would move not simply from being persecuted to being tolerated but from being persecuted to being favored and essentially to be on the road to becoming the state religion? Yet that is what happened—and Constantine made it happen. It is almost impossible to exaggerate his importance.

His father, Constantius Chlorus, was the emperor in the West. When he died in 306, Constantine was in Britain with his troops, who immediately acclaimed him emperor to succeed his father. Constantine made his way to Italy and then to Rome and finally, in 312, engaged his rival, Maxentius, in a decisive battle at the Milvian Bridge, a short distance north of the city walls. At the time of the battle Constantine saw a vision in the heavens with the message that "In this sign you will conquer" (*In hoc signo vinces*). Was what he saw a pagan symbol or a symbol of Christ? It is impossible to know, but Constantine attributed his victory to the divinity. The next year, moreover, he issued his famous Edict of Milan, an official guarantee of toleration for Christians. Although Christians had been able to practice their religion publicly since the retirement of Diocletian, the Edict indicated and symbolized the beginning of a new era for the church and for its status in Roman society. It deserves therefore the place in history traditionally accorded it.

Was Constantine at this point already a Christian? Within a few years most people seemed to think so. His mother, after all, was not only a Christian but would come to be revered as Saint Helena. He put Christian symbols on his banners, even on his coins, but he also kept the pagan symbols. Was he a syncretist, or just a political opportunist? If Diocletian saw Christians as divisive, Constantine seems to have seen the church as a force that could bring cohesion to the empire.

Christians were now the largest single religion in the empire. Despite their internal divisions, they on balance held themselves together rather well and had institutions for dealing with their problems. Among those institutions councils or synods (the words are synonyms) were especially important and were by the year 250 held with some regularity in most parts of the empire—in Alexandria, for instance, in Antioch, Arles, Rome, and, as mentioned, many times in Carthage. They made decisions that were binding in their locality and sometimes even beyond them. The bishops, who now numbered in the many hundreds, had established a remarkable network of communication among themselves across the empire. The church continued, moreover, to have an effective system for dealing with its poor and needy members. Here was a structure within the imperial structure that was not a threat to it but a potential boon.

Whether Constantine early in his career as emperor was a Christian or not is almost beside the point. What is important is what he did in favor of the church. He continued the policy initiated by Maxentius of restoring to individuals and to the churches property that had been confiscated, and he did this without recompense to the interim owners. He made it possible for Christians to compete for high public office and he, indeed, favored them. He put the clergy on the same fiscal basis as the pagan clergy. This meant, principally, that they were exempt from certain taxes. Provisions like this made the clerical state attractive for financial reasons, especially in an era like this one where the distinction between private property and public trust was not always clear.

The clergy began to assume at least a semiofficial public role. They are not quite employees of the empire, but they have close ties to it as well as high status. For bishops Constantine recognized the jurisdiction and the decisions of their courts and of their councils, which judged the behavior especially of the clergy and imposed penalties for misdeeds. These ecclesiastical institutions soon began in some measure to be part of the judicial system of the Roman empire.

Most impressive was the stunningly lavish building program throughout the empire in favor of the Christian church—in Jerusalem, Bethlehem, Antioch, and elsewhere. He wrote to Bishop Macarius of Jerusalem about the church to be built there at the emperor's expense:

It befits Your Sagacity to make such arrangements and such provision of every necessary thing, that not only shall this basilica be the finest in the world but that everything else, too, shall be of such quality that all the most beautiful buildings of every city may be surpassed by this one. . . . Concerning the columns and marbles of whatever kind you consider to be the most precious and serviceable, please inform us yourself in writing . . . that they may be delivered from every quarter. . . . As for the vault, if it is to be coffered, it may also be adorned with gold.

Constantine rebuilt as a Christian city the old city of Byzantium on the Bosporus that came to bear his name. He could not quite do that in Rome itself, but his church-building program there was greater than in any other city—Saint Paul's Outside the Walls, Saint John Lateran's,

Santa Croce in Gerusalemme, Saint Peter's basilica, and others. The interiors of his churches glittered with the precious metals and mosaics that adorned them and with the jewels inset into the sacred vessels and furnishings.

The Lateran basilica with its free-standing baptistery became by Constantine's designation and has remained the cathedral of the bishop of Rome. It went up quickly, finished before Constantine died, and consisted of such massive proportions that it was larger than any other public building in the city. It could hold up to ten thousand people. The emperor's first donation to it included 4,390 *solidi* for the purchase of lamps, 82 kilograms of gold for liturgical vessels, and 775 kilograms of silver for seven silver altars weighing over 150 kilograms apiece, plus a life-sized statue of Christ enthroned, and a hundred silver chalices!

Although the church of the Lateran was their cathedral, the bishops of Rome always had a special relationship to Saint Peter's—for the obvious reasons. As mentioned, Constantine went to extraordinary trouble and expense to build the church where he did. That church too was of massive size, longer than an American football field and proportionately as wide. It too could easily hold many thousands. Constantine's basilica lasted for over twelve hundred years and, had it been properly cared for, could probably have lasted for another twelve hundred. To maintain these massive buildings, Constantine made incredibly generous grants of land to the church from places all around the empire.

If anything argues to the sincerity of Constantine's conversion to Christianity, it is this unbelievably sky's-the-limit expenditure and mobilization of resources for the church. The result was that the face of the city of Rome, as well as of Jerusalem, Antioch, and other places, was rapidly transformed. In their very physicality they became Christian cities, without destruction of their already existing buildings and monuments. If there ever was an era of "the church of the catacombs," it was over now.

In 321 Constantine declared Sunday, the day Roman Christians celebrated Christ's resurrection, a public holiday in the empire, a tradition that is with us still. He mitigated the brutality of some aspects of Roman criminal law and the treatment of slaves. He made grants to support poor children and in this way discouraged abortion and the exposure of children to die. He freed celibates and unmarried persons from special taxation at a time when celibacy and virginity had become a Christian ideal. Surely some of this legislation was Christian inspired.

Constantine began to refer to himself as the "common bishop" (*koinos episkopos*), a kind of super-bishop whose function was to ensure order and orthodoxy in the church, to do what was necessary to enable the church to function and flourish. The term meant that his influence extended over all bishops. Those bishops, including the bishop of Rome, paid him deference, no questions asked. He in turn respected the bishops' authority and realized that they had a sphere properly their own, but he was not above taking the initiative in particular cases. The church began to function within the Roman system but was not absorbed by it.

Constantine at first seemed not to reckon with the fact that, though Christianity might be a force for cohesion within the empire, it was itself torn by doctrinal and disciplinary quarrels. The emperor generally left the settling of the disputes to the clergy, but he sustained their decisions and, when appropriate, implemented them. In 319–320 the greatest controversy to date broke out in Alexandria when the bishop summoned a synod of all the bishops of Egypt, which condemned a priest named Arius. Arius, to put it in its simplest terms, denied the divinity of Christ. According to him, the Son of God was a creature—a preeminent creature created before the beginning of time but not of the same substance as the Father.

Arius did not accept the synod's condemnation and continued to preach his ideas, which spread rapidly and widely especially in the East. It sparked incredibly bitter controversy. Bishops took sides. Arius was a clever publicist for his ideas and promoted them by composing little chants, slogans, and ditties that could easily be remembered and repeated by ordinary folk, which resulted in the controversy taking hold even in the lower strata of society.

This situation led to Constantine's most important measure in supervising the church, his convocation of the first church-wide, or "ecumenical," council in the city of Nicaea (present-day Iznik in northwest

Turkey) near his capital in Constantinople. He invited all the bishops of the empire, a number estimated at well over a thousand by this time, of whom more than 250 attended the council. The council-pattern for settling disputes had been in place for at least a century and, indeed, the bishops of the empire prepared for Nicaea in 324 with a series of local councils.

The council of Nicaea, held in the imperial palace, opened on May 20, 325, the year Constantine became sole emperor. Constantine delivered the opening address, exhorting the bishops to harmony and fraternal union among themselves. The purpose of the council was to bring peace to the church—and thus to the empire, especially in the East. The president of the council was a bishop, Ossius (or Hossius) of Cordoba, one of the very few Western bishops present. Constantine seems to have allowed the bishops full freedom in arriving at their decisions but made it known that he would implement them. The law of the church was on its way to becoming the law of the empire.

The council lasted about a month and made important decisions. For instance, it ratified the Roman and Alexandrian position on the date for Easter. It also published a number of disciplinary canons (ordinances) that included prohibiting women from living in priests' houses unless they were near relatives, imposing punishment on clergy who practiced usury, and forbidding kneeling during Sunday mass (the custom was to stand).

Towering above everything else, however, was the condemnation of Arius and the formulation of a confession of faith or creed that is still used today, along with some later additions to it, by all the mainline Christian churches. The anti-Arian section of the creed says about Jesus Christ: "[He is] the Son of God, born of the Father, that is, from the substance of the Father, God from God, light from light, true God from true God, begotten not made, consubstantial with the Father." At Nicaea the Arians were condemned but not convinced. The council did not succeed in stamping out the heresy, which continued to trouble the church for centuries, but it set the standard of orthodoxy for dealing with it.

Beyond its specific measures the council of Nicaea had further significance. It functioned in ways strikingly similar to the Roman

Senate. Like the Senate it assumed both a legislative and a judicial mode. It made laws, to which penalties were often attached for non-observance, and it judged cases, issuing sentences against ecclesiastical criminals, in this case, Arius. Moreover, Constantine behaved toward the council much as late Roman emperors behaved toward the Senate. He convoked it, in effect ratified its agenda, and committed himself to enforcing its decisions. When the council closed, he threw a magnificent banquet for the bishops in his palace. In his own name he sent a letter to "all the churches" informing them of the outcome and assuring them that all questions had been thoroughly considered.

In comparison with Constantine, the bishop of Rome during these years seems like a minor official. Probably in 310 Pope Eusebius succeeded Marcellus but lived only a short time. The next pope, Miltiades (or Melchiades), reigned until 314. To him Constantine presented the palace of the Empress Fausta as his residence near where the Lateran basilica would soon be built. When in a disputed election over the bishopric of Carthage the contenders appealed to the emperor (not to the pope) for resolution, Constantine commissioned Miltiades along with three Gallic bishops to adjudicate the case. This is the first instance of a direct intervention by an emperor in internal church affairs. Miltiades deftly changed the character of the proceedings into a regular church synod by adding fifteen Italian bishops, but he nonetheless accepted without question the emperor's initiative in the affair.

The party that lost the case again appealed to the emperor, who himself summoned a council to meet in 314 in Arles. Miltiades died in the meantime and was succeeded by the long-lived Silvester (314–331). The new pope attended neither Arles nor Nicaea. At least the former council communicated its decisions to him, which was a recognition of his special status. Silvester, invited of course by the emperor to Nicaea, pleaded old age and sent two priests to represent him. The priests were not shown any special signs of respect during the council, but they were the first to sign the official acts, right after Ossius, the president.

Silvester, pope for one of the most earth-shaking periods in the history of the church and the history of Rome, seems to have been passive through it. His reputation was richly embroidered in later legend. He supposedly converted Constantine, baptized him, and cured him of leprosy. He also received from him temporal domination over Rome and all the provinces and states of the West (known as the Donation of Constantine). There is no truth in any of it.

Constantine's actions in favor of the church needed no embellishment or exaggeration. For that reason he is known in some Orthodox churches as "the thirteenth apostle." Along with his mother Helena he is venerated in those churches as a saint, and mother and son share the same feast day, May 21. Because of him the church was now securely public, impressive in its sheer physicality, and ever more responsible for providing civic services of various kinds. Constantine was not only the greatest patron the church would ever see, but he felt responsible for its well-being and acted accordingly. Constantine and the bishops were partners. Unresolved was the question of which of the two was the senior partner.

PROSPERITY TO CRISIS:
DAMASUS AND LEO THE GREAT

B y the time Constantine died in 337, twelve years after Nicaea, the church had entered a golden era, with its hand held firmly and appreciatively by its great patron. That does not mean its course was untroubled. Of all the troubles, Arianism headed the list and generated bitter controversies. Constantine never formally wavered in his support for the council's anti-Arian stance, but he came more and more under the influence of Arian bishops, who were able to persuade him of the ill will or malfeasance of leaders of the orthodox party, which led him to exile a number of them. Included among the exiles was Saint Athanasius, bishop of Alexandria, who had been the most important opponent of Arius at the council and had become the very emblem of Nicene orthodoxy. By the time Constantine died the Arians, despite Nicaea, were stronger than ever.

Constantine arranged for a division of the empire among his three sons after his death. Although raised Christians, they were a brutal brood. The eldest, Constantine II, was soon eliminated, which by 340 left Constans as emperor in the West and Constantius II in the East. The young emperors soon departed from their father's tolerant attitude toward the traditional religions of the empire. In 341 Constantius issued a decree, "Let superstition cease" (*Cesset Superstitio*), which encouraged a bellicose attitude and in some places the wanton destruction of statues and temples. In Arethus in Syria, for instance, Bishop Marcus had a pagan temple demolished and replaced it with a church on the same site.

Before his death Constantine II gave permission for the exiled bishops who adhered to the Nicene Creed to return to their sees. This conciliatory gesture backfired because the Arians adamantly refused to give ground. Disorder broke out almost everywhere the exiled bishops returned, but nowhere more confusedly and persistently than in Alexandria, which forced Athanasius into exile once again. In an ill considered move Arian bishops brought the pope into the fray by implicitly asking his judgment on Athanasius. The pope was Julius I.

Elected the year Constantine died, Julius had a long reign of fifteen years. A forceful leader, born in Rome, he was a striking contrast with the bland Silvester. Among his other accomplishments was the reorganization of the papal chancery in imitation of the procedures of its imperial counterpart, another instance of ecclesiastical institutions conforming to patterns set by the secular power. He also built at least one important church in Rome, Santa Maria in Trastevere.

Julius is most remembered, however, for his unwavering support of Athanasius. He emphatically declined to endorse the Arian bishops and at the same time gave Athanasius and other exiled bishops refuge in Rome, where they were safe under his protection. In 340 or 341 he held a synod in Rome, which cleared Athanasius and the others of the charges the Arians laid against them. The Arians reacted fiercely and at a certain point issued a letter excommunicating Julius and the Western bishops who supported him. Toward the end of Julius's pontificate, his position seemed to prevail because in 346 Athanasius was for a second time able to return to Alexandria.

By the time Julius's successor Liberius was elected in 352, however, the Arians were again in the ascendancy in the East. Constantius II, now sole emperor and residing in the West at Arles, had fallen increasingly under their influence and had turned into a determined opponent of Athanasius. He put pressure on the Western bishops, especially

Liberius, to conform. He called a council at Arles of Western bishops, whom he bullied into condemning Athanasius. When Liberius protested, insisting that it was not so much the person of Athanasius that was at stake as the Creed of Nicaea, Constantius in 355 called another council at Milan, which not surprisingly ended with the same result.

Through it all Liberius steadfastly held out in the face of threats and bribes. Constantius then had him seized, brought by force to Milan and, when he continued to resist the emperor's will, banished to Beroea in Thrace. Under constant pressure as the months slowly passed into years, Liberius finally capitulated in 357. He agreed to the excommunication of Athanasius and signed a creedal statement that was at odds with Nicaea. In his absence, however, the emperor with the connivance of some Roman clergy had a new pope, Felix II, installed and had him consecrated bishop in the imperial palace in Milan by three Arian prelates.

The Romans resisted Felix, and Constantius became convinced that public order in Rome could be restored only with the return of Liberius which, with Liberius's capitulation, he was ready to allow. The emperor entertained the absurd idea that Liberius and Felix could function in the same city as co-bishops, which was not only unthinkable from a canonical viewpoint but politically unworkable. Although Liberius had badly compromised himself with the church at large and was held in some disdain, he still commanded the loyalty of most of the clergy and faithful of Rome. When he returned in 358, the popular reaction against Felix boiled over and forced him to leave the city. The Romans' battle cry against Felix was "One God, one Christ, one bishop!"

Felix, still supported by the emperor and a minority of the clergy, installed himself in a suburban town, while Liberius took hold of the Lateran palace for himself. From 358 until 365, when Felix died, Rome had, it seems, two bishops. Liberius, who upon the death of Constantius in 361 reasserted his support of Athanasius and Nicaea, died the year after Felix.

The troubles had not ended. Clergy loyal to Liberius met in the new church of Santa Maria in Trastevere and elected a Roman deacon, Ursinus. Meanwhile clergy loyal to Felix elected Damasus. Violence

broke out, instigated for the most part by Damasus's supporters. Ursinus, now pursued by the city prefect favorable to Damasus, had to
withdraw from the city. At a certain point a group of thugs favorable
to Damasus, and seemingly with his approval, stormed a meeting of his
rival's followers, which left over a hundred dead. Damasus, who seems
to have had majority support within Rome, was soon regarded at home
and abroad as the legitimate pope, recognized by the emperor. But the
rivalry continued until Ursinus's death about eight or nine years later.

This was, to say the least, an inauspicious beginning, and
Damasus's fellow bishops, shocked by reports of the violence that accompanied his election, never quite forgot it. Nonetheless, Damasus
went on to a long, prosperous, and important pontificate (366–384).
He was a Roman, which stood him in good stead, and his father was a
bishop, which gave him an early entree into clerical circles. A man of
refined tastes, he for a while employed Saint Jerome as his secretary.
He encouraged Jerome to undertake a new translation of the Bible into
Latin, which eventuated in the so-called Vulgate, the standard biblical
text in the West into the sixteenth century—and for Roman Catholics
into the twentieth.

Damasus earned criticism for his lavish lifestyle and for currying
favor with the old Roman aristocrats, especially the women, many of
whom were still pagans. At one point he had to defend himself against
charges of adultery. Despite the annoyance he suffered from his rival,
Damasus managed to survive quite well, as suggested by the number
of churches he built in the city and his exaltation of the burial places of
the martyrs, whom he wanted to be regarded as the true heroes of the
city. The real glory of Rome was Christian.

As pope he took a firm anti-Arian stance. He tried, for instance, to
dislodge from Milan, now the capital of the empire, the Arian bishop
Auxentius. Although he was unsuccessful, he saw his goal accomplished when, upon the death of Auxentius in 373 or 374, the clergy
and faithful of Milan acclaimed Ambrose their bishop. Ambrose, an
unbaptized layman at the time of his election/acclamation, immediately set himself to study the Scriptures, at which he was extraordinarily successful. After his death he became recognized as one of the
four doctors of the church along with his two contemporaries—saints

Jerome and Augustine—and the later Saint Gregory the Great. In his *Confessions* Augustine recounts how Ambrose's homilies influenced his conversion.

Ambrose had a sometimes tense relationship with the emperor Theodosius, a Spanish career soldier who ascended the throne in 379. Theodosius was a devout and orthodox Christian who despised Arianism. Like many other emperors, he had a brutal side. Ambrose several times confronted him, most famously after Theodosius ordered a massacre of civilians in Thessalonica in retaliation for the murder there of an imperial official. Theodosius accepted the penance Ambrose imposed. Ambrose was thus important for being among the first to challenge imperial authority and successfully to assert the prerogatives of a higher one. Ambrose therefore, not Damasus or his successor Siricius, was the dominant ecclesiastical figure in the West in the fourth quarter of the fourth century.

Theodosius's zeal for the Christian faith was real, and he tried to make it effective. He outlawed Arianism and other heresies. In 380 he issued the Edict of Thessalonica, which with some exaggeration is generally interpreted as a declaration of Christianity as the state religion. In it he specified the form of Christianity as what the Romans received from Peter and what Damasus now professed. In Theodosius, therefore, Damasus had an ally and one that was in line with Damasus's increasing insistence on the preeminence of "the Apostolic See," a term he favored, over the other sees. In that regard Damasus had another ally in Ambrose who, independent though he was, paid deference to Damasus and supported without question the Roman claims. In the East those claims were resented, especially when Damasus addressed the bishops there not in the traditional formula as brothers but as sons. Damasus and his successor initiated the custom of replying to questions from fellow bishops in the form used in imperial rescripts, thus suggesting that the reply had the force of law.

In 381 Theodosius convoked a general council in Constantinople, the first since Nicaea to be recognized as such. It reaffirmed, as Theodosius expected it to, the earlier council and somewhat reformulated the Nicene Creed to produce the formula that is recited at mass every Sunday and at corresponding services by other Christian churches.

Not a single Western bishop was present, and Damasus did not even send envoys.

The pope, although pleased with the doctrinal affirmation of the council, rejected a disciplinary decree that hit right at the heart of the relationship between the East and the West. The decree gave primacy of honor among bishoprics to Constantinople, the "new Rome," after the primacy of the old Rome. The decree implied that Rome's primacy derived from the same imperial status as Constantinople's and not from its apostolic origins. The next year a Roman council rejected the decree and insisted that Rome's primacy came from Christ's words, "Thou art Peter, and upon this rock I build my church."

In the middle of the next century Pope Leo the Great carried Damasus's claims for the papacy to a new level. He was a renowned preacher, and in his sermons he hammered home Peter's mystical presence in Rome and presented himself as able to act with Peter's authority. He wrote long letters to bishops of Africa, Gaul, Spain, and Italy admonishing them, settling disputes, and letting them know he expected them to follow Roman customs. When Bishop Hilary of Arles began to behave as if his see were a patriarchate independent of Rome, Leo got a rescript from Emperor Valentinian III confirming that he had jurisdiction over all the western provinces. He later clipped Hilary's wings in a practical way by dividing the bishopric into the two sees of Arles and Vienne.

The pope gloried in his orthodoxy and the orthodoxy of his see and kept a keen eye out for heresy. His greatest triumph in that regard came with the Council of Chalcedon, 451, called by the emperor Marcian, much assisted by his wife Pulcheria. Monophysitism (sometimes called Eutychianism after one of its promoters) was the heresy in question. If Arianism denied the full divinity of Christ, Monophysitism denied his humanity by insisting that he had only a divine nature instead of the orthodox belief that he had both a human and divine.

Eutyches had earlier appealed to Leo to enlist him in his cause. Leo, now alerted to the problem, then spearheaded the opposition to him. He hoped that the council dealing with the matter would be held in the West. Although that did not happen, Paschasius of Lilybea, head of the Roman delegation to the council, presided over it, even though nineteen envoys of the emperor sat on a raised platform in the center of the assembly and ensured orderly procedure. The council was especially well attended—perhaps as many as six hundred bishops were present.

A letter that Leo had earlier written denouncing Eutyches, known as Leo's *Tome*, was accepted at the council as clearly setting forth the orthodox position—"true God and true man"—and was included in the council's profession of faith. This was certainly Leo's most impressive doctrinal achievement. According to reports, the fathers at the council exclaimed, "Peter has spoken through Leo!"

But Leo had to face the same problem Damasus faced with an earlier council. In a disciplinary decree, canon 28, the council, despite the protests of Leo's legates, accorded Constantinople the same patriarchal status as Rome. Both were imperial cities. As did Damasus, Leo found this utterly unacceptable and, despite his triumph at Chalcedon, he withheld for a time his approval of it. He later accepted the doctrinal stance of the council to become one of its great champions, but he continued to repudiate canon 28. As is obvious, assertions of Roman primacy, in the terms the popes had begun to formulate it, continued to meet resistance in the East. Nonetheless, Leo's faith in his prerogatives was impregnable: "Who is so ignorant as to underestimate the glory of Saint Peter and believe that there would be parts of the church that escape the solicitude of his governance?"

Leo reigned for twenty-one years (440–461), an extraordinarily long pontificate for those days. He was elected *in absentia* while on an imperial diplomatic mission in Gaul. This extraordinary circumstance suggests the esteem in which he was already held in the city. He was active during the pontificates of his two predecessors and acquitted himself well. Forceful and energetic, he was more a doer than a thinker, and even his *Tome* was notable for its clarity and precision rather than for its subtlety. Ninety-six of his sermons and a hundred and forty-three of his letters survive, and they provide a precious window into the pope and into the world in which he lived.

That world was far less safe for Rome than it had been in Damasus's time. No emperor had resided there since Constantine. At the beginning of the century Alaric, leader of the Visigoths, who were Arian Christians, marched back and forth over Italy, three times laid siege to Rome, and extracted tribute from it. Incredible as it might seem, Alaric and his forces did not set fire to the city as expected when they finally penetrated it in 410, though of course pillage, burnings, and rape took place.

Saint Jerome wrote of the event, "The city that had captured the whole world was itself captured. Indeed, it perished by famine before it perished by the sword, so that few were found to be taken captive." Alaric then continued his march south. From this point forward the vulnerability of Rome was obvious for all to see.

Leo, who as a youth had witnessed Alaric's sack of Rome, twice assumed the role as defender of the city against mortal threats to it, a clear sign that upon the pope had devolved duties formerly borne by the emperor and secular officials of the city. In Rome the bishop was now something more than head of its church. In 452 Attila the Hun, who already had a brilliant military career behind him and commanded large forces, landed in Italy and threatened to march south on Rome (see fig. 4.1).

At the urging of Emperor Valentinian III, Leo along with two officials of the city raced north to meet him near Mantua. Attila, "the scourge of God," withdrew, possibly more influenced to do so because of imperial victories in the East than by Leo's entreaties.

Attila died shortly afterward, but another threat just as severe loomed within three years. Geiseric (or Genseric), king of the Vandals, who like Attila commanded an extensive army, invaded Italy and appeared at the gates of the city. Leo pleaded with him not to put the torch to it and to spare the population. Geiseric agreed. But he inflicted extensive damage and carried off the dowager empress, the widow of Valentinian. Alaric, Attila, and Geiseric were not fly-by-night leaders of small marauding bands. They were professional soldiers, skilled leaders of disciplined armies who successfully challenged the Roman forces in both the East and the West. Constantinople was able to hold out against them. Rome was not, and it would continue from this point forward to be a vulnerable military target. Jerome was right: it had long ago ceased being mistress of the world.

Leo is one of only two popes on whom posterity with unanimity conferred the title "great." He was not a genius, not even a particularly

4.1: Leo I with Attila the Hun

Algardi, Alessandro (1602–1654). Pope Leo I meeting Attila. St. Peter's Basilica, Vatican State.

© Scala / Art Resource, NY

profound thinker. But he was decisive, a person of integrity and courage, which he showed in a number of situations but nowhere more strikingly than in his confrontations with Attila and Geiseric. In taking upon himself the responsibility for the defense of the city of Rome, he provided a precedent for his successors that they would for a millennium and a half interpret as their sacred duty.

GREGORY THE GREAT

Gregory became pope at the end of the sixth century (590–604). By now the Germanic peoples ruled much of the West—the Visigoths in Spain, the Lombards in northern Italy, the Franks in present-day France and further east, and the Saxons even further east, and so forth. Of these peoples all except the Franks were Arians, which for Catholics was almost as bad as being pagan. Most dangerous to Rome were the Lombards, centered in Pavia south of Milan and generally located in the part of Italy today known as Lombardy. Unlike the Huns and Vandals, the Lombards came and stayed, and they had their hearts fixed on expanding their territory. In 569 they captured Milan, the erstwhile capital of the empire, and their king took the title of Lord of Italy. They soon occupied much of northern Italy.

Since 476 there had been no emperor in the West, only an exarch (imperial representative) in Ravenna on the Adriatic coast south of present-day Venice. The exarch, weakly supported by the emperors in Constantinople because they had problems of their own at home, could muster little resistance to the Lombard threat. The Lombards had, moreover, practically cut connections between Ravenna and Rome. To add to the problem the population in the cities of Italy, and indeed throughout the empire, had declined due to plague, war, and the difficulty of provisioning them as travel and shipping became more dangerous. The population in Rome at one point dipped as low as thirty thousand but then climbed to about ninety thousand, a growth due in part to the influx of refugees. This was a far cry from the million inhabitants at Rome's peak of prosperity. Everywhere in the empire much of the old infrastructure had been destroyed, damaged and not repaired, or was gradually eroding due to neglect.

It was into this world probably in 540 that Gregory was born of an old and wealthy patrician family. Despite all the disasters Rome had suffered for almost two centuries, families like Gregory's had managed to survive and maintain standards that hardly seem possible under the circumstances. The family owned a beautiful palace on the Caelian hill in Rome and extensive properties outside the city. Gregory's father, Gordian, was a senator, which suggests how the great families continued to dominate the city despite the vicissitudes it had suffered. The influence of the family becomes even more apparent in the fact that two of Gregory's relatives had been pope. Felix III (483–492) was his great-grandfather, and Agapetus I (535–536) was a more distant relative.

The family was devout. Gregory had two or three aunts who were nuns, and his mother Sylvia, regarded as a saint, also became a nun when Gordian died. An early biographer, John the Deacon, said that Gregory was a saint brought up among saints. His family ensured that he receive an excellent and traditional Roman education in which along with training in eloquence (and probably in Gregory's case some legal training) went the inculcation of the virtues of prudence, constancy, moderation, and magnanimity That education above all inculcated a sense of responsibility for the public weal and was aimed at producing civic leaders and statesmen. With Gregory the education took, so that as an adult he seemed an embodiment of the old Roman virtues, which he combined with Christian humility and charity. For him and his family service to the city and service to the church were intertwined.

From 572 until 574 Gregory was prefect of the city of Rome, a position roughly equivalent to mayor. He was in his early thirties at the time. He acquitted himself well, but when his father died in 574

Gregory resigned and became a monk. His brother succeeded him as prefect, which is another indication of the family's influence and high standing in the city. Gregory converted the family palace on the Caelian into a monastery under the patronage of Saint Andrew and founded six more monasteries on family estates in Sicily. He was, obviously, a man who had ample resources at his fingertips even at this point in history when the great Roman fortunes were generally in sharp decline.

Gregory's actions fit, however, into a pattern mentioned earlier: the propensity of wealthy Christian families in Rome to give large properties "to Saint Peter" for pious purposes. It was this pattern, exemplified here by Gregory, that by his time already made "the patrimony of Peter" extremely wealthy. The patrimony comprised vast areas of real estate in and around the city of Rome but also in other areas of the empire—in Sicily, southern Italy, Sardinia, Africa, and Gaul. The patrimony was a splendid resource for the church in its efforts to succor widows and orphans and to maintain its churches in a worthy fashion, but it also posed a temptation for the unscrupulous.

Gregory was a fervent monk, as indicated by a regime of fasting he imposed upon himself, a regime that negatively affected his health. He lived at Saint Andrew's under an abbot or prior that he had not appointed. He later maintained that his years in the monastery were the happiest of his life. They were short-lived. He later said of his monastery days, "I sigh as one who looks back and gazes at the shore he has left behind."

Probably in 578 Pope Benedict I ordained him a deacon and appointed him to look after the temporal administration of one of the city's districts. In August of the next year the Lombards laid siege to Rome. The new pope, Pelagius II, was desperate for help, and he chose Gregory to be his *apocrisiarius* ("envoy" or "ambassador") to the court of Emperor Tiberius in Constantinople. Even though Gregory knew no Greek and seems to have learned none while in the East, he had a background and personality that made him ideal for the mission.

He remained in Constantinople for six years, which was an invaluable experience for somebody like him, now almost forty years old, who had until then never lived outside Rome. In his official residence he tried as best he could to maintain a monastic regimen with the other monks he had taken with him from Saint Andrew's, but he was of course drawn into the activities of the court, which is precisely what Pelagius intended to happen. He became godfather to the new emperor Maurice's eldest son.

The purpose of Gregory's mission was to persuade the emperor to send military and material help to Italy in face of the Lombard threat. He had little success, not because of lack of skill or effort but because of the straitened circumstances of the emperor. Recalled to Rome in 585 or 586, he returned to his monastery, where he was elected abbot. His major responsibility at this time, however, was acting as trusted adviser to Pelagius.

In the winter of 589 the Tiber overflowed its banks, as it often did, but this time it caused even more damage than usual, contaminating food supplies and causing general havoc. Pelagius died in the plague that ensued, in February 590. It came as no surprise that Gregory, long an important figure in the city, was elected his successor. The vote in his favor was virtually unanimous, an unusual occurrence, and he was enthusiastically supported by the laity. Appalled at the outcome, he declined and even appealed to Emperor Maurice, whom he of course knew well from his years in the capital, to withhold his approval. (Take note of the imperial prerogative in that regard that Gregory took for granted.) His protests were in vain, and finally in September he was consecrated bishop and assumed the papacy, an office he held for fourteen years.

With Gregory, unlike others who have protested their reluctance to assume high office, the dismay was genuine. He had no ambition to be pope. While he held the papacy he consistently referred to himself as "the servant of the servants of God," and he did not use the expression lightly. Despite his reluctance, he, in accordance with the tradition in which he had been raised, fully accepted all the responsibilities of his office and proved to be perhaps the most successful and respected pope of all times.

Although he disliked administration, he had talent for it. Building on structures already traditional, he made his bishopric into an organization efficient in providing multiple services. Seven deacons, assisted by subdeacons, had responsibility for the social services required in the seven religious districts of the city. Gregory had a list of every indigent person in the city that indicated the amount of food they were allotted by the deacons every week. A story circulated that from his resources as bishop of Rome he fed some three thousand persons a day. The story could well be true, but just as consonant with his personality is the story that every day he invited a dozen poor men to dine with him. Gregory employed a large corps of notaries and secretaries, who preserved and organized the archives, drew up official letters and documents. He dictated to them almost daily. He created a council of advisers to help him in his decision-making and to keep things running smoothly when he was unavailable.

He fulfilled in an extraordinarily effective way, in other words, the duties that had long been standard for bishops as religious figures, but he also had to tend to duties now incumbent upon them as civic officials. In Rome, as in many other cities, responsibility for the physical upkeep of the city had gradually passed to the bishop, who filled the vacuum left by the erosion of the imperial administration. Gregory found himself responsible for paying accounts due for civic services, and he sometimes ironically referred to himself as "treasurer" of the state.

Out of the revenues of the patrimony he drew money to bribe the Lombards to keep their distance and, though wary, tried to influence them in positive ways. He reorganized the far-flung and extensive estates that made up the patrimony (the church was now the largest landowner in Italy) and installed rectors in them who were directly responsible to him. With the rectors he insisted on humane and effective management. He cooperated with the generals in trying to ensure Rome's safety, sometimes paid the soldiers, and in 595 signed a treaty with the Lombards because he was more present on the scene than either the exarch or of course the emperor. He noted in a letter, "Under the pretext of being made a bishop, I have been brought back into the world, and I devote myself to secular things to a much greater extent than I recall ever having done when I was a layman."

He had good relations with the king of the Franks and of course was delighted when he heard in 591 that Recarred, king of the Visigoths in Spain, had converted from Arian Christianity to Catholicism.

His relationship to England has long been recognized as special. According to one story, he wanted to go to England himself as a missionary, but the Romans raised such a protest that he could not do as he wanted. According to another that became almost canonical, Gregory, while still a deacon, saw on a visit to the Forum in Rome some young Anglo-Saxon slaves. When he inquired who they were and was told they were "Anglos," he replied that they rather should be called angels, and later as pope he determined to see to the conversion of England. The story is a distortion of something that in fact happened. In 595 Gregory endorsed the purchase of Anglo-Saxon slaves in Gaul, probably in Marseille, so that they might be educated as Christians and then employed as missionaries in their homeland.

In 596 he sent to England an unprecedented mission of forty monks headed by Augustine, his successor as abbot of Saint Andrew's. He did this, it seems, in response to requests from the Catholic queen of Frankish origins or from her husband, King Ethelbert of Kent. In one of his letters he said that "the people of the Angles, that is, its leaders, wish to become Christians." Ethelbert converted, and shortly thereafter, it is said, ten thousand of his subjects did the same. On the way to England Augustine had been consecrated a bishop, and once in England he founded, with Ethelbert's assistance, Christ Church, the cathedral in Canterbury.

Five years later Gregory dispatched another corps of missionaries led by Melitus, who later became bishop of London, and Paulinus, later bishop of York, and he made Augustine archbishop of the English. The newly established church was to be independent of the Gallic church and the papal vicariate of Arles, but it was to be united with the Celtic British churches, a solution that eventually led to problems over whose customs were to prevail. Despite future troubles, Augustine's mission has to be counted as a remarkable success for him and for the pope who sent him. The venture was unprecedented. Never before had a pope sent out a delegation of missionaries to convert a pagan people.

Like Damasus and Leo before him and every pope since, Gregory was a staunch defender of the special prerogatives of the Apostolic See and quick to respond to any infringements of them. He was challenged on that score even in the West, where the bishops of North Africa proved particularly recalcitrant. In the East he was able to maintain a certain measure of Rome's claim to act as the appellate court in disputed ecclesiastical cases. He felt compelled to challenge the bishop of Constantinople's application to himself of the term "universal [or ecumenical] patriarch," which he thought implied an authority over the churches identical with Rome's. Emperor Maurice chided him over making such a fuss over the words, but Gregory saw implications that Maurice did not and resented his interference. Maurice, for his part, resented Gregory's dealings with the Lombards, enemies of the empire, and let his feelings be known. If there is a blot on Gregory's record, it is the satisfaction with which in 602 he greeted the news that Maurice had been murdered and his throne usurped.

Gregory continued to promote monastic life. When in 593 Maurice issued an edict forbidding soldiers to resign in order to enter a monastery, so desperate were the needs of the military, Gregory sent him a stinging criticism. Even though in his own monastery he did not adopt the Rule of Saint Benedict, he was a great admirer of "the founder of Western monasticism." He is almost certainly the author of a collection of stories about Benedict, as well as some other saints, called the *Dialogues*. The fanciful nature of many of the stories, coming from such a respected and well-educated person, has generated considerable discussion through the centuries. It is important to remember in that regard that hagiographical accounts like these already had a tradition as a catechetical genre meant to edify and instruct children and illiterate adults through entertaining stories. This does not mean that Gregory doubted the truth of the stories.

Gregory was a voluminous writer. While like Leo not an original thinker, he was an effective communicator, which meant his works were carefully studied and came to be esteemed to the point that, along with Ambrose, Jerome, and Augustine, he, as earlier mentioned, ranks as one of the four original doctors of the Latin Church. Included in the corpus of his writings are the 850 letters that survive, which is only a small percentage of his original correspondence. Even as they stand they reveal the remarkable scope of his interests and concerns. For most of them Gregory dictated the subject matter and the general approach to be taken, but highly trained notaries/secretaries put them into the technical and legally precise language the papal chancery had by this time adopted as its own.

He wrote his *Pastoral Care* in 591, shortly after he had assumed office. In it he set forth his ideal of the bishop. Preaching plays such a major role in the book that it can be considered a treatise on preaching, the only one on this central Christian ministry composed in Latin antiquity beside Saint Augustine's *On Christian Doctrine*. Both these works were read avidly in the Middle Ages until they were displaced in the twelfth and thirteenth centuries by the great outpouring on the subject by the manuals called the *Ars Praedicandi* (the Art of Preaching). Gregory's book had the special distinction of being translated into Greek, quite a compliment at a time when Greek-speaking Christians looked down on their Latin counterparts as only half-educated. It was later translated into Anglo-Saxon by King Alfred himself.

Both Gregory and Augustine assumed that preaching is based immediately on the text of Scripture and to a large extent is nothing other than a practical commentary on it. This means that it is sometimes difficult to pronounce whether one of Gregory's books is a Scriptural commentary or a collection of homilies on a book of the Bible. This is true of Gregory's extant works: forty short *Homilies on the Gospels*, twenty-two longer *Homilies on Ezechiel*, a *Commentary on 1 Samuel*, and two homilies on the *Song of Songs* (Song of Solomon). His *Moralia*, among his most popular works, is a mystical rumination on the book of Job. Although Gregorian chant bears his name, it seems almost certainly to be a somewhat later development. Its precise origins and early history are still not clear.

Since his early monastery days Gregory suffered from ill health, and by the end of his life he was so afflicted with gout that he could not walk. When he lay dying Rome, once again under siege, was in the midst of severe famine, for which the desperate population blamed the man who had done everything he could during his lifetime to alleviate such suffering. He was buried in Saint Peter's, with the fitting epitaph, "The Consul of God."

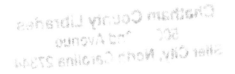

PART

II

BRINGING ORDER
OUT OF CHAOS

GREEKS, LOMBARDS, FRANKS

I n your mind's eye imagine three scenes. The first takes place in Rome about fifty years after Gregory's death. Picture for yourself a pope, desperately ill. He is in the cathedral of Saint John Lateran, where he has taken refuge as a place of sanctuary for protection against the agents of the emperor. The agents violate the sanctuary, seize the pope, strip him of his pontifical robes, and smuggle him onto a ship heading for Constantinople. Once in Constantinople, the pope, Martin I, is put on trial on trumped-up charges of treason. He is found guilty, dragged in chains through the streets, publicly flogged, and sentenced to death, which is commuted to life-imprisonment. The pope dies six months later from cold, starvation, and harsh treatment.

Fast-forward a hundred years. The second scene takes place in what was once Gaul, now the kingdom of the Franks. Picture for yourself a pope and his entourage in penitential garb in the presence of the king of the Franks. They fling themselves on the ground before the king, beseeching him, for the sake of Saint Peter, to deliver them and the people of Rome from the Lombard threat. The situation, they insist, is desperate.

The third scene. In the same location picture the same king. Picture the same pope, not in penitential garb but seated on a horse with

Pepin, king of the Franks, on foot holding the horse's bridle as if he were a mere groom, servant of the pope. The pope is Stephen II, the first pope in history to cross the Alps into northern Europe. He has sought protection by turning his efforts not to Constantinople in the East but to the kingdom of the Franks to the north and west. His plea, unlike so many identical pleas to the court of Constantinople, has been heard and will be acted upon.

These three scenes dramatically illustrate the revolution that took place in the century and a half after Gregory's death. The revolution was slow, gradual, and painful, but by the middle of the eighth century it had been accomplished. The relationship between the pope and the emperor in Constantinople that had prevailed since Constantine's day was transferred to another ruler in northern Europe. Pope Leo III will solemnize and ritually proclaim it a few decades later when in Saint Peter's basilica on Christmas Day, 800, he crowns Pepin's son Charlemagne as emperor and then kneels in homage before him.

The two centuries leading up to that momentous coronation were filled with conflict and confusion. During Gregory's time and even during Martin I's, the traditional center of authority continued to be Constantinople, still the capital of the empire, still glorying in the prestige of Constantine, and still insisting on its traditional roles regarding the Western church. In actual fact, however, its effective political and military presence in the West had come close to disappearing. Moreover, by Martin's pontificate in the middle of the seventh century, it had its hands full with war against the Persians, with Slavs raging against its authority in the Balkans, and with the new threat from Arab Muslim forces that would overrun the Middle East, North Africa, Spain, and even southern France.

Imperial impotence in providing the papacy and Rome with the protection they needed is the context that made the revolution almost inevitable. Fraying the relationship on another level were the claims by the patriarchate of Constantinople of equal, or almost equal, standing with the see of Rome, claims that the emperors implicitly or explicitly supported. The alienation between the Greek-speaking and the Latin-speaking churches that achieved its symbolic expression only in 1054 with the Great Eastern Schism had been in the making for centuries and was another factor in the alienation between the papacy and the emperors.

The doctrinal disputes that wracked the East in ways they did not wrack the West but that implicated the popes exacerbated the problem, as the case of Martin I makes clear. In the East the Monophysite heresy, which postulated Christ had only one nature, divine (just the opposite of Arianism), had for two centuries divided the church and endangered the empire, which needed to rally all parties to deal with the military threats to it. In an effort to conciliate the Monophysites while still affirming the orthodox view that Christ had both a human and a divine nature, a doctrine sprang up asserting that he had only a divine will, into which his human will was absorbed—Monothelitism. The compromise only worsened the situation, and finally in 648 Emperor Constans II forbade the use of formulas expressing either view.

In the early stages of the controversy, Pope Honorius (625–638) had embraced Monothylitism, but his successors, Pope John IV (640–642) and especially Pope Theodore I (642–649), emphatically repudiated it. Theodore, a Greek, born probably in Jerusalem, son of a bishop, had come to Rome most likely as a refugee from the Arab conquests. He excommunicated two patriarchs of Constantinople for their teaching on the subject, in retaliation for which imperial troops in Rome looted the papal treasury.

When Martin came to the throne in 649, he faced a tense situation. Born at Todi in Umbria, he had served Theodore as his *apocrisiarius* in Constantinople, where he became thoroughly familiar with the issues and with the personalities involved in the controversy. He showed his independence immediately upon being elected by going ahead with his installation without waiting for approval from Constans II.

He then organized a synod in Rome attended by over a hundred bishops as well as some Greek clerics exiled because of their stance on the doctrinal issue. The synod, one of the most theologically sophisticated to be held in the West, lasted a month. It repudiated not only Monothylitism but also Constans's decree forbidding discussion of the matter. The emperor, infuriated at these challenges to his authority, ordered his exarch to arrest Martin, but the attempt failed because of Martin's widespread support in Rome. Having learned his lesson, the emperor subsequently sent an armed force and achieved his goal, which led to Martin's bitter death in exile. The church in Rome, although it remained utterly passive during Martin's ordeal and made no effort to help him, soon afterward began to venerate him as a martyr.

The next two popes exhibited none of Martin's courage in facing the emperor, and when Constans visited Rome for twelve days in 663 Pope Vitalian (657–672) showed him every honor and orchestrated a gift-bearing procession for him and his soldiers at the tomb of Saint Peter. During his visit Constans had the Pantheon and other public buildings stripped of their bronze tiles and adornments, which were melted down to be taken back to Constantinople. Few things he did made his memory more roundly hated in Rome. When five years later Constans was brutally murdered in his bath, the Romans shed no tears.

During the next fifty years relations between the two authorities seesawed back and forth between recriminations and reconciliations. Constans's successor repudiated Monothelitism, and in 680–81 the Third Council of Constantinople affirmed the orthodox teaching. Nonetheless, in the West the conviction grew stronger and stronger that the emperors could not be trusted—they failed to honor their obligations to Rome, they espoused heresy, and they exacted heavy taxation from the West, in return for which they gave nothing. The popes, by contrast, expended tremendous care on the city, upheld orthodoxy, and bore the heaviest burden of imperial taxation.

Meanwhile an amazing thing had happened in Rome. Because of the many problems in the East—political, military, and doctrinal—more and more refugees from there flocked into the city. Pope Theodore was one of the first to come to public notice. Of the thirteen popes elected between 687 and 752 only two were Latin-speaking. These popes tended to be even more anti-imperial than their Italian counterparts, which led to further deterioration in the East-West relationship. They brought with them Greek icons and liturgical practices, which resulted in a new era of church building and decoration in Rome, some of it absolutely splendid and still visible today. Into the ceremonies, liturgical and other, of the papal court infiltrated more sumptuous and symbolically mystical elements that were reminiscent of court rituals in Constantinople and that suggested the sacredness of the person of the pope.

In 726 the emperor Leo III further damaged imperial prestige by embarking in his dominions on a campaign of icon-smashing that for a century was carried on with varying degrees of intensity by most of his successors. A complicated and bitter affair, the campaign was related to the declining fortunes of imperial prestige. The major protagonists for the iconoclasm were the emperors, beginning with Leo who, looking for a scapegoat for his troubles, found it in the sin of idolatry practiced by his people, that is, their veneration of icons.

Just how much actual image-smashing took place during the long Iconoclast period is not known, but occur it did, with the stripping of mosaics and frescoes from churches, the destruction or expropriation of altars and church furnishings, the burning of relics, and the destruction of icons outside church precincts. The phenomenon confirmed Western conviction that the emperors had once again become heresiarchs, a conviction strengthened by the laments of Greek refugees from iconoclast persecution streaming into Rome. Leo could not have done more to worsen the situation than when in 732 or 733 he, in dire financial straits, confiscated all the estates of the Patrimony of Saint Peter in Sicily and southern Italy, a major source of papal income.

The fact that the Lombards had become Catholic Christians did not quench their ambition to consolidate and expand their political domination of the northern half of the Italian peninsula and much of the southern half. By 751 they had captured Ravenna and thus put a definitive end to the exarchate, the emperor's only post in the West. In less than a year the Lombard king Aistulf appeared at the gates of Rome and demanded an annual tribute. Pope Zachary, the last of the Greek popes and the last pope to feel any allegiance to the emperor, died at this crisis point. He was succeeded by Stephen II (752–757), a Roman from a wealthy and aristocratic family, the man who would effect the great turn from Constantinople to the kingdom of the Franks.

In that kingdom earlier in the century Charles Martel, officially Mayor of the Palace, had emerged as the unquestioned political leader. A brilliant general, he in a series of wars united the Franks in a way they had never been united before, and he cast into an obscure shadow the kings in whose name he served. The Arab Muslims had by the third decade of the century conquered all of Visigoth Iberia, crossed the Pyrenees, and were threatening Poitiers. In 732 Charles defeated them decisively in the famous battle of Tours, which marked the end of Muslim advance there. Here in Martel was a political and military leader, a Catholic Christian, who had the resources to aid the ever more desperate popes.

Pope Gregory III (731–741), a Syrian by birth and equally fluent in both Latin and Greek, had seen in Charles a potential champion, and in 739 and again in 740 he sent embassies to him with impressive gifts and the offer to confer upon him the title of consul and the rank of patrician if he would but come to the aid of the church. Charles received the envoys graciously but had no interest in going to war with the Lombards, erstwhile allies of his in his northern campaigns. Into the lap of the next pope, Zachary, fell, however, a golden opportunity. Charles and Pepin, his son and successor, though they ruled the kingdom, had no official title indicating the legitimacy of the authority they exercised de facto. In 750, after Charles's death, Pepin sent a chaplain to Zachary to ask the loaded question of who deserved the title of king, to which Zachary replied that the royal title belonged to the person who performed the office. The next year Saint Boniface, the English missionary to Germany, crowned Pepin king of the Franks, and with that a new dynasty was born—with papal approval and blessing.

Zachary died the next year, but the stage had been set for Stephen's fateful trip across the Alps in 754. Stephen was elected with the Lombards at the gates of Rome. Although Aistulf withdrew, Stephen realized that the city would never be safe until some way was found to contain the Lombards, and he fully realized that it was useless to implore help from Constantinople. He turned to Pepin and asked to visit him to discuss the situation. Pepin responded with unexpected alacrity and generosity, surely in gratitude for the great benefit that Zachary had conferred upon him. He sent Bishop Chrodegang of Metz and his own brother-in-law Autcar to lead the entourage that ensured the pope's safety during the trip and accompanied him into his kingdom.

On January 6 Stephen and Pepin met at Ponthion, south of Châlons-en-Champagne in the northeast of present-day France, where

Stephen got a warm reception. The next day, the penitential procession and prostration of the pope and his party took place. Stephen soon received a response from the king that surpassed his wildest expectations. The two men continued to meet for the next several months, which culminated at Easter with a meeting near Laon. Pepin promised to aid the pope and the people of Rome in their distress, a promise he was fully capable of keeping.

But he went far beyond that. In writing he guaranteed that Saint Peter had rightful possession of the Duchy of Rome (a large territory surrounding the city), which was astounding enough. He further guaranteed possession of Ravenna and the territory of the old exarchate, and seemingly other extensive territories north and east of the duchy held by the Lombards and reaching to the exarchate. This guarantee became known as the Donation of Pepin, the origin and foundation of the Papal States. The moment marked the beginning of an era of papal history that would continue for more than eleven centuries, during which the popes claimed they were rulers in their own right over an extensive territory. It was about this time or a little later that the "Donation of Constantine," one of the most famous forgeries of all time, was composed and began to circulate. The document, mentioned earlier, was at least in part an attempt to give Pepin's action a precedent in a supposedly similar act by Constantine (see fig. 6.1).

On July 28 Stephen solemnly anointed Pepin, his wife, and his sons, putting the final seal of approval on the dynasty and proclaiming to all its legitimacy in the eyes of the church and of God. He bestowed on the king and his sons the exalted title "patrician of the Romans," a title formerly held by the exarch. Besides being an honor, the title seemed to make this Germanic king a Roman, which was the beginning of a lot of confusion for centuries.

Pepin tried to negotiate with Aistulf to hand over the territories he had promised the pope, but, not surprisingly, Aistulf refused. In a swift campaign Pepin invaded Italy and by August that same year, 754, had defeated Aistulf and forced him to comply. The pope, who had accompanied Pepin's army, returned to Rome after the campaign and received a jubilant welcome. Stephen had accomplished the impossible.

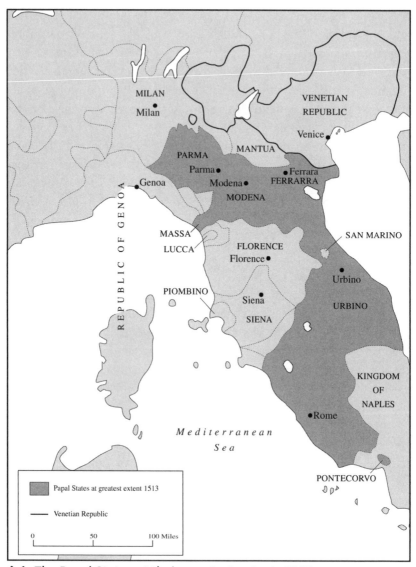

6.1: The Papal States at their greatest extent, 1513.

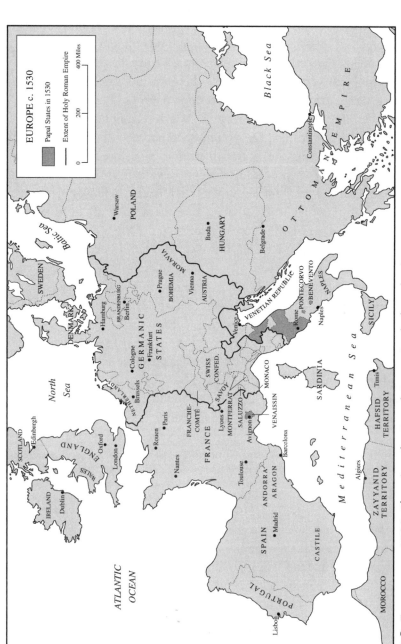

6.2: Europe, ca. 1530, Showing the Papal States in darker shading.

The celebration was, however, premature. When Pepin withdrew, Aistulf repudiated his agreement and in 756 laid siege to Rome. Stephen was forced to appeal to Pepin who, though unwilling to cross into Italy again, finally acceded to the pope's repeated entreaties. He met Aistulf's forces and defeated them. This time there was no immediate Lombard resurgence, partly because of the crushing nature of Pepin's victory and partly because Aistulf died shortly afterward, leaving no heir.

Stephen moved into the vacuum and successfully backed Desiderius of Tuscany for the Lombard throne, a gesture of support that Desiderius repaid by promising the pope several more cities, including Bologna, for his growing dominions. It was easier, however, to lay a claim to all these territories than to rule them successfully or even to hold onto them, as Leo's successor found out. When Stephen died in 757, his younger brother Paul was elected. Paul immediately, though only briefly, had to deal with an anti-pope, elected by a group of clergy unhappy with the Frankish alliance. Before he was consecrated, Paul announced his election to Pepin and used the same protocol traditionally reserved for informing the imperial exarch.

It was obvious Paul intended to follow in the path so brilliantly laid out by his brother. He had been Stephen's trusted adviser and right-hand man, but he did not enjoy Stephen's good fortune. Desiderius soon made it clear that he did not feel bound by the promises made to Stephen, and he set about trying to recover lands Pepin had donated to Saint Peter. Paul had to beg Pepin to intervene once more, but the king of the Franks, though willing to bring pressure to bear on Desiderius, did not cross the Alps himself or send troops. Both Desiderius and Paul had to compromise, an uneasy peace.

Meanwhile Emperor Constantine V, shocked that lands he considered his own had fallen into the hands of the pope, posed a menace as he tried to forge alliances with both the Lombards and the Franks. He continued the iconoclast policy initiated by Emperor Leo III, which drove more Greek-speaking refugees into Rome and confirmed once again Western perceptions of the emperors as enemies of orthodox faith. Constantine tried to sway Pepin and his bishops to his iconoclast policy, but the Franks resisted, to the great relief of the pope.

When Paul died in 767 after a reign of ten years, twice as long as his brother's, a surface calm prevailed. Rome was secure enough to allow the pope, following the example of Gregory the Great, to turn his family palace into a monastery for the benefit of refugee Greek monks, near which he built a new church, San Silvestro in Capite. But the situation in central Italy was unstable, made worse by resentment of Paul's harsh rule. Six or seven centuries after Paul's death his name began to appear on lists of saints. It still appears there today, though why he merits the honor has never been clear.

CHARLEMAGNE: SAVIOR OR MASTER?

The year is 800. Picture Saint Peter's basilica during mass on Christmas Day. At a certain point Pope Leo III takes a crown in his hands and places it on the head of Charlemagne, Pepin's son and the king of the Franks. This crown does not signify mere kingship but the imperial dignity, an interpretation confirmed immediately when the congregation, obviously prepared for what happened, broke into words reserved for the emperor, singing three times, "Charles, most pious, Augustus, crowned by God, great and peace-loving emperor, long-life and victory!" According to accounts from Charlemagne's court, the pope kissed the ground in front of him, a gesture reserved for the emperor. Papal accounts omit that important detail but noted, instead, that Leo anointed Charlemagne and called him his "excellent son."

Everything in the scene is unprecedented. A pope crowns an emperor, having seemingly determined who that emperor was to be. The new emperor is not from old Latin or Greek stock but is a Frank—that is, a German, from a race formerly referred to as barbarian. Moreover, a presumably legitimate emperor—rather, empress (Irene)—is sitting on the throne in Constantinople. She was not consulted or even informed until after the fact. When the imperial court at Constantinople learned about what had happened, it was stupefied.

Aside from an inner circle, therefore, Leo's contemporaries were altogether unprepared for what took place. The Frankish court tried to pass off the story that even Charlemagne was taken by surprise (see fig. 7.1). Although Leo's action was far from an inevitable culmination of events that began with Pope Stephen's meeting with Pepin, it obviously developed out of the close relationship Stephen had established with the king of the Franks. The implications of that relationship became ever clearer as the years passed after the death of Pope Paul, Stephen's brother.

Even as Paul lay dying, Duke Toto (or Theodore) of Nepi was plotting to manipulate affairs so as to make his brother Constantine pope. Constantine was a layman. Especially with the great lands the papacy now claimed, the papal office had become even more attractive than before to the unworthy. Immediately upon Paul's death, Toto with his three brothers seized the moment. They arranged for armed contingents to enter Rome, take possession of the Lateran, and there have Constantine acclaimed pope, after which he was hastily ordained subdeacon, deacon, priest, and, finally, bishop. The new pope informed Pepin of his election but never received a reply, probably because the king was busy conducting a campaign in Aquitaine but also possibly because he learned of the strange circumstances of the election.

The "election," in which the clergy played little or no part, was engineered by laymen for their own benefit. The clerical party in Rome regrouped around its leader, Christopher, chief notary of the city, the only important figure openly to oppose Constantine. Christopher with his son Sergius fled the city. They made their way to Pavia to appeal to Desiderius, the Lombard king, to set things right. The appeal could not have fallen on more willing ears. Desiderius was all too happy to settle the matter in a fashion favorable to himself. Lombard troops accompanied by Christopher and Sergius swooped into the city. In the ensuing confusion Toto was killed in street fighting and Constantine seized in the Lateran palace and arrested. He had been pope for a year. He was later officially deposed by a Roman synod, paraded through the

7.1: Charlemagne's coronation
Charlemagne crowned as emperor, c 1325–c1350. From "Chroniques de France ou de Saint Denis." Roy 16 G VI. Folio No: 141v.
British Library, London, Great Britain.
©HIP/Art Resource, NY

streets of Rome on the back of an ass, and imprisoned in a monastery. Many of his supporters were executed. During his imprisonment a gang attacked him and gouged out his eyes

Meanwhile, Christopher helped organize a legitimate election, at which on August 7, 768, Pope Stephen III, Christopher's candidate, was chosen. Sergius headed an embassy to the Frankish court, where Pepin's two sons, who were now co-rulers—Carloman and Charles (Charlemagne)—agreed to send a delegation of thirteen bishops to Rome for a synod to mop things up after the great confusion. This synod, held on the day after Easter 769, besides condemning the anti-pope Constantine, decreed that henceforth only the Roman clergy would elect the pope, a decision that outraged the Roman aristocracy and that, as the following centuries showed, they did not observe.

Stephen was pope, but Christopher and Sergius were the power. Unfortunately those two had earned the fierce enmity of Desiderius, who had gained nothing from responding to Christopher's plea. By a strange turn of fate, moreover, the Franks and the Lombards entered into an era of good feeling, which raised questions about how committed the Franks were to holding the line against Desiderius's encroachments on the lands given by Pepin. Stephen vacillated in his policies and, chafing under Christopher's domination, in 771 found an opportunity to betray him and his son to Desiderius and thus send them to their certain deaths. When Stephen, neither loved nor respected, died the next year, the situation in Rome and central Italy was dangerous.

The right man appeared on the scene. In striking contrast to the chaos that broke out upon Paul I's death, Hadrian, a deacon under both Paul and Stephen III, was in 772 elected easily and without notable opposition. He would have a long reign of twenty-two years (772–795). The major problem facing him, of course, was the tangled and dangerous relationship with Desiderius, now further complicated by the death of Carloman and the dispute over the succession to the Frankish throne. The nobles rallied around Charlemagne, but Carloman's widow appealed to Desiderius for help. Hadrian was, however, not at all keen on furthering the designs of a house that lately had seemed to draw back from the commitments made by Pepin.

When in the winter of 772–773 Desiderius marched on Rome and was held back only by Hadrian's threat to excommunicate him (the first time excommunication was ever used for a political goal), Hadrian secretly appealed to Charlemagne for help. Charlemagne, now secure in his brother's succession, responded favorably and tried to persuade Desiderius to abide by earlier determinations. The failure of those negotiations provided Charlemagne with the excuse he had probably been waiting for. He invaded Italy and by the next spring had captured the Lombard capital, Pavia. With this expedition Charlemagne destroyed the Lombard kingdom once and for all.

He decided to visit Rome for the Easter celebrations, during which he and Hadrian met for the first time. To show his deference for Saint Peter, Charlemagne kissed every step at the entrance to the basilica, inside which the pope awaited him. It was a fateful moment, the beginning of a long personal friendship that had its difficult moments but that in the long run served both men well. In Saint Peter's on April 6, 774, Charlemagne signed a document that not only confirmed everything in Pepin's original Donation but added to it vast territories formerly held by the Lombard king. Hadrian's understanding of the significance of what happened is revealed in the fact that he now began to have coins struck with his own effigy on them, rather than the emperor's, and to date them accordingly, that is, according to the years of his pontificate. In Hadrian's mind there was no doubt that he was a king in his own right.

Once Charlemagne mopped up his campaign against Desiderius a few months later, he thought better of his open-handedness and, with Desiderius his prisoner, not only took for himself the title of King of the Lombards but held onto Lombard territory included in his donation to Hadrian. Nonetheless, Hadrian, who was in no position to protest, still ended up a winner, and he knew it. Charlemagne made two more visits to Rome during Hadrian's lifetime, the occasions of further and reasonably amicable negotiations.

The two men worked especially well together in Charlemagne's campaign to reform and bring order to the Frankish church. For both men this meant in large part making it conform to canonical standards and liturgical usages that prevailed in Rome. Hadrian sent Charlemagne an important collection of canon law, biased of course toward papal claims of primacy, and also a sacramentary, a book containing the prayers and rubrics for mass, which helped standardize Frankish liturgical practice. The net result was a Frankish church more Roman than before.

In Rome itself Hadrian built, restored, or embellished a number of churches. He repaired the city walls and completely rebuilt four great aqueducts. Under him, with Charlemagne's help the city enjoyed a peace and prosperity it had not known for a long time. In keeping with the long-standing tradition of special care the papacy felt for the poor of the city, Hadrian established a system whereby a hundred people were fed daily, and he provided resources for other institutions dedicated to the same aim.

On one religious issue Hadrian and Charlemagne or his court had a misunderstanding. In 780 emperor Leo IV died and was succeeded by his young son, which meant a regency under Leo's widow, the empress Irene. The empress was a determined enemy of the iconoclasts. She besought Hadrian's cooperation in convoking a council at Nicaea to assert the legitimacy and praiseworthiness of image veneration. Hadrian responded enthusiastically. He did not object, please note, to the fact that a woman called the council.

Nicaea II met in 787, reaffirmed the traditional practice and teaching, and in its decree on the subject incorporated a document drawn up with much care by Hadrian's curia in preparation for the council. The council marked a rare moment of accord between East and West during these centuries. Charlemagne was insulted that he had not been invited to send bishops to the council. When Hadrian sent him a poor Latin translation of the council's decrees, Charlemagne and members of his court were dismayed when, because of the faulty Latin of the text, they came to the conclusion that a council had ratified image worship instead of image veneration. But even this misunderstanding did not seriously damage Charlemagne's relationship with the pope, at whose death in 795 he was said to grieve as if he had lost a brother or a child.

Leo III, a priest of humble origin who had risen high in ecclesiastical rank, was elected pope the day Hadrian died and consecrated bishop the next day. The speed with which these events took place suggests a carefully planned preemptive strike by his supporters against other contenders. What is certain is that from the beginning Leo had enemies among the Roman aristocracy who were determined to unseat him. It is ironic, therefore, that, like Hadrian before him, he had an unusually long pontificate that lasted almost twenty-one years, 795–816.

He sent word of his election to Charlemagne along with the keys to Saint Peter's tomb and the banner of Rome, seemingly sensing at this early date that he would need the protection of the king of the Franks. Charlemagne replied politely but let the pope know that the papal office was strictly spiritual, whose essential duty was not much more than praying for the good of the church and for its protector, himself. "Your task, Holy Father, is to raise your arms to God in prayer as Moses did to ensure the victory of our arms." Many subsequent emperors (and kings) subscribed to this understanding of the pope's role in the church.

Four years later, on April 25, 799, Leo's enemies staged a vicious coup against him. While the pope was leading a procession through the streets of Rome on the way to Saint Peter's, a gang led by a nephew of Pope Hadrian attacked him, threw him from his horse, beat him, and attempted unsuccessfully to gouge out his eyes and cut out his tongue. Leo somehow lived to tell the tale but then was accused of adultery and perjury, deposed, and imprisoned in a monastery. He managed to escape and make his way to Paderborn to plead his cause with Charlemagne. Not to be outmaneuvered, his enemies sent envoys to the king to justify their actions and to lay out a list of charges against the pope in which the most serious were adultery and perjury.

Charlemagne, advised by the learned monk Alcuin, proceeded cautiously, though his entourage was inclined to believe the accusations. He had Leo conducted back to Rome, protected by guards, where an investigation was carried out by Frankish agents that tended to confirm the major charges. But the matter was again referred to Charlemagne, who decided to come to Rome himself to settle the affair. He arrived in late November 800, and was greeted with great pomp that Leo was able to orchestrate. Charlemagne convoked a meeting of Roman and Frankish bishops, abbots, and notables to review the case once again and then to decide the fate of the pope, but the assembly demurred at the prospect of sitting in judgment on a pope.

At that point Leo volunteered to take a solemn oath to purge himself of the charges, and this was the solution agreed upon. On December 23, in the presence of a large and solemn assembly, Leo swore his oath, whose text survives to this day. The emperor was satisfied. Leo was thus vindicated against his enemies. Two days later the extraordinary event took place in Saint Peter's that gave the world a new emperor.

From that time forward until Charlemagne's death in 814, Leo, though secure in his position, knew his place. He acted more as Charlemagne's agent in Italy than as an independent bishop, let alone as the bishop of Rome. On one crucial point, however, he resisted the emperor's wishes. The Frankish church had inserted an addition into the venerable and sacrosanct Creed formulated at the first council of Nicaea, 325, and somewhat elaborated upon by the next council, Constantinople I. Not only was such tampering unprecedented, it was also expressly forbidden by the council of Ephesus, 431.

The Creed said simply that the Holy Spirit proceeded "from the Father." The Franks had added "and from the Son," the famous *filioque* that would later cause such contention between the Greek and Latin churches when the West later accepted it into the Creed. The problem was not only the doctrine of the *filioque* but as well the unilateral and illegitimate insertion into the Creed. When in 809 Charlemagne sent to Leo the opinion of his bishops favoring the *filioque*, Leo responded sharply and reprimanded the bishops.

Leo, despite his subservience to the emperor he had created and his continued unpopularity with much of the Roman clergy, showed himself an able administrator of the old papal patrimony. He further strengthened the network of assistance to the poor and needy in the city and took the initiative in constructing and restoring churches and in adorning some of them lavishly. He constructed a great hall for the Lateran palace that could be used both for social occasions, like banquets, or as a place to conduct business that required a large assembly.

When Charlemagne died in 814, Leo lost his protector. He at that point discovered a serious conspiracy to assassinate him. By this time, however, he had enough control of the city to rout out the conspirators and bring them to trial. A large number of those found guilty were executed—sources give the almost certainly exaggerated figure of three hundred.

Leo himself did not have long to live. He did not die a beloved pope. The Romans were ready for somebody less harsh and more conciliatory, whom they found in Stephen IV (816–817), a Roman aristocrat. The new pope was firmly devoted to the house of Charlemagne. Almost immediately after his election he made the people of Rome swear allegiance to Louis the Pious, Charlemagne's son. Shortly thereafter he crossed the Alps to anoint and crown Louis at the cathedral in Rheims. Although neither he nor his predecessor had a voice in who was to succeed Charlemagne, this anointing was important because it gave rise to the conviction that the exercise of full imperial authority was not legitimate without some form of papal recognition.

During his sojourn at Rheims Stephen and Louis held long conversations together. The newly crowned emperor renewed his commitment to defend the Apostolic See and assure canonical elections of the pope. Stephen also won from the new emperor a pardon for the conspirators against Leo III whom Louis's father had exiled in 800 after the pope vindicated himself by his oath. He returned to Rome laden with lavish gifts from Louis, but he died three months after reaching the city.

Between the pontificate of Stephen II and Stephen IV, a period of some sixty-five years, a politico-ecclesiastical revolution of almost titanic proportions had occurred with ramifications almost beyond counting. Why and how it happened is clear, but one aspect of its ramifications requires comment: the popes' easy acceptance of responsibility for the vast territories included in Pepin's Donation. Unfortunately, no pope from the era left us a document in which he spelled out the reasons for this remarkable acquiescence. The rationale for it must be patched together through inference and consideration of circumstances.

From the appearance around this time of the Donation of Constantine it can be inferred that, as mentioned, contemporaries of the fateful decision also required justification or explanation. The forgery originated in Rome probably sometime in the mid-eighth century but certainly no later than 850. It purported to be a grant from Constantine to Pope Silvester in which the emperor conferred upon the pope and his successors primacy over all other churches and political dominion not only over Rome but over the entire West. In it Constantine also offered the pope the imperial crown, which he humbly refused. Later popes used the document to validate some of their claims and, although doubts about the Donation's authenticity were sometimes expressed, it was not definitively unmasked as a forgery until the fifteenth century.

Unquestionably among the reasons that prompted Stephen II to accept Pepin's gift with so much enthusiasm was that it promised to give the papacy resources to deal with the Lombard threat, resources that were vastly increased by the promises Charlemagne later made as he dismantled the Lombard kingdom. The popes saw what developed into the Papal States as a line of defense for the city of Rome itself, a buffer state that could absorb the shock of aggression against it.

The popes surely also saw their role over the new territories as consonant with their traditional oversight of the extensive and scattered lands of the old papal patrimony. From that perspective the new situation was just more of the same—lots more! Just as the patrimony provided revenues to allow the popes to fulfill their many and seemingly ever expanding responsibilities, so would these new lands.

Not to be discounted, finally, is a persuasion made explicit by a few later popes that Saint Peter was pleased to be in charge through his vicar of an earthly kingdom. That is a mentality so far removed from the twenty-first century that it is difficult to take it seriously, but the evidence for it is clear. One thing is absolutely certain: the popes came to look upon the Papal States as a sacred trust which, along with ambition and greed, explains why they clung to them for the next millennium with such uncompromising tenacity.

8

THEIR DARKEST HOUR

I n the first half of the ninth century during the reign of Charlemagne and even the reign of his son Louis the Pious, the Christian West looked perhaps as well as it had for two centuries. In
Rome a series of mostly short-lived and not particularly noteworthy
popes succeeded one another, sometimes encumbered by the now
rather frequently disputed elections, but they did not have to deal with
major upheavals or crises. Charlemagne's empire by the end of his life
extended from southern France as far east as Saxony and south into
Italy. His cultural and religious achievements were just as impressive.
Although he himself probably could not write, he gathered in his court
such a brilliant group of scholars, at whose head was the great Alcuin,
that it was the center of what is called the Carolingian Renaissance.

Charlemagne's zeal for a literate clergy devoted to their pastoral
tasks was extraordinary. He assumed without question that it was his
prerogative to appoint bishops and especially archbishops, whose loyalty to himself was essential for holding the empire together. While
these prelates' fidelity was the nonnegotiable requirement, he wanted
men who were worthy of their office, and he acted accordingly. He
was just as concerned with the lower clergy, whom he insisted be able
to read, and even possibly understand, the Latin of the mass and the

sacraments, and he wanted them to conduct themselves in ways appropriate to their status. He encouraged bishops to hold synods to determine disciplinary matters, most of which concerned the behavior of the clergy. When Charlemagne died in 814, his son Louis carried these policies forward and, as his sobriquet "Pious" suggests, was more willing than his father to take guidance from bishops.

Louis was incapable, however, of holding his father's empire together, built as it was on the strength of Charlemagne's character, his military prowess, and the personal loyalty he elicited and demanded. Louis began as early as 817 to partition administration of the empire among his sons, but only after his death was a somewhat stable tripartite division agreed upon by the Treaty of Verdun, 843: Louis the German got the eastern portion of Charlemagne's domains, essentially Teutonic in speech and blood and extending from the Rhine River to the easternmost frontier. Charles the Bald got the westernmost part, basically Romance in speech and roughly covering the area of later medieval France. Lothair got the "middle kingdom," the amorphous territory between the other two stretching down into Italy, and he got as well the titles of emperor and king of Italy.

The Treaty of Verdun is crucially important because in its provisions it sketched the territories that later developed into France, Germany, and the disputed areas between them that led to so many wars. The kingdoms developed, moreover, their own royal dynasties, with which the popes had to deal. To the individual bearing the imperial title the popes showed special deference, but they conducted themselves according to the effective power any one of them held. The days of a single ruler like Pepin, Charlemagne, or even Louis the Pious were over for good. When Lothair died in 855, for instance, his lands were in turn parceled out among his sons.

Just as the political scene became more complicated, Nicholas I emerged as the most capable and important pope since Hadrian, a person of truly international significance. His pontificate (858–867) is a high-water mark for the century, and it stands in contrast to the depths into which the papacy soon sank. Born in Rome into an important family, Nicholas was a trusted confidant of his predecessor, Benedict III. He was elected easily in the presence and with the support of the new emperor, Louis II, son of Lothair, who had sped to Rome to be present for the occasion. Louis and other rulers soon learned that Nicholas was not only a person of commanding personality but somebody who had an exalted view of papal authority even in relationship to secular authorities like themselves. He would not tolerate actions on anybody's part that he thought infringed on the powers Christ bequeathed to Peter and to Peter's successors.

On a trumped-up charge of incest, Louis's brother, Lothair II, king of Lorraine, repudiated his wife Teutberga, who had failed to provide him with an heir. A synod of bishops at Aachen in 862 and another at Metz the next year upheld the king and ratified his new marriage to his mistress, by whom he had already begot three children. Teutberga appealed to Nicholas. When the archbishops of Cologne and Trier brought to Rome the synodal decrees in favor of Lothair, Nicholas rejected them out of hand and then deposed and excommunicated the two archbishops for what he considered aiding and abetting bigamy. At that point emperor Louis took up his brother's and the archbishops' cause and marched on Rome with his troops, forcing the pope to take refuge in Saint Peter's. Even with this extreme measure Louis was unable to make the pope budge. Nicholas stood his ground, Louis did not dare kill him, and Lothair was therefore forced to take back his wife.

Nicholas took on other archbishops who he believed misused their authority, including Hincmar of Rheims, the most powerful archbishop north of the Alps, who had been as opposed to the repudiation of Teutberga as had Nicholas. Hincmar, however, deposed Bishop Rothad of Soissons and tried to block his appeal to Rome for justice. Nicholas reinstated Rothad and, when Hincmar resisted the decision, threatened to suspend him from celebrating mass. Hincmar backed down. The pope reproached John, the archbishop of Ravenna, who acted in ways that indicated independence from the jurisdiction of Rome. John made matters worse by seizing lands that Nicholas considered papal. The pope excommunicated, deposed, and then reinstated him only after he promised to behave properly in the future.

There were other important instances of Nicholas's asserting his authority over archbishops in the West and of his coming to the aid of bishops who challenged them. He possibly found grounds for his actions in what became known as "The False Decretals," another medieval forgery. These documents, a purported collection of canon law, strengthened the rights of bishops against their archbishops and emphasized the authority of the papacy as the guarantor of those rights. They had been generated in France about the year 850 by clerics opposed to Hincmar and, more generally, resentful of the increased authority with which Charlemagne had invested archbishops at bishops' expense. At the time a few persons challenged their authenticity, but for most of the Middle Ages the documents were considered genuine. It is not absolutely certain Nicholas knew of them, but they certainly bore a message he and his successors were ready to hear: final authority in the church flowed from the papacy.

Nicholas's most famous, important, and controversial exercise of papal authority came with his action against Photius, patriarch of Constantinople, whose predecessor, Ignatius, had been deposed at the instigation of the emperor. Nicholas sent envoys to Constantinople to investigate, refused to recognize Photius, whose election was in fact irregular, and then at a synod held at the Lateran in 863 demanded Photius step down. When emperor Michael III protested, Nicholas propounded to him all the exalted prerogatives the papacy enjoyed over the whole church. Further complications ensued. In 867 Photius in turn held a synod in Constantinople that deposed and excommunicated Nicholas, who died before the news reached Rome. For the Greek-speaking church the so-called Photian Schism became the burning symbol of popes badly overreaching themselves, and it became another of the classic sore points in the relationship between the two churches.

For Nicholas's immediate successors the problems with Constantinople paled before a new menace. The Saracens had not only captured Sicily but had moved up the peninsula so as to threaten Rome itself. John VIII (872–882), who succeeded the elderly and vacillating Hadrian II, had been a close collaborator with Nicholas and like him had high views of his office. But his back was against the wall as he fought off the Saracens and at the same time tried to protect himself from the intrigues and plots of power-hungry nobles within the city. John turned desperately from one ruler to another for assistance against the Saracens, but their promises of aid were empty. He had to take military matters into his own hands. He reinforced the walls around the Vatican area of the city built by his predecessor, Leo IV, built a defensive wall around Saint Paul's basilica, and founded and took command of a papal fleet.

His most lasting claim to fame is his steadfast defense of Saint Methodius, missionary and then archbishop of Pannonia in south-central Europe. Methodius and his brother Cyril were later celebrated as the "Apostles to the Slavs." Clerics reported to the pope that the archbishop sang the liturgy "in a barbaric tongue." John summoned Methodius to Rome and was soon convinced that he was on the right track. He then authorized him to translate the Bible into Slavonic and, more astounding, to sing mass in that language. "He who made three main languages—Hebrew, Greek, and Roman—also made all the other languages to sing his praise and glory." For the first and the last time until Vatican Council II, a pope ratified a liturgy not in Latin.

It is almost certain that John VIII was murdered by one or more of his own clerics—poisoned and then clubbed to death, according to a credible report. If true, this horrible crime can stand as the formal opening of the darkest period in all papal history. Bereft of effective support from powerful protectors from outside the peninsula, the popes became ever more victims of the ambition and greed of the local nobility. Even during this scandalous era that lasted well over a hundred years, there were some decent and hard-working popes, but they were outnumbered by mediocrities, toadies, or much worse. Papacies were ominously short, and the list of popes who died violent or suspicious deaths ominously long.

There were some notorious and well-documented cases. The enemies of Pope Stephen VI (896–897) seized him, stripped him of his papal insignia, cast him into jail, where he was strangled to death. Leo V, pope for a few months in 903, suffered an almost identical fate—seized, thrown into a dungeon where he was promptly murdered. Just a few years later John X saw his brother murdered before his eyes in the Lateran cathedral. The next year his enemies seized him, cast him into prison where they suffocated him with a pillow. In 998 the anti-pope John XVI, incredible though it might seem, survived having his eyes gouged out, his tongue cut out, and his nose, lips, and hands hacked off, after which he was dragged through the streets of Rome and thrown into prison.

Nothing in this period reveals more undeniably the depths to which the situation had sunk than the macabre trial of Pope Formosus, which is sometimes called "the cadaver synod." When Stephen VI (who as just mentioned himself had a bad end) became pope, he had the corpse of his hated enemy Formosus exhumed, placed on a throne in his full pontifical robes, and made to stand trial for perjury, for coveting the papacy, and for many other crimes. Formosus replied to the charges as best he could through the mouth of a deacon standing beside his rotting corpse. His defense was, not surprisingly, judged inadequate, and he was convicted. Three fingers of his right hand, the ones used for blessing, were hacked off, his robes were stripped from him, and his body thrown into the Tiber (see fig. 8.1).

8.1: Cadaver Synod
Laurens, Jean-Paul (1838–1921). Pope Formosus (891–896) and Stephen VI (896–897). Ca. 1870. Oil on canvas, 100 x 152 cm. Photo: Gérard Blot. Pope Stephen had the body of his predecessor exhumed and presented before a Roman synod in 897. Musée des Beaux-Arts, Nantes, France.
©Rénuion des Musées Nationaux / Art Resource, NY

The plots, counterplots, bribes, threats, choreographed violence, and shifting alliances that centered on the prize of the papacy in Rome and central Italy during this period almost defy description. Control of Rome and its bishopric was the goal of many factions and families, but the counts of Tusculum (Frascati) deserve special mention because of the control long exercised by Marozia, the notorious matriarch of the family. She was the daughter of the Roman consul Theophylact, count of Tusculum, and Theodora, the real power in the city. At the age of fifteen Marozia allegedly became the mistress of Pope Sergius III (904–911), by whom she had a son, the future Pope John XI. The allegations about her relationship to Sergius have been largely discounted, but it is certain that she was John's mother. There is, in fact, good reason to think John's father was Marozia's husband, Alberic I, duke of Spoleto.

When Alberic died, Marozia married again. By 920 she had become almost omnipotent in Rome. She and her husband organized the revolt against Pope John X mentioned above and saw to his murder. She then maneuvered the election of the next two popes—Leo VI and Stephen VII. By the time Stephen died, her son had reached his majority, and the moment of her greatest triumph arrived. She secured his election as John XI (931–936 or 937). He was in his early twenties.

This great coup ended badly, however, for both mother and son. Upon the death of her second husband, Marozia married a third time. Alberic II, her son by her first husband, at least a half-brother of the pope, led a revolt against the new couple and in 932 stormed the Castel Sant'Angelo in Rome where his mother, her spouse, and the pope were installed. He easily captured the stronghold and took his mother and the pope prisoners. (Marozia's husband had managed to escape.)

Alberic II eventually released John XI from prison but kept him under house arrest until his death. Nothing further is known about Marozia. From this point forward Alberic II dominated the city and secured the successive election of all his candidates as pope—Leo VII, Stephen VIII, Marinus II, and Agapitus II. On his deathbed, 954, he still exerted enough authority and instilled enough fear successfully to oblige the Romans to elect his bastard son Octavian pope when Agapitus died, which happened the next year. Octavian, barely eighteen years old, was duly chosen. For only the second time in history up to that point, the pope-elect took a new name for himself. (The first was Mercury, 553, who because his name was that of a pagan god changed it to John.) Octavian is known in history as John XII (955–964).

With John XII the papacy took another of its unexpected turns and, not because of any virtue on John's part, it began a slow and very uneven ascent out of the scandalous depths in which it wallowed. The turn was due, as had been the case two centuries earlier, to an intervention from northern Europe. Emperor Otto I descended into Italy to set things straight. His intervention initiated another century in which the Roman emperor in the West (the German king!) would act as protector, savior, senior partner, and master of the popes.

The years between 850 and 950 had been catastrophic not simply for the papacy but for the West more generally. Not only had Charlemagne's empire disintegrated and public order collapsed as a result, but from south, north, and east external enemies battered Europe. The Muslims, driven back from France into Spain, kept fighting and, as mentioned, launched aggressive campaigns from Sicily and southern Italy northward. As early as 846 their fleet carrying five hundred horsemen sailed up the Tiber and sacked Rome. The Norsemen or Vikings set out in a series of devastating raids into the coasts of northwest Germany, the Low Countries, Spain, England, and France. Around the year 843 they sailed up the Seine and repeatedly attacked and looted Paris and Rouen. At about the same time the Magyars pressed against the eastern frontier and eventually reached as far west as Augsburg.

The Saracen raids against Italy would continue intermittently for centuries, but in the next century they lost their strongholds in Sicily and the southern part of the peninsula. The Norsemen, perhaps the fiercest of the lot, were also the most quickly assimilated. In 911 Rollo, one of their leaders, was invested with a duchy, and the Norsemen became Normans, their duchy Normandy. Then in "France," the western kingdom, a new dynasty took over in 956 that its first king, the capable Hugh Caput, put on a new path to prosperity and stability. Just a little later in the east Otto, duke of Saxony, had been able to gain control of the factions warring with one another off and on for a century. Then in 955 he decisively defeated the Magyars and turned them back. That sealed his control. Although he was not related to Charlemagne by blood, he saw himself as his successor.

Thus by the middle of the tenth century the external enemies of Europe had been contained, assimilated, or rolled back, and an era of strong and capable rulers in northern Europe dawned. Most of these rulers were genuinely concerned for the well-being of the church and felt a responsibility to promote it. Among them the German kings, beginning with Otto I, would for the next hundred years be especially important for the measures they took to put the papacy back on its feet.

John XII scandalized even the Roman society of his day with his addiction to pleasure and debauchery. His political situation gradually deteriorated in the city, largely because, with his powerful father dead, he lacked the resources to defend it and himself. His enemies capitalized on his weakness, and by 959 his situation was desperate. He appealed to Otto for help and in return promised him the imperial crown. It seems almost like a replay of the drama enacted by Leo III and Charlemagne a hundred and fifty years earlier. There was, however, a significant difference. While the papal legates dutifully transmitted to Otto the pope's message, they also expressed disapproval of his conduct.

Otto gladly accepted the invitation, arrived in Italy with his troops, and easily brought it under his domination. On January 31, 962, John imposed the imperial crowns on the heads of Otto and his wife Adelaide in Saint Peter's basilica. With that ceremony the Holy Roman Empire was born, even though it was not named that until centuries later. From this time forward, in any case, the imperial dignity would be linked with the German crown. While Otto was in Rome, he confirmed the Donations of Pepin and Charlemagne, but he stipulated that after a pope was freely elected he was to take an oath of fealty to him and his successors as emperor. In Otto's presence a synod was held that admonished John for his behavior and settled some matters concerning the German church.

Both Otto and John, though distrustful of each other, had every right to be pleased. But upon Otto's departure John connived with some of the new emperor's enemies, which brought Otto back to Rome to preside over a synod that deposed John, who with the papal treasury in hand had fled the city, and installed another in his place. The emperor this time laid down that in the future the consent of the emperor was required for the validity of a papal election With this stipulation he raised the stakes considerably.

Otto departed. John had sufficient resources to retake the city and through a synod, over which he presided in Saint Peter's in February 964, he deposed the anti-pope and had himself reinstated. But his triumph was short-lived. A few months later he suffered a stroke, allegedly while committing an act of adultery, and died almost immediately. He was about twenty-seven years old.

SAVING THE PAPACY FROM ITSELF

Almost in the very same year Rollo became duke of Normandy and his followers became Christian, William the Pious, duke of Aquitaine, founded the monastery of Cluny in Burgundy in east-central France near Mâcon. The monastery and the network of monasteries in its tradition that eventually spread widely in Western Europe were an especially powerful engine in a religious revival that positively affected the higher ranks of society. Important though Cluny was, it was only one in a new outburst of monastic fervor that would last for two centuries. This phenomenon was now possible because of the newly stable political conditions that began to take hold by the middle of the century after the containment of the Saracens, Huns, and Norsemen.

Those conditions were also the prerequisite for a resurgence of scholarship that paralleled the religious revival. At Rheims around the year 975, for instance, the monk Gerbert d'Aurillac had a mastery not only of the logical works of Aristotle, translated into Latin long ago by Boethius, but of the classical poets and dramatists Virgil, Statius, Terence, Juvenal, Persius, and Horace. Gerbert later became Pope Silvester II (999–1003), appointed by emperor Otto III, an instance of a rare break in the hold of the Roman families on the papacy during this period and of the reforming aspirations of the emperors. Otto III, by the way, openly expressed his doubts about the authenticity of the Donation of Constantine.

Important for church life was the upsurge in the study of canon law. Burchard, bishop of Worms for twenty-five years from 1000 to 1025, compiled an especially important collection entitled the *Decretum*. As these sources were studied, discrepancies between present practice and earlier traditions emerged. Three points in those traditions became ever clearer: celibacy was the standard discipline for the clergy; simony, especially the buying of church offices, was a crime severely punished; and bishops were freely elected by the clergy of the city.

Duke William was precocious in stipulating that the monks of Cluny freely elect their abbot rather than have him imposed by an outside authority, lay or clerical. This stipulation was extraordinary for an era in which the custom in that feudal society was by now well established that bishops and abbots were vassals under a liege lord who "nominated" them for their office. Free election of the abbot was surely responsible for the remarkable series of abbots who ruled Cluny and who for the next century and a half became the leading religious figures in Europe, far more important in that regard than any pope.

The secular leaders in Europe had not the slightest inclination to give up their right of nomination for the higher ecclesiastical offices. Bishops and abbots were great landholders and could muster badly needed troops. Their cooperation was essential for defense against outside enemies and for maintaining internal peace. But now a keen sense of responsibility for seeing that bishops and abbots were worthy spread among dukes, counts, and kings. Nowhere was this truer than in the German, that is, the imperial court. At the beginning of the next century Emperor Henry II appointed bishops and abbots in as autocratic a manner as any medieval ruler before him, but he made sure, as best he could, that they performed their religious duties faithfully and were a credit to him and to the church. No more eloquent testimony to his service of the church is possible than his canonization in 1146 and his wife Kunigunde's in 1200.

Although the papacy in Rome was still in the hands of local families, the quality of its occupants had risen. Henry had nothing to do with the election of Pope Benedict VIII (1012–1024), but the two men formed a partnership in which both benefited. Benedict, a member of the Theophylact family, was elected while still a layman. More a politician and leader of armies than a spiritual leader, he nonetheless admired the abbots of Cluny and cooperated with the emperor at an important synod at Pavia, 1022, that imposed drastic penalties on subdeacons, deacons, and priests who married or kept concubines. Henry incorporated measures like these into the imperial code, a sign of things to come. He also persuaded Benedict to incorporate the *filioque* into the Creed in the masses celebrated in Rome, a northern innovation that until then the popes had resisted.

When Benedict died in 1024, his family connived and bribed electors to get his younger brother elected, who in a single day was elevated from layman to pope, bishop of Rome. John XIX, not quite as bad a pope as the circumstances of his election suggest, crowned the next emperor, Conrad II, who treated him with the disdain he deserved. Upon John's death in 1032 the family, never at a loss for candidates, bribed the electorate to have a nephew of the two former popes elected. Still a layman, the pope-elect, Benedict IX, went through the same rushed series of ceremonies comprising ordination as subdeacon, deacon, and priest that culminated in his consecration as bishop of Rome, successor to Saint Peter. He was probably in his late twenties.

Even with allowances for exaggeration in the contemporary accounts, Benedict's personal life was violent and dissolute. He was, nonetheless, a competent executive and managed church affairs with some success until in 1044 a revolt against him broke out in Rome, partly caused by his scandalous behavior and partly by resentment of his family's dominance and arrogance. Things went rapidly from bad to worse, and by 1046 two other men laid claim to the papacy— Gregory VI and Silvester III. At this moment emperor Henry III arrived in Italy with his entourage to receive from the pope the imperial crown. Young, a skillful leader of armies, and as sincerely devout as his namesake, Henry II, he surrounded himself with learned and dedicated churchmen.

The great turning point had at last arrived. The beginnings of a thorough rehabilitation of the papacy date from Henry III's actions in 1046, when the seeds for the Gregorian Reform were sown. Upon arriving in central Italy and learning of the situation, Henry convoked in December 1046, a synod of bishops at Sutri, a small town near Viterbo north of Rome. To it he summoned the three contenders. Once he heard the cases, he through the synod deposed all three and nominated a reforming bishop from his entourage, Suitger from Bamberg in Bavaria, who took the name Clement II. The new pope had no relationship with the papacy-hungry Roman nobility, and his nomination challenged their hold on the office. He was above and beyond the contending parties. Enthroned in Saint Peter's on Christmas Day 1046, he at the same ceremony placed the imperial crowns on the heads of Henry and his wife Agnes. Two weeks later he held a synod that issued sharp legislation against simony, especially the buying and selling of ecclesiastical offices—such as the papacy.

This was certainly not the first time an emperor appointed a pope. What was different this time was that Clement was the first in an almost continuous series of reformers that would break the prevailing pattern. By choosing the name of one of the immediate successors of Peter, the author of the famous letter to the church at Corinth, Clement insinuated a determination to return to an earlier and purer model for the conduct of the papacy. Clement's appointment reveals another change taking place: until about this time only priests, deacons, or laymen were elected bishop of Rome because an ancient tradition stipulated bishops not move from their original see to another. But Clement was bishop of Bamberg.

Clement died after less than a year, and Benedict IX tried again to reinstate himself with a powerful military force. The emperor, in no mood to tolerate the nonsense, nominated another German confidant, the bishop of Brixen, and successfully intimidated Benedict into surrender. The new pope, Damasus II, was in office only twenty-three days when he died, allegedly of poison but probably of malaria. With that came Henry's most momentous nomination, his cousin, Bruno, a skilled military leader who also happened to be bishop of Toul. As Pope Leo IX, Bruno would be one of the most important popes in the whole of the Middle Ages. The five years of his papacy, 1049–1054, were decisive.

Although named by the emperor, he insisted that he would not enter Rome until the clergy and people accepted him, an important gesture toward the old tradition of free election. He arrived at the city in pilgrim garb, saying he had come to venerate the tombs of Peter and Paul. The city in fact received him almost with jubilation, and he was ready to begin. His name choice, like Clement II's, recalled a venerated pope from an earlier age, Leo the Great.

The new pope hit the road. He went to France and three times to Germany, as well as to southern and northern Italy, thus dramatizing the international scope of the papal office. He broke the image of popes enmeshed in the politics of the Duchy of Rome. Almost everywhere he went he held synods. Leo had a program to sell that consisted essentially in three points: reinstate free elections to ecclesiastical offices, eliminate simony in all its forms, and insist on celibacy for the clergy. The synod in Mainz, 1049, over which both he and emperor Henry III presided, denounced two of the abuses—simony and clerical marriage.

That same year he held an important synod at Rheims. The French king, anticipating Leo's insistence on free elections, forbade his bishops to attend, so that only twenty showed up. Leo nonetheless plowed ahead. The first two canons of the synod were explicit about elections and simony: "[1] That no one shall be advanced to the rule of a church without election by clergy and people. [2] That no one should buy or sell sacred orders or ecclesiastical offices or churches." The pope demanded to know of the bishops and abbots present if any of them had received their office through any exchange of money, and he proceeded to denounce and depose those who had. This was an extraordinarily bold show of determination to initiate a new order of things.

The three points in the reform program, however, flew in the face of the social reality of the day. Clerical concubinage and even marriage was widespread and in many places accepted as normative. And lay magnates, while they might pay lip-service to free election, understood it as a routine confirmation of their candidate. Everybody was ready to denounce simony as long as it was an abstract concept but balked when the stigma was attached to accepted practices. Leo's program, the distillation of reform sentiments brewing in certain circles for a long time, could not but run into trouble.

Leo gathered around himself other like-minded reformers who would provide continuity with the program for the next several pontificates. Among them was Saint Peter Damian, a monk, an ascetic, a fearless preacher against simony, and an expert in canon law. Another was Humbert of Silva Candida. He too was a monk but, unlike Damian who was Italian, was from Lorraine and had come down to Rome with Leo in 1049. Learned, but an uncompromising zealot in moral and canonical matters, he caused more problems than he solved. The youngest and eventually the most important by far was Hildebrand, a native of Tuscany, who later became Pope Gregory VII. Leo also fostered close relations with religious leaders elsewhere, most notably with the great and saintly Hugh, abbot of Cluny.

Besides trying to implement a program of internal reform, Leo faced two external problems. The most immediate was a new danger from south of Rome. The Normans had successfully driven the Muslims out of Sicily and moved up the southern part of the peninsula to occupy it as their own. Although they were now Christians, they were still fiercely bellicose and threatened Rome, its environs, and lands Rome claimed in the south. Leo himself led an ill-fated military campaign against them in 1053, which ended with him being taken prisoner for nine months and yielding to Norman demands. Even so, for the moment Rome itself was safe.

Constantinople laid claims to southern Italy, and against the Normans Leo sought the East as an ally. In 1054 he unfortunately confided leadership of the mission to Constantinople to the hot-headed Humbert, who brimmed over with ideas about the absolute superiority of Latin discipline and practices and about the supreme power of the bishop of Rome over all churches. He inevitably clashed with the patriarch of Constantinople, Caerularius, and pronounced against him an excommunication. The patriarch, as bigoted against the West as Humbert against the East, responded in kind. This unfortunate incident, just one of course in a tradition of similar exchanges, grew in the telling. In the memory and imagination of both churches it achieved the status of a definitive break—the Great Eastern Schism.

In reality it was almost a temper tantrum between two individuals, but it dramatized the deep resentments that had long been festering.

As subsequent events would show, despite this "schism," relations between Constantinople and Rome would for the most part continue for centuries in their traditional on-again off-again pattern. Leo IX had no opportunity either to approve or disapprove of Humbert's actions because he had died by the time Humbert returned to Rome.

Upon Leo's death the reform party at Rome sent a legation to the emperor headed by Hildebrand. After lengthy discussions at Mainz, Henry III named another relative to succeed Leo. The new pope, Victor II, the last of Henry's four appointments and the last German pope until Benedict XVI, followed Leo's policies. In company with the emperor he held an important synod of over a hundred bishops in Florence at which simony, clerical unchastity, and the alienation of church property into private hands were all anathematized. Henry died shortly afterward, leaving his empire to his five-year-old son, another Henry, for whom his mother Agnes was to act as regent. For a while, therefore, the reformers could not look to the imperial court for effective support, embroiled as it often was with intrigue during the regency of the devout but weak Agnes. Then Victor died. He had been pope for barely two years.

The reformers, without making any contact with the imperial court, quickly organized the election of the abbot of Monte Cassino, Stephen IX. When Stephen died after just six months, a clique of Roman nobles saw their chance, and through bribery and swift action it elected and enthroned its own candidate, who took the name Benedict X. The tight-knit reform party fled the city to Siena, where they proceeded to elect Nicholas II, originally from Lorraine or French Burgundy but at the time of his election bishop of Florence. The new pope and his electors successfully sought the approval of the imperial court and then obtained military aid against their enemies from the powerful rulers of Tuscany, the Countess Matilda and her spouse, Duke Godfrey. The reform forces marched on the city, drove Benedict from it, and installed Nicholas in his place.

From a canonical viewpoint Nicholas's election looked just as questionable as Benedict's, but possession was even then nine-tenths of the law. This short pontificate of only two years, 1059 to 1061, furthered the reformers' agenda in three extremely important ways. First of all, Nicholas made peace with the Normans by offering them political legitimacy in exchange for an oath of fealty to Saint Peter. He also granted these former "usurpers" the principality of Capua, the duchies of Apulia and Calabria, and the lordship of Sicily as papal fiefs. In their oath the Normans explicitly bound themselves to ensure proper procedures at papal elections and to provide military help when needed. The pope and the Normans, former enemies, thus became allies.

The imperial court was much displeased, partly because it regarded the Normans in southern Italy as enemies, partly because the provision about the elections seemed to usurp a function reserved to the emperor, and partly because the pope had no right to create such fiefs out of territory that did not belong to him. Nicholas benefited immediately from the alliance because the Normans stormed the stronghold of anti-pope Benedict outside Rome and handed him over to Nicholas as a prisoner. Benedict renounced his claims, retired to his family estates, but was later imprisoned.

Secondly, the synod Nicholas held at the Lateran in 1059 for the first time forbade "lay investiture," that is, the investing in his office of a prelate-elect by a lay person using crosier (staff) and ring to do so. The crosier and ring were symbols of pastoral responsibilities. The problem the reformers had with this ceremony, which had grown up and become normative over the past several centuries, was that it implied that a layman had the power to impart spiritual authority. To some reformers, moreover, the ceremony looked like thinly veined simony. The bishop-elect or abbot-elect often gave the ruler who nominated him a large sum of money. The synod's enactment and its follow-up within a few years ignited a terrible conflagration between the reformers and lay rulers, especially the emperor.

Thirdly, the synod of 1059 set down rules concerning papal elections. The decree for the first time put the election into the hands of the cardinal-bishops. It was vague on the rights the emperors had traditionally exercised, it reduced the role of the cardinal-priests and cardinal-deacons to assent to a choice already made, and it reduced the role of the people (in effect, the aristocracy) to acclamation. It also failed to stipulate what constituted a majority—one-half or two-thirds—a failure that led to many disputed elections.

With this decree the cardinals for the first time in history emerged from the shadows to begin to play determining roles in the history of the popes and in the history of the church. Until this point cardinals were essentially liturgical figures. Rome was peculiar among cities in that it had, besides its cathedral, John Lateran, four other major basilicas whose dignity and vast spaces required that somebody of greater dignity than a mere priest preside at their sacred functions. The practice grew of bringing into Rome at least for great occasions the bishops of the small towns of the surrounding area such as Ostia and Palestrina. Although still bishops in their own right, they for liturgical functions were looked upon as incorporated into—"incardinated" into, to use the technical term—the diocese of Rome. By a kind of legal fiction, therefore, they were Roman clergy and hence had a right to elect the Roman bishop. This fiction is kept up today in that every cardinal, no matter where in the world he might permanently reside, is attached to a church in Rome.

A similar legal fiction prevailed even in the city itself regarding certain senior priests and deacons—twenty-eight of the former and nineteen of the latter. Although they were attached to individual churches in Rome, they too were often required for service in the five great basilicas, which as a group formed almost a church within the churches of Rome. These priests and deacons in time were also considered cardinals in a sense similar to the cardinal-bishops. This distinction of rank among cardinals continued until the middle of the twentieth century when John XXIII raised (practically) all cardinals to the episcopate.

By 1059 the seven suburban bishoprics were in the hands of the reformers. But beyond the immediate occasion the decree had obvious and momentous repercussions. It was a radical break with the past. It created a new and powerful class within the church, a new force to be reckoned with. It certainly did not eliminate contested elections, yet it was the first time that real procedures were laid down that would in their essence pass the test of time. The history of papal elections from this time forward is a history of amplifying, strengthening, and manipulating the basic program established by the synod of 1059. At the time the decree was enacted not everybody was pleased with it or intended to abide by it.

GREGORY VII:
WHO'S IN CHARGE HERE?

Picture for yourselves an emperor in penitential garb standing in the snow outside a castle begging forgiveness of a pope who is a guest inside. The year is 1077, the place is Canossa (a small village in the Apennines), the emperor is Henry IV (son of Henry III), and the pope is Gregory VII (formerly known as Hildebrand). This scene is a stunning contrast to the scene at Sutri in 1046 when Emperor Henry IV's father sat proudly in judgment on three claimants to the papacy, saw to their deposition, and then placed his own candidate on the throne. In the thirty years that intervened between these scenes a revolution had occurred and a huge controversy had exploded.

This complex phenomenon goes by two names that indicate two aspects of the same reality. It is known as the Gregorian Reform when interpreted from the viewpoint of the changes that a small but determined group of reformers in Rome tried to effect in the church. The Reform begins with Leo IX, but it gets its name, quite properly, from one of his successors, Gregory VII. The phenomenon is known as the Investiture Controversy when interpreted from the viewpoint of the political ramifications of especially one element of the reformers' program, the relationship in church leadership between the lay rulers and the higher clergy. Put anachronistically, the Investiture Controversy was about the relationship between church and state. The basic question was—who's in charge?

If Leo IX initiated the Reform, Nicholas II set the immediate stage for the Controversy with the decree on lay investiture. When he died in 1061, relations with the imperial court were tense. The reformers at that point therefore sought a candidate acceptable to the court but one at the same time firmly in their camp. They found him in Anselm, bishop of Lucca, who took the name Alexander II. The reformers conducted the election according to the new provisions. Eager though they were to soothe relations with the imperial court, they did not request its assent to the election, an omission that did not go unnoticed. Meanwhile the Roman nobility stirred up so much opposition to the pope chosen according to provisions hateful to them that they were able to block access to Saint Peter's, and Alexander had to be crowned under cover of night in another church in Rome dedicated to the same apostle, Saint Peter in Chains.

For four years Alexander had to contend with an anti-pope, Honorius II. He won the support of the reform-minded Anno, archbishop of Cologne, who had replaced Agnes as regent for the young Henry. Alexander finally prevailed and was able to establish himself for an important reign of twelve years, but the phenomenon shows that the reformers were still in a precarious position and that they were in no position to discount the authority of the imperial court, which in this instance saved Alexander's papacy.

Alexander pursued the reform program already under way and at first, after the anti-pope problem was settled, did so without serious conflict with the court. But, in 1066 when Henry IV achieved his majority, trouble began to stir. The teenaged monarch was intelligent, resourceful, arrogant, and undisciplined, and he was much aware of the German kings' tradition of pope-making. He was not somebody to be cowed by papal claims. When he came to the throne after a decade of regency, much of it under his mother, he found his domains in disarray. They would soon be in revolt. He had to assert himself strongly if he were going to keep his throne.

Henry's chief and richest fief in Italy was the archbishopric of Milan. When Archbishop Guido died in 1071, Henry tried to force his candidate on the Milanese without any regard for elective procedures. The Milanese reacted against his moves, and Alexander could not stand by and let such a notorious flouting of the reform program happen in the second most important bishopric in Italy after his own. The Milanese meanwhile elected another archbishop, who had to flee to Alexander for protection against Henry's supporters. The problem dragged on for almost two years. Alexander dared not confront the young emperor-elect directly, but instead in 1073 he excommunicated for simony five of Henry's councilors involved in the affair. When Alexander died that year, the problem hung ominously in the air for his successor to handle.

Who would that successor be, and how would he be chosen? During Alexander's funeral a cry arose from the crowd, "Hildebrand pope! Hildebrand pope! Hildebrand pope!" The cardinals immediately took matters into their own hands and gave their assent to the popular will. Was the outburst premeditated? There is no way of knowing, but there is also no doubt that Hildebrand was the reformers' ideal candidate. Under Alexander he had risen to unquestioned leadership among the reforming party and served the pope well during those crucial years.

The mode of Gregory's election was irregular according to the protocol laid down by Nicholas II, a fact that would later be thrown up at him and open him to charges of usurping the office. He himself never questioned the legitimacy of the election process. Although he expressed surprise and dismay at being chosen in words that have the ring of truth, we must in such cases make generous allowance for self-deception. In a letter to Wibert, archbishop of Ravenna, he described what happened:

"But then, suddenly, while our late master the pope was being borne to his burial in the church of Our Savior [John Lateran], a great tumult and shouting of the people arose and they rushed upon me like madmen, leaving me neither time nor opportunity to speak or to take counsel, and they dragged me by force to the place of apostolic rule, to which I am far from being equal. So that

I might say with the prophet . . . 'Fearfulness and trembling are come upon me, and horror hath overwhelmed me.'"

Thus began one of the most important and tumultuous pontificates of the entire Middle Ages. About Gregory nobody is neutral. For one extreme he was a power-hungry cleric who would let nothing stand in the way of his achieving domination. For the other he was a holy man, a prophet, who did his duty no matter what the cost to himself. (He was canonized in 1606, but his feast was not celebrated in the Austrian empire until the mid-nineteenth century.) German-language historians have until relatively recently consistently criticized him as a pope who interfered in internal German politics, humiliated the emperor, and contributed heavily to the subsequent weakness of the empire. Gregory's contemporaries were just as divided in their assessment of him. Saint Peter Damian, one of his closest collaborators, at one point called him "my holy Satan."

Gregory came from relatively modest origins but had a good education in monasteries in and around Rome. He probably spent time as a monk, and some of his contemporaries considered him one. As pope he surrounded himself with students of canon law. Although he sometimes showed a surprising flexibility and compassion in dealing with difficult situations, he saw things in terms of black and white. Like the prophets he took justice as his war cry. His task was to ensure it prevailed, cost what it may. He liked to quote Isaiah, "I cannot be a mute dog afraid to bark "(Isaiah 56.10). When it was objected to him that lay investiture had become the established custom, he replied, "Jesus said, 'I am the truth,' not I am the custom."

Gregory was utterly dedicated to the Roman church and believed all its claims with every fiber of his being. He saw himself a mystical extension of Peter into time. He not only exercised his authority as Peter's vicar and in Peter's name, but he embodied the saint in his person. This was certainly not a new idea for a pope, but few of Gregory's predecessors felt it as passionately and intensely. Gregory had a dark view of the world in which he lived. It was a world where the devil held sway, where the righteous were few. In that world Gregory believed that he was among those few who had truth and right on their side. Since that was the case, he could not possibly lose in his contest against Henry and in his contests against other monarchs of the day.

Monarchy, in Gregory's view, sprang from greed and ambition, unlike priesthood, whose origin was spiritual. He thus pitted secular and sacred against each other with a new and uncompromising starkness and in so doing denied the quasi-sacramental understanding of kingship that had long held sway. Moreover, implied in Gregory's viewpoint was the principle that it was the pope's prerogative to decide who was fit for kingship. No king of the eleventh century (or any century!) was ready to accept such outlandish ideas.

Gregory described the issue at stake in his dealings with monarchs, who besides Henry included King Philip I of France and William the Conqueror of England, as "the liberty of the church" (*libertas ecclesiae*). He fought for it as part of his mission to see justice done. From this point in history forward "the liberty of the church" became the slogan the church has habitually used to justify its prerogatives and its independence of action in struggles against unfriendly governments.

In the Vatican archives rests a document, *The Memorandum of the Pope* (*Dictatus Papae*) from 1075, of which Gregory is the author. It consists in a series of twenty-seven affirmations or axioms, perhaps meant to be headings for a reorganization of canon law. No matter what Gregory intended them to be, the axioms reveal how exalted his opinion of papal authority was. Here are a few samples:

No. 3. "That the pope alone can depose and reinstate bishops."

No. 8. "That he alone may use the imperial insignia."

No. 9. "That the pope is the only one whose feet are kissed by all princes."

No. 12. "That he may depose emperors."

No. 14. "That he has the power to ordain a cleric of any church he may choose."

No. 19. "That he may be judged by no one."

No. 22. "That the Roman church has never erred, nor ever, by the written word of Scripture, shall err to all eternity."

No. 23. "That the Roman pontiff is undoubtedly sanctified by the merits of Saint Peter."

No. 27. "That the pope may absolve the subjects of unjust men from their oath of fealty."

Most of the claims made in the Memorandum had been made by earlier popes. They were, however, surely not accepted by everybody even in the West. In the Memorandum they were given a more absolute quality by being expressed so starkly, and the orchestration of them in the one document imbued them with a newly radical character. Some claims, however, were new and struck at the heart of the institutions that guaranteed order in a feudal society like that of the eleventh century. Among them was the claim that the pope could absolve subjects of their fealty.

But of the twenty-seven the most daring and unheard-of was number 12, that the pope may depose emperors. Gregory thought he had historical precedents for it, but many of his contemporaries thought, correctly, that he misunderstood the record. No pope had ever deposed an emperor. The claim that most blatantly flew in the face of the historical record, however, was number 23, that upon becoming pope a man was made holy.

Henry and Gregory carried out their bitter contest on two levels. The first was on the level of action. The deeper but less obvious was on the level of theology. It is interesting that they both used the same arguments to defend their positions. They were both theocrats. They saw themselves as chosen by God (or Saint Peter, in Gregory's case). They were anointed, and their persons were sacred. They both acknowledged that the office the other held had a role in the well-being of church and society. They very much disagreed, however, on which of the offices had the dominant role—the king or the pope (*regnum* or *sacerdotium*).

The very personalities of Henry and Gregory might make it seem inevitable that they would clash. But the fight broke out over quite specific actions of the young emperor, beginning with his high-handed actions in Milan, a problem Gregory inherited from Pope Alexander. Henry installed his own candidates not only in Milan and sees in Germany but then used the same high-handed procedures in installing bishops at Fermo and Spoleto, right under Gregory's nose. Henry was feeling strong and invincible because he had just put down a rebellion in Saxony.

As early as 1074, just after he was elected, Gregory wrote to the German bishops complaining that they were not enforcing reform decrees. The next February, 1075, he held a synod of bishops in Rome that in strenuous terms once again forbade lay investiture. Then on December 8 that same year he for the first time wrote Henry reproaching him for his conduct. He reminded the emperor that he, like everybody else, was bound to obey papal decrees. If Henry did not, he would have to suffer the consequences.

Henry, furious at such insolence, summoned at Worms a synod of German bishops, who were themselves smarting under Gregory's reprimand to them. The synod denounced Gregory as a usurper of the papacy and accused him of perjury, immorality of various kinds, and abuses of papal authority in the dioceses of Germany. It pronounced Gregory deposed, a sentence confirmed by bishops of Lombardy. Henry himself wrote to Gregory asserting in the most extreme terms his theocratic view of his office. The letter began, "Henry, king not by usurpation but by the pious ordination of God, to Hildebrand, now not pope but false monk." He went on:

You threatened to take the kingship from us, as though we had received it from you, as though kingship and empire were in your hands and not in the hands of God. Our Lord Jesus Christ has called us to kingship but has not called you to the priesthood. For you have risen by these steps, namely by cunning, which the monastic profession abhors, to money, by money to favor, by favor to the sword. Your have destroyed the peace. You have dared to touch me who, though unworthy, have been anointed to kingship. The true pope, Saint Peter, exclaims in his first epistle, "Fear God, honor the King." . . . Descend, therefore, condemned by this anathema and by the common judgment of all our bishops and of ourselves. Relinquish the Apostolic See that you have arrogated. . . . I, Henry, king by the grace of God, together with all our bishops, say to you, Descend! Descend!

Gregory responded in kind. A few weeks later, February 1076, he held a synod in Rome that excommunicated Henry and all the bishops who had sided with him, released Henry's vassals from their oath of fealty, and declared him deposed. Henry had badly overestimated his strength in Germany, where his vassals, including the bishops, were all too happy to curtail his authority, and their release from their oath freed them to do so. Moreover, at least with some of them the word of the pope commanded their respect and obedience. Henry was put on the defensive and his throne endangered. He had to agree to allow Gregory to come to Augsburg in Germany to settle the affair. Gregory accepted the invitation, set out, had difficulty getting through Lombardy because of the strong sentiment against him. He took temporary refuge in early 1077 in the castle at Canossa of the Countess Matilda. There a seemingly penitent Henry met him and for three days begged forgiveness and reinstatement (see fig. 10.1).

Gregory had won the first round. Canossa was Gregory's great victory, but he paid for it dearly. He felt that as a priest he had to forgive any penitent person, no matter how high-born or low-born he might be, no matter what the offense. After Henry spent three days of penance in the snow outside the castle, Gregory forgave him and lifted the excommunication. He found his passage to Germany, however, still blocked by the Lombards, and Henry was able to present to his subjects his absolution as the definitive settlement of the affair.

The Germans could hardly believe their ears when they heard the news. Gregory had betrayed them! They had violated their oaths to their liege lord and now had to be reconciled with him on terms not their own. Some rallied to Henry's side, but others continued to oppose him and, without consulting Gregory, went ahead to elect a new king, Rudolph of Swabia. Gregory, who had not foreseen such a turn of events, was dismayed at having to choose between the two candidates but, finally, three years later, in 1080, as civil war raged in Germany between the forces of the two claimants, decided for Rudolph and again excommunicated and deposed Henry.

O blessed Peter, chief of the Apostles, and thou, Paul, teacher of the gentiles, deign, I pray, to incline your ears to me and mercifully

R ꝰⲬꝝⲞꝝⲀⲦ ꜲꞵꞵⲀⲦ Ꜳꝺ / ꞷⲀꝱꜧⲓⲖꝺⲓꝱꝱ ⳊⲩⲣⲣⲖⲓⲥⲀⲦ Ꜳⲧꝱ ;

10.1: Henry IV

Emperor Henry IV on his knees before Matilda of Canossa, Countess of Tuscany, imploring her to intercede on his behalf to Pope Gregory VII in their struggle over lay investiture. Abbot Hugo of Cluny, another of the pope's supporters, is present. Miniature from the Vita Mathildis by Bonzio. Ca. 1114 CE. Facsimile. Photo: Dietmar Katz.

to hear my prayer . . . [remember] most unwillingly and unworthy as I was, to my great grief and with groans and lamentations I was set upon your throne. I say this because it is not I that have chosen you, but you that have chosen me and laid upon me the heavy burden of your church. And because you have commanded me to go up into a high mountain and denounce their crimes to the people of God and their sins to the sons of the church, those limbs of the Devil have begun to rise up against me and have dared to lay hands on me even unto blood.

The Germans had responded to the first excommunication and had paid the price. They were in no mood to worry about the second. They blamed Gregory for the plight into which they had fallen. And by then Henry had emerged victorious, with Rudolph dead on the battlefield. He had no reason to pay heed to anything Gregory said and, indeed, was eager to take him on again. He first summoned synods in Germany and Lombardy, which again declared Gregory had unlawfully usurped the papacy. This time they went on to elect another in his stead, Clement III, an old ally of Henry, former archbishop of Ravenna whom Gregory had excommunicated in 1076. From that point forward things moved fast. Henry, now feeling secure in Germany, marched into Italy with his troops in 1081 and soon laid siege to Rome

For the next two years Henry and his troops were for the most part kept at bay. By the summer of 1083, however, Henry took over the area around Saint Peter's and by 1084 easily controlled the whole city. Gregory and a small force held out in Castel Sant'Angelo. Thirteen of Gregory's cardinals deserted him and ran to Clement's side. They along with other bishops solemnly enthroned Clement in Saint John Lateran, where Clement then crowned Henry emperor.

In desperation Gregory appealed to the Normans, with whom he had renewed the alliance first established by Nicholas II. Robert Guiscard, their leader, responded positively and arrived at the city with his troops. Henry's forces withdrew without giving battle. The Normans thus freed the city from the emperor but then lived up to their reputation for viciousness by looting and burning at least a third of it. The result was one the worst sacks in the history of Rome.

The Romans held Gregory responsible, and he was therefore now in danger from them. He managed with Guiscard's help to get out of the city unscathed, though cursed, and made his way to Salerno where the Normans ensured his safety. When the Normans withdrew from Rome, Clement reentered the city, where he was greeted as pope, a welcome replacement for the now despised Gregory. Henry IV's triumph was total. The old pope, defeated, exiled, broken in body and spirit, did not have long to live. As he lay dying in Salerno a few months later, still thoroughly convinced of the righteousness of his actions, his last words, paraphrasing the psalm, "I have loved justice and hated iniquity, and therefore I die in exile."

PART

III

DEVELOPMENT,
DECLINE,
DISARRAY

COMPROMISES, CRUSADES, COUNCILS, CONCORDATS

No pope ever died hated by more people than Gregory VII. Both the partisans and the enemies of Henry IV blamed him for the chaos in the empire. The Italians held him responsible for Henry's descent into the peninsula with his troops, and the Romans despised him for the devastation his Norman allies inflicted on their city. By the end of his pontificate he had managed to divide even the reform party, until then able to march in serried ranks. While it is true that he enjoyed a good relationship with William the Conqueror in England and treated Philip I of France with moderation, despite fulminations against him, rulers and bishops outside Germany and Italy were wary and had come into conflict with him.

In 1085, therefore, Saint Peter in his vicar had fallen low, and the triumph of Canossa had turned into a prelude to disaster. More important, the reform program was, partly as a consequence, meeting such resistance as to seem impossible ever to implement. Rulers balked at the idea of surrendering their right, now long-established custom, to designate bishops and abbots, who were among their most important vassals and whose loyalty was essential for the stability of their rule.

The strictures against clerical concubinage and marriage seemed un-realistic in the extreme and were resisted in many places by both the clergy and their flocks. Otto, bishop of Constance, refused outright to enforce them and, when Bishop Altmann of Passau tried to, his clergy drove him out of his diocese with armed force. The conflict between Henry and Gregory ignited a propaganda war that lasted for two gen-erations, until a compromise on the key issue of lay investiture was finally reached in 1122 with the Concordat of Worms.

Meanwhile, Clement III had established himself firmly in Rome and had won respect even from former foes for his learning, eloquence, and his obviously upright character. He commanded the allegiance of a majority of the cardinals. The clergy and nobles in and around Rome supported him so faithfully that they ensured his hold on the city for twelve years, from 1086 until 1098, when Pope Urban II was finally able to gain his last stronghold, the Castel Sant'Angelo. Not the pup-pet of the emperor he was expected to be, Clement acted with consid-erable independence and in a Roman synod of 1089 legislated against simony and clerical marriage. Clement III was a figure to reckon with, and he campaigned vigorously with rulers throughout Europe to have his pontificate recognized as legitimate.

The choice of a successor to Gregory was of course critical. Car-dinals loyal to him were with the help of Countess Matilda for a brief period able to drive Clement from the city, and in May 1086, a year after Gregory's death, they elected Desiderius, the respected abbot of Monte Cassino, who tried to decline the office. Four days after the election, rioting broke out in the city and the pope-elect was forced to flee for Monte Cassino. Not until another year passed did he finally yield to pressure and accept his election. He was duly consecrated, tak-ing the name Victor III. To no avail. He died four months later.

The cardinals faithful to Victor had difficulty regrouping, but finally on March 12, 1088, they elected the cardinal-bishop of Ostia, Eudes of Châtillon-sur-Marne, who took the name Urban II. By the time Urban died eleven years later he had accomplished a miracle. He regained Rome, won almost universal recognition of the legitimacy of his papacy, and at the Council of Clermont in 1095 emerged as one of the most heeded leaders of all Europe.

A member of a noble French family, he had an excellent education at Rheims, entered the monastery of Cluny, where he rose to be grand prior under the revered abbot Hugh. Probably in 1080 he obeyed Gregory VII's summons of Cluniac monks to Rome, where the pope named him to the see of Ostia. Throughout Gregory's many travails, Eudes remained faithful to him and served him in a number of capacities. He was thoroughly committed to Gregory's program, but his strategy for forwarding it was considerably less confrontational. The strategy was due in part to his personality, in part to lessons learned from Gregory's mistakes, and perhaps in largest part to the precarious situation in which he found himself.

He was a realist. With steadfast military allies in the Normans and Countess Matilda, he entered upon a deliberate policy of soothing antagonisms. Although he was never able to mollify Henry IV, he was able to use Henry's increasingly difficult political, military, and even marital situation to his own advantage. By 1092 he helped rally important cities like Milan and Cremona against the emperor, and by 1093 he profited from the defection of Henry's son Conrad from his father to become the pope's protector. By 1094 he similarly profited by the defection of Henry's wife, daughter of the grand-prince of Kiev, to Henry's enemies. The Normans, as mentioned, had supported Urban from the beginning, and they provided him with the military backing he often needed on the local scene. He was therefore able through bribery, force of arms, and persuasion bit by bit to regain Rome. In 1094 he took possession of the Lateran and shortly controlled the rest of the city except for the Castel Sant'Angelo. Clement III, who died two years later, was never able to return to Rome.

With the kings of England and France and the great nobles, he held the line on principle, but he was flexible in concrete circumstances and did his best to avoid open conflict. Urban made important concessions to William II of England and, fearing William's possible defection to Clement III, he refused to settle the king's conflict with Anselm, archbishop of Canterbury. In France he tried to adopt a cautious, soft-spoken approach to the problem of Philip I's marriage, widely denounced as adulterous, but he eventually excommunicated the king. He therefore took a firm stand when alternatives were exhausted, but his more generally conciliatory policy won him heavy criticism from the zealots among the reformers. He prevailed.

At home he proved an able organizer. For the first time in papal documents the word curia begins to appear. It was simultaneous with the ever-increasing importance of the cardinals in decision-making. They now formed an inner circle around the pope, similar to a royal or imperial court. The cardinals, who began their ascendancy by being invested with pope-making authority, now became the chief counselors of the pope and assumed ever more responsibility for determining policy and acting as agents of the papacy to the church at large.

With his position secure by 1095, Urban held an important synod at Piacenza, which pronounced all ordinations performed by Clement and the bishops who sided with him invalid. Like Gregory VII, Urban hoped to ameliorate relations with the East and undo the schism of 1054. At the synod, therefore, Urban asked Christian warriors to respond to an appeal from emperor Alexis I Commenus of Constantinople for military aid against his enemies, the Seljuk Turks. Envoys from the emperor were present at Piacenza. The emperor's situation was in serious jeopardy ever since in 1071 he lost the Battle of Manzikert, which meant the collapse of his eastern frontier.

Almost as soon as the synod at Piacenza was over, the pope traveled to Clermont in central France for another. At it occurred something totally unexpected, one of the most famous and momentous events in the entire Middle Ages. Urban, surely with Alexis's appeal in mind, issued a passionate call to Christians to take up arms to help relieve the military pressure on Alexis and, even more important, to free the Holy Land from the "infidel." (The Turks had captured Jerusalem in 1076.) He, according to one account, detailed the atrocities the Muslims were supposedly committing against Christians.

With that call the pope launched the First Crusade, a holy war willed by God. The cry thus arose, "God wills it!" With the cry arose the persuasion that taking up holy arms wiped out one's sins and any punishment they deserved in this life or the next. It was out of this phenomenon that the seed for the doctrine of indulgences, later developed at length by theologians, was sown, which would be the spark that ignited the Reformation.

There were precedents for the crusades. Early in his pontificate, for instance, Gregory VII several times called upon Christian leaders, including his later enemy, Henry IV, to run as "soldiers of Christ" (*milites Christi*) to the aid of Alexis. But then he got so enmeshed in his problems in the West that he was not able to press his point further. By 1095 Urban was in a much stronger position. Despite the precedents, it was Clermont that set in motion the crusading movement that would from this point forward be a major preoccupation of the popes well into the seventeenth century. A new task was added to the popes' ongoing agenda.

Urban meant the call for the young French nobility, which in fact took it up in great numbers. Military command fell to Count Raymond IV of Toulouse, who was joined by other important nobles. But Urban's words fell upon other ears as well. In an age when preachers were able to rouse crowds to a frenzy, Peter the Hermit, who may or may not have been present at Clermont, was among them. Peter stirred the enthusiasm of tens of thousands of peasants and minor nobility—men, women, and children—to set out for the East without thought for the morrow. Many in this horde, which was devastated by disease and starvation, never made their way outside western Europe, and many of those who did left behind a trail of desperate pillage. Those who reached Constantinople were faced with a startled emperor, whom they expected to feed and provision them. Finally Alexis sent them on their way. The Turks ambushed, slaughtered, or enslaved many of these holy warriors. Peter survived and for a while played a role once the real forces arrived from the West.

Those forces traveled in several armies from France and southern Italy across the Balkans and Asia Minor under capable leadership, and they captured Antioch in 1098. The next year they captured Jerusalem and in a blood bath ruthlessly murdered the infidels, Jews, and even some Christians they found inside. Godfrey of Bouillon was then appointed the first Latin ruler of Jerusalem. Upon his death shortly afterward his brother Baldwin succeeded him, and on Christmas Day 1100, was crowned king of Jerusalem. Within the next twenty years the crusaders established themselves firmly in Palestine and Syria and formed a Latin Kingdom there that would last for two centuries but with ever decreasing strength. This First Crusade was the only one of the many modeled after it that "succeeded," that is, the only crusade that defeated the enemy and gained the territory the crusaders sought.

Urban, who surely had no idea of the profound import of what he had set in motion, died two weeks after the crusaders took Jerusalem. He left the papacy in an incomparably stronger position than he found it when he was elected. He had accomplished a great deal, but the controversy over lay investiture required something more than his *ad hoc* solutions. That problem he left to his successors.

Sixteen days after Urban's death the cardinals elected, without incident, Pascal II. Although the new pope, formerly a monk and then a cardinal, had held important missions under Urban, he was a timid, yet sometimes stubborn, personality for whom the complicated political situation of the day was beyond his powers. Pope for nineteen years (1099–1118), he was hardly the man to carry forward a solution to the problem. He made the abolition of lay investiture the very core of his program, which meant conflict was inevitable.

In 1105 Pascal made a big mistake in supporting Henry V, another of Henry IV's sons, in his revolt against his father. Henry V eventually carried the day, but he turned out to be a brutal and treacherous ruler, as arrogantly insistent on royal right of investiture as his father had been. In 1110 he led an expedition into Italy with the purpose of attaining the imperial crown from Pope Pascal, and by the next year he had occupied Rome.

In February 1111, at Sutri north of Rome Henry agreed to a radical, if unrealistic, solution Pascal proposed to him: that the bishops, abbots, and other ecclesiastical vassals of the emperor renounce all their resources in land and men and turn them over to the emperor. The prelates would retain only those revenues, such as tithes, that came to them from strictly ecclesiastical sources. In exchange the emperor was to renounce investiture and guarantee that the future election to ecclesiastical offices would be free. For what more could Henry ask? He immediately accepted it, and agreed that the decision be announced during his coronation ceremony in Saint Peter's.

The announcement sent tidal waves of shock through the assembly, brought the liturgy to an abrupt and disorderly halt, and then sent the same waves into the outside world. The cardinals immediately denounced it, and the German bishops in Henry's entourage who up to this point had loyally supported him were outraged and loudly announced their refusal to be bound by it. Pascal's solution—essentially a monk's solution—was a solution that turned their world upside down. There was no way they could or would abide by it. Henry withdrew his assent to the proposal, and Pascal refused to crown him.

In the ensuing confusion Henry carried the pope and his cardinals off as his prisoners and then extracted from Pascal the right of investiture with crozier and ring and a promise that he would never excommunicate him. Two months after the aborted coronation ceremony Henry and Pascal returned to Saint Peter's, where Pascal crowned Henry emperor. Every prelate committed to the principles of the Gregorian Reform reacted with fury. They accused the pope of heresy. When Pascal was finally free of the emperor, he himself renounced what he had done, saying he agreed to it only under duress. Such vacillation and obvious bowing to pressure further weakened the already weakened prestige of the pope.

Harassed now by reformers who felt he was not to be trusted and in 1116 forced by rioting to flee Rome, Pascal considered abdicating. He was able to return to Rome, but when he died shortly afterward in Castel Sant'Angelo, the city was once again in rebels' hands. The cardinals hastily elected the cardinal-deacon John of Gaeta, at one time a monk of Monte Cassino but who later had served with distinction as chancellor of the Roman church under both Urban and Pascal. He as Gelasius II had a short but unusually turbulent reign.

Already elderly when he became pope, he had hardly been elected when he was brutally attacked and imprisoned in Rome by the head of the patrician Frangipani family, who detested Pascal and everybody in any way associated with him. Soon released, he fled Rome upon hearing that Henry V was approaching with demands to settle the investiture problem—of course in his own favor. Henry, convinced he could make no headway with Gelasius, installed an anti-pope in Rome, which led Gelasius to excommunicate both of them. Henry departed, leaving Rome in the control of Gelasius's enemies, which included the anti-pope, Gregory VIII.

Gelasius managed to get into Rome but was again set upon by the Frangipani. He escaped their clutches and again fled the city. He set sail for France, where he hoped he would be safe and able to conduct the business of the papacy in peace. Upon his arrival there he almost immediately fell ill, retired to the monastery of Cluny, where he died after a pontificate that lasted barely a year.

Only two cardinal-bishops had accompanied Gelasius to France. Upon his death they elected Guy de Bourgogne, archbishop of Vienne and son of Count William of Burgundy. They notified the cardinals in Rome, who quickly ratified the election and had it publicly acclaimed by the clergy and people of the city assembled in John Lateran. They believed this hasty and doubtfully canonical procedure was required because the crisis demanded swift action and because they had in Guy an excellent candidate. On that last point they were absolutely correct.

The new pope, Callixtus II, was related to the English, French, and German royal houses. He knew and understood how that class thought and felt, and he recognized the legitimacy of some of their concerns about the abolition of lay investiture. He was a member of the secular clergy, not a monk as recent popes had been, and he was known and respected among his clerical peers. Never having lived in Italy, he was outside and above all factions there, including the factions among the cardinals themselves. Already recognized for his learning and diplomatic skills, he had all the strictly secular requirements for the job. He was, as well, fully committed to the principles of the reform. It is he who would bring the controversy to an honorable close, which meant compromises on both sides.

Callixtus was crowned at Vienne in central France on February 9, 1119, a week after his election. Even Henry V was ready for a settlement and began to see, from precedents gaining ground in France and England, that it was possible to renounce use of the ring and crozier and still retain some control over the choice of the candidates. The German princes and bishops, tired unto death of the controversy, applied pressure to Henry to seek a solution. Negotiations were opened, faltered, and resumed. In early 1122 an embassy came to Callixtus from Germany, which the pope received favorably, and in response to it he sent three cardinals to Worms to work out an agreement.

The result was the Concordat of Worms, the first such formal agreement between the papacy and a government or ruler. Beginning with this document the concordat became a standard instrument in papal policy-making. It thus had many successors through the centuries, some of them of great importance, such as the Concordat of Bologna, 1516, which for centuries regulated especially the mode of nomination of French bishops. During the years between the two World Wars the Holy See negotiated more concordats than at any other single time because of the way the map of Europe was rearranged by the Treaty of Versailles.

The terms of the Concordat of Worms were straightforward. Bishops (and abbots) would be freely elected by their clergy. The emperor gave up the right to invest them with ring and crozier. He was, however, allowed to be present at the election and receive homage from the new prelate as his vassals. Since he could refuse to receive homage, he in effect had veto rights and thus continued to exercise considerable control over the election. In balance, the emperor won the advantage, as did other rulers, as this solution became standard. The church had, however, successfully asserted a principle, had it enshrined in a solemn document, and had a trump card in deciding the validity of the election.

To ratify the Concordat and fully to solemnize it, Callixtus convoked a synod in the Lateran the following year. This synod was not much different from the many other synods that popes had been holding regularly, especially since the days of Leo IX. But as the centuries passed this synod began to be invested with greater authority and eventually became recognized as ecumenical, on a par with the great councils held in the East beginning with Nicaea in 325. But as an "ecumenical council" it and those that followed it were strikingly different. They were held in the West. They were exclusively Western in the makeup of the prelates who participated in them. Their language was Latin not Greek. Most important, they were convoked by the pope not the emperor. The pope set their agendas and in person or through his legates presided over them. Another great revolution and enlargement of papal authority was taking place.

INNOCENT III: VICAR OF CHRIST

The first crusade. The first concordat. The first papal council.
The evolution of a workable solution to the investiture controversy. The emergence of cardinals not only as pope-makers
but as the members of a curia. The twelfth century opened a new era
for the papacy as it did for Europe more generally. Real monarchs had
by now emerged out of the feudal muddle, and they were ruling countries that we can begin to identify as England, France, and, at least to
some extent, Germany (better known as the empire). Other monarchs
emerged as well in eastern Europe, for instance, and in Spain.

These rulers paid a certain deference to the emperor, but they
knew they were monarchs in their own right who could deal with the
emperor on equal footing. Two powerful emperors made their mark—
Frederick I and Frederick II—but after that a decline set in. Whereas
in England and France, as well as other places, the crown had become
hereditary, in Germany it remained elective, which contributed to its
weakness and to the failure of a consistent pattern of strong leaders to
emerge who could bring the nobility to heel. Until the middle of the
thirteenth century the popes suffered a great deal of grief at the hands
of the emperors, but after that they had more to gain and more to fear
from the king of France.

119

The revival of literature and learning in the twelfth century was just as noteworthy as the emergence of monarchy. Vernacular poetry flourished among the troubadours. The sermons and treatises of Saint Bernard of Clairvaux, who spearheaded a reform of the Benedictines, circulated widely and were esteemed for their passion and warm devotion. From this time forward until at least the seventeenth century, he will be the most frequently read and highly esteemed Christian writer after Saint Augustine. Monk though he was, he projected a powerful public image. In the first half of the twelfth century, he was better known and exerted more moral authority than any pope.

A passion for learning gripped young men, who were ready to travel hundreds of miles and live in unfamiliar cities to sit at the feet of a renowned master. The study of canon law, which had never completely died out and had begun to revive even before the Investiture Controversy now entered its golden age, with an especially impressive center in Bologna. Application to Christian doctrines of the logical works of Aristotle, available in the important libraries in Latin translations, received impetus from Saint Anselm early in the century and from Abelard later. They were precursors of the great intellectual enterprise known as Scholasticism, which was well on its way a generation after Abelard as more and more ancient Greek and Arabic works were translated and assimilated.

Roads were repaired, travel was easier and safer. Trade therefore revived, as did cities. With the revival of cities, learning moved from monasteries, those holy castles in the countryside, to the bustle of the city. Urban schools sprang up, which by the end of the century had developed in several places into sophisticated universities—organized according to disciplines (philosophy, law, medicine, theology), held together by a corps of full-time faculty, and regulated by careful statutes. The universities offered degrees, which were public and official certification of professional competence.

As the great Romanesque and then Gothic churches rose in the cities, universities also became an impressive part of the urban complex. Although the students in them (all male) represented only a tiny percentage of the population, they became leaders in secular and ecclesiastical society. For ambitious churchmen, professional competence in canon law was more important than in theology. Bologna was the recognized center for the former, Paris and then Oxford for the latter. Impressive schools like these overshadowed others, but the lesser ones were many (about eighty by the sixteenth century) and forces to be reckoned with.

The twelfth-century revival of learning and high culture differed in one important regard from the similar phenomenon at the court of Charlemagne in the early ninth century and at the court of the Ottos in the tenth. The earlier revivals lasted not much more than a generation, after which, due to the worsening political and military situation, the surge lost its strength. The twelfth-century revival launched a trajectory that has continued unbroken up to the present. It has taken all sorts of twists and turns and has radically changed character, but it never suffered a real interruption.

All these developments had an impact on the papacy. Jurisdictional claims the popes had long been making could in these new circumstances be more readily reduced to practice. Although canon law recognized the autonomy of ecclesiastical institutions that filled the medieval landscape, it had a bias toward supporting the papal claims. The new ease in communication facilitated recourse to Rome for the settling of disputes. The papal tiara, a crown-like headdress, began to take on its definitive form and symbolize supreme papal authority. The papal curia grew in sophistication and complexity. The office of cardinal became ever more prestigious. The cardinals not only elected the pope but they, with a few exceptions, elected the pope from their own number.

What were formerly papal synods of local significance grew into general councils that legislated for the whole of Christendom. Although the medieval church continued to be radically local in character, it was unmistakably on the path to greater centralization. As secular monarchies more distinctly and distinctively emerged, so did the papal monarchy.

The story of the twelfth-century popes is a story of lights and shadows. As mentioned, putting the election in the hands of the cardinals did not eliminate contested elections. The cardinals were often bitterly divided among themselves on policy and politics. Most of them were Italian, which meant they were often embroiled in local rivalries and lacked the big vision of popes like Leo IX and Callistus II. In the decades after Callistus, however, what divided the cardinals was still the resolution of the investiture issue. The old-line, hard-core Gregorians, who were still a majority, had not fully reconciled themselves to the Concordat of Worms, whereas their opposite numbers considered the matter settled and wanted to move on. The Schism of 1130 between Anacletus II, who represented the former faction, and Innocent II, who represented the latter, became a pan-European affair and was not fully settled in favor of Innocent until Anacletus died eight years later.

In 1139 Innocent held the Second Lateran Council in which it became clear that, although the cardinals might differ among themselves on just how the principles of the Gregorian Reform were to be put into practice; those principles had by now worked their way into almost unquestioned acceptance among large numbers of churchmen. This was nowhere clearer than with clerical celibacy. Although cohabitation with wives and concubines was expressly forbidden in canon 7 of Lateran Council I, the five hundred bishops assembled for Lateran II gave the matter a fuller formulation, which would become classic. Canons 6 and 7 forbade all those in major orders (subdeacons, deacons, priests) from taking wives and, further, forbade the faithful from assisting at masses of priests they knew to have wives or concubines. The legislation did not stamp out the practice, but the law had been clearly laid down.

Among the popes of the twelfth century Alexander III is particularly important. He had an unusually long reign (1159–1181). As a young man he won renown as a professor at the emerging university of Bologna and as author of an important theological work and an even more important work on canon law. He had therefore assimilated the new learning, and his election signified that the technical proficiency he represented had become a new desideratum in the profile of church leaders. As pope he faced many tribulations, none more serious and ongoing than his conflict with the German king Frederick I (Barbarossa), who announced his intention of restoring the splendor of the empire. Frederick meant, in other words, to interpret the Concordat of Worms in terms favorable to himself and to establish his authority in Italy.

Alexander's anti-imperial policy meant that, besides his other conflicts with Frederick, he had to face a succession of four anti-popes. At one point Frederick seemed invincible. He took Rome in 1167, installed his own pope, and forced Alexander to flee. Within a decade, however, Frederick was on the run. Alexander backed the northern Italian cities against Frederick, which led to his defeat in 1176 at the Battle of Legnano. Frederick's defeat provided the conditions that allowed Alexander to make peace with him and then to hold the impressive Third Lateran Council in 1179, which further strengthened the prestige of the Apostolic See.

When King Henry II of England in 1164 promulgated a series of measures known as the Constitutions of Clarendon that asserted royal prerogatives over episcopal appointments, restricted certain privileges of the clergy, and put hindrances in the way of appeals to the pope, he ran into conflict with the archbishop of Canterbury, Thomas Becket. Alexander tried to remain aloof from the affair, partly because he wanted Henry's support against Frederick but also partly because he held more moderate views than Becket on the relationship between the spiritual and the temporal powers. Finally drawn into the conflict, he worked successfully, it at first seemed, to achieve a reconciliation. Becket returned to England from exile—only to be assassinated by four henchmen of the king. With that Alexander acted decisively by imposing a personal interdict on Henry, who was forced to submit, do penance, and rescind the Constitutions.

After Alexander came five popes in seventeen years. The last of them, Celestine III was eighty-five when elected. He lived for another five years, vigorous to the end. Well educated as a young man at Paris, where he studied under Abelard and later defended him against Saint Bernard, he had a deserved reputation for an unusual combination of integrity and political finesse. Like Alexander III he had to expend his energies trying to hold at bay an emperor—Frederick's son, Henry VI. In 1197 Henry died, leaving his young son as his presumptive heir. The pope himself died the next year and was succeeded by Lothar of Segni, who took the name Innocent III (1198–1216).

Although Innocent's decisions sometimes backfired, with him the medieval papacy reached an apogee of authority and respect. Only thirty-seven when elected, and thus a dramatic contrast with his pre-decessor, he came from a noble family of central Italy, which provided him with good connections in the upper strata of European society. It was a papal family *par excellence*. From it had come his uncle, Pope Clement III, predecessor to Celestine III. Innocent's own successor but one would be his nephew, Gregory IX, after whom about a decade and a half later his grandnephew would be elected as Alexander IV.

As a young man Innocent received a cosmopolitan and first-rate education at the best institutions of the day—theology at Paris and then, at least for a short while, canon law at Bologna under the cel-ebrated scholar Huguccio. He at some point made a pilgrimage to the shrine of Thomas Becket at Canterbury. Ordained to the diaconate and made a cardinal when he was probably in his late twenties, he stood on the sidelines during Celestine III's pontificate. He used the time to write an ascetical treatise on the misery of the human condition (*De Miseria Humanae Conditionis*) and on the mass (*De Sacro Altaris Myste-rio*), valuable as a window into the liturgy of the time. Both of them had wide circulation.

Like all the popes of the era, he was drawn into political imbro-glios, the most immediate and long-lasting of which was the contest in Germany over three candidates for the imperial crown, which dragged on for most of his pontificate. A dreary, dangerous, and complicated affair, in which Innocent supported now one, now another candidate, ended in 1215 with the crowning of Henry VI's young son, Frederick II. Innocent's consistent concern was to give his approval to the person most likely to safeguard the rights of the church and least likely to en-croach upon the territories of the Papal State and of the old Patrimony of Saint Peter. Frederick would later severely disappoint Innocent's successors in both regards.

In 1208 the pope put England under interdict and then excommu-nicated King John for refusing to recognize Stephen Langdon, whom Innocent had nominated as archbishop of Canterbury. John submitted, made his Anglo-Irish domains a fief of the Holy See, and recognized the pope as his overlord. A few years later, in 1215 Innocent sided with the king and declared the Magna Carta void because it had been extorted from the king by his barons without papal consent. Elsewhere

in Europe he intervened in royal matrimonial disputes, which brought
him into conflict with the kings of Aragon, León, and France.

Innocent wanted to reestablish good relations with Constantinople
and at the same time wanted to reestablish Christian control over the
Holy Land. The Latin Kingdom founded after the First Crusade was
by now little more than a vestige, and both the Second and Third
Crusades had been failures. Innocent encouraged yet another attempt
at helping Constantinople and conquering the territories lost to the
Muslims. Largely due to his impetus a Fourth Crusade was launched
from Venice in 1202. Planned and to a large extent executed as a big
expedition, the crusade ran into serious difficulties even before it left
Europe, and it soon got enmeshed in a bitter struggle for the imperial
throne in Constantinople.

As a result of confusion, intrigue, and betrayals, the crusaders di-
verted their energies to Constantinople itself, to which they first laid
siege, then invaded, and finally in the "Great Fire" of 1204 burned
down a large part of it. This tragic episode made the Fourth Crusade
for Greek-speaking Christians a horrid symbol of Latin aggression
and barbarism. It became a major obstacle to reconciliation between
the two churches, an atrocity never forgotten or forgiven. For the
next four centuries further crusades were launched, none of which
ever achieved its objectives; none of which was as ignominious as the
Fourth.

If Innocent's crusading effort was a disaster, he was more successful in north-central Italy. He is sometimes considered the real founder
there of the Papal States in the sense that he was the first to bring
them, if only temporarily, under effective papal control. They lay in
the hands of local families and factions, some more loyal to the emperor than to the pope. Through his own authority and through his
family connections, Innocent was able to place men loyal to himself
in major cities and centers such as Bologna, Ancona, and Parma and
thus ensure the States' stability and the flow of income into Rome. He
campaigned for allegiance with the motto, "My yoke is easy, and my
burden light."

Innocent, resolutely in the tradition launched by Gregory VII,
held exalted views of papal authority. He is the first pope to divest

himself of the title vicar of Peter and appropriate the title Vicar of Christ. "We are the successor of the prince of the Apostles, but we are not his vicar or the vicar of any man or Apostle. We are the vicar of Jesus Christ himself."

This was a promotion of such magnitude as to defy comment. It was self-conferred. Through the centuries until the present it has wielded enormous rhetorical power, and when invoked it silences all opposition. Nonetheless, Innocent was a careful canonist and, despite what his political interventions might suggest, held fast to the distinction between the spiritual and temporal orders. Secular rulers had authority in their own right, independent of the church, but they could not exercise it in ways detrimental to the church. When they thus transgressed, the church had to step in.

Important though Innocent's interaction with the great monarchs was, his pontificate had a much broader scope. For its long-range effect on the ministry and spirituality of Catholicism, nothing Innocent did can compare in importance with the encouragement he gave to the religious orders founded during his pontificate by Saint Dominic and Saint Francis of Assisi. Dominic gathered a group of priests to preach against the dualistic heretics known as Albigensians or Cathars in southern France, and Francis gathered clerics and laymen into a loose association to live in the poverty they imagined Jesus lived in and to preach a message of repentance, peace, and joy.

In encouraging these two groups Innocent provided the church with a new set of ministers besides the local clergy, who exercised care of souls in parishes and other local institutions. The Dominicans, Franciscans, and then the other orders that followed them, performed their ministry outside the parish structure as directed by their own superiors rather than the local bishop. They soon began to occupy important chairs in the universities, establish their own theological schools (*studia*) usually open to other clerics, and undertake evangelizing missions to exotic lands. They produced famous preachers and by their preaching zeal revived this fundamental Christian ministry that for a half dozen centuries had lain almost dormant. The official name for the Dominican order is, therefore, truly significant, the Order of Preachers (see fig. 12.1).

12.1: Innocent III with Saint Francis

Saint Bonaventura, Legenda major: 1457. Brescia, Italy. Pope Innocent III
approving the Franciscan order.
©Alinari / Art Resource, NY

Innocent's encouragement of the Dominicans and Franciscans is
only one indication of his concern for the betterment of the internal
life of the church. Although insistent on papal oversight of bishops, he
deliberately strengthened their authority by limiting appeals to Rome
and by encouraging them to hold frequent councils on the local level.
He reformed the procedures of the curia to make them more efficient
and less susceptible to bribery and other abuses. More than six thousand letters from his curia are still extant, many of which bear signs of
his personal touch.

Perhaps the most reliable indication of the prestige he enjoyed
and the authority he wielded was his marvelous success in convoking
the Fourth Lateran Council in 1215, the year before his death. The
council was one of the largest and most impressive assemblies in the
Middle Ages and the largest council in the history of the church up to
this point. Innocent intended it to be an assembly representative of the

whole church, lay and clerical. To it came some four hundred bishops, some eight hundred abbots and other ecclesiastics, royal ambassadors from England, Germany, France, Hungary, Aragon, and Portugal, plus a number of representatives from smaller political units. In preparation for it Innocent had called for and received reports and suggestions from bishops in the field.

The council lasted only twenty days yet passed a large number of important decrees. To a great extent, therefore, it was a rubber stamp, simply ratifying materials prepared for it. Yet those materials had been drawn up using previously solicited information that had come from the bishops. Among the decrees none was more important for the life of piety of all Christians or would have a greater influence for centuries to come than *Omnis utriusque sexus* ("Everybody of both sexes"), which required annual confession and communion of every adult.

Innocent was pope at the head of a century that produced Saint Dominic and Saint Francis, Saint Bonaventure and Saint Thomas Aquinas, Saint Clare of Assisi and Saint Elizabeth of Hungary, Saint Anthony of Padua and Saint Louis IX, king of France. Though a man of unquestioned integrity, Innocent was not himself a saint and never pretended to be one. He made some colossal mistakes, such as the Fourth Crusade and the crusade he promoted against the Albigensians in southern France. But he won for the Apostolic See greater respect and deference than any of his predecessors since Gregory the Great in the sixth century. His brilliance was too bright to last.

BONIFACE VIII:
BIG CLAIMS, BIG HUMILIATION

B y the end of the century that opened so propitiously with
Innocent III, the papacy was about to enter two extremely
difficult and scandalous periods, the so-called Babylonian
Captivity, which segued into the Great Western Schism. The vestibule
to those periods was the back-to-back pontificates of Celestine V and
Boniface VIII. In his *Divine Comedy* Dante, who was the popes' contemporary, placed both of them in hell.

After Innocent III a series of capable and spiritually minded popes
followed, all of whose pontificates were severely troubled by conflicts
with Emperor Frederick II, who was determined to establish himself
in Sicily and in southern and central Italy. Matters reached a climax
when in 1244 Innocent IV secretly fled Rome to France. The next
year he convoked the First Council of Lyons, whose agenda was broad
but whose center was Frederick. The council summoned Frederick to
answer charges of perjury, breach of the peace, sacrilege, and heresy.
The emperor did not appear but was allowed a defense attorney who,
not surprisingly, was unsuccessful for his client.

The council deposed Frederick, released his vassals from their oaths of fealty, and invited the Germans to elect a new king. Although somewhat weakened by the council's action, Frederick was able to defy it. Only his unexpected death five years later resolved the conflict. It was the end of a long era. Frederick was the last of the emperors to inflict such havoc upon the papacy, which now had to begin contending, instead, with other rulers.

Despite the disruptions Frederick caused in the first half of the century, the popes managed to function and, under the circumstances, function well. They continued to give support to the Dominicans and Franciscans and encouraged the development of similar orders, such as the Augustinians and the Carmelites. They also fostered the development of lay associates of these orders, the "tertiaries" (a *third* level of membership after the friars and the nuns), which was extremely important for the spread of a deeper piety among the laity and would produce a number of saints, including Saint Catherine of Siena. Even after the disaster of the Fourth Crusade, they in this period launched three more, with the usual frustrating results. They tried to stamp out the vestiges of the Albigensian heresy that still persisted. They supported the universities, now fully mature institutions, and they were especially instrumental in fostering the development of canon law.

Meanwhile, as the empire declined after the death of Frederick, the French monarchy grew ever stronger. In 1262–1263 Charles, count of Anjou, ambitious brother of the saintly Louis IX, moved into southern Italy at the invitation of Pope Urban IV, himself a Frenchman, to establish an Angevin kingdom there (*Angevin* meaning "from Anjou"). His presence near Rome divided the cardinals into pro-French and anti-French camps, a division further exacerbated by rivalries among the great Roman families, especially the Orsini and the Colonna.

Although the caliber of popes continued generally high, the second half of the century saw thirteen popes in forty-four years, an average of three years per pontificate. Practically all were elected outside Rome—at Viterbo, Perugia, Arezzo, Naples—either because of a particular political situation or because Rome was deemed too unhealthy for a lengthy meeting. There were often delays of many months, even years, between the death of one pope and the election of another.

After the death of Clement IV in 1268, for instance, the cardinals who assembled at Viterbo took three years to elect a successor, Gregory X. As public resentment against them mounted, the civic authorities of Viterbo finally locked them in the papal palace, then removed the roof, and finally threatened to cut off their food supply if they did not come to a decision. The learned and devout Gregory, not a cardinal and elected in absentia, was as scandalized as everybody else by the long interregnum and as pope decreed that henceforth the cardinals would be sequestered until they elected a pope and suffer a carefully calculated reduction of food and drink as the deliberations dragged on. Although the cardinals had been put under lock and key for the first time at the election in 1241, Gregory's decree is conventionally considered the origin of the papal "conclave" (*con clave*, "with a key"). Gregory's provisions were observed loosely, intermittently, or not at all in subsequent papal elections, but they put on the books a basic procedure still operative today for papal elections.

By the end of the century the prestige of the papacy had declined from the high level achieved by Innocent III. The popes' constant involvement in political and military conflicts took its toll on their reputations, even though they often, given the assumptions of the age, could hardly have stayed aloof from them. They faced growing criticism because of levies they imposed for financing crusades and for other causes and faced it as well for what sometimes seemed the ostentatious wealth of churchmen, especially the cardinals and the pope himself. A radical branch of the Franciscan order, the "Spirituals," preached a poverty for the church and the papacy that sounded suspiciously like destitution and especially on this issue they became dangerous antipapal propagandists. Even outside Franciscan circles expectations that God was about to send an "angel pope" to rescue the church from worldliness circulated fairly widely

This was the sour context in which the legend of Pope Joan emerged. According to the story, which, though it has absolutely no basis in fact, was accepted as true in the Middle Ages and later, a learned woman in male disguise managed to get herself elected pope. She reigned for two years. During a procession on its way to the Lateran Joan gave birth to a child, which in the most dramatic fashion imaginable unmasked the deception. She died immediately afterward. Versions differed of course in detail, including the years when Joan reigned, though it was never set in the present or near-present. What the legend indicated was how ready the faithful were to believe the worst (see fig. 13.1).

When Nicholas IV died at the end of the century, 1292, the twelve cardinals—ten Italians and two Frenchmen—were hopelessly divided, split this time as much by personal and family rivalries as anything else. They took twenty-seven months to elect a new pope. The conclave (such as it was) first met in Rome, then transferred to Perugia, and then back to Rome, where the bickering continued. When Charles II, the Angevin king of Naples and Sicily, arrived there in March 1294, he applied pressure for a resolution of the impasse, but even that expedient did not work. After the king's departure the meeting, again transferred to Perugia, dragged on into July.

The king meanwhile urged a hermit, Pietro del Morone, to write to the cardinals, warning them that dire calamities would befall the church if they delayed any longer. The letter had an impact and moved the cardinals to elect no other than the letter's author, a complete outsider to the conclave and a complete outsider to organized ecclesiastical life. The new pope-elect, startled by this turn of events, was only with difficulty persuaded to accept the cardinals' decision. He took the name Celestine V. He was in his mid-eighties.

Pietro del Morone had as a much younger man organized a small brotherhood of hermits and gained a reputation for holiness. Although an ordained priest, he had only a rudimentary education and could barely read Latin. The Spiritual Franciscans greeted his election with jubilation, expecting him to be a pope who would put things aright according to their radical program. Here was a pope who stood for poverty, austerity, and holy simplicity.

Celestine's election broke the deadlock in the conclave, and the cardinals could congratulate themselves on choosing somebody who had no worldly attainments, a purely spiritual candidate. They had risen above all pettiness, they believed, and made a holy choice. After the election and coronation, Charles II made himself Celestine's guardian and installed him in his capital in Naples, to the great dismay

13.1: Pope Joan

Pope Joan giving birth to a child during a procession. Des Clercs et Nobles Femmes, by Giovanni Boccaccio. Ms.33, 69 verso. Vellum. France, c.1470. Spencer Collection. Astor, Lenox and Tilden Foundations.

of the cardinals who had elected him. Celestine took his orders from Charles, appointed Charles' favorites to key positions in the curia and Papal States, and created twelve cardinals who were Charles's nominees. On his own, however, he showered privileges on his congregation of hermits and showed similar favors to the Spiritual Franciscans.

It soon became obvious to everybody close to him that Celestine had not the slightest idea of what was expected of him and that he lacked every skill required by the highly responsible position to which he had been elected. His ignorance of Latin was simply his most obvious deficiency. Soon even he realized that a mistake had been made. On December 13, 1294, after a pontificate of five months during which he never set foot in Rome, he abdicated. In the presence of the cardinals he read his statement, laid aside his pontifical robes, and donned once again his gray habit as hermit. He was now once again simply Pietro del Morone. As a contemporary chronicle put in, "On Saint Lucy's day, Pope Celestine resigned, and he did well."

Eleven days later, on Christmas Eve, the cardinals assembled in Naples and elected one of their number, Benedetto Caetani, who took the name Boniface VIII. It is not clear what led to such swift action, in striking contrast to the previous conclave. The cardinals' choice, in any case, fell on a man who could not have been more different from his predecessor. Boniface came from a family of the minor aristocracy located in the countryside south of Rome near Anagni. As a young man he studied law at Bologna and elsewhere, now almost the prerequisite for rising in secular or ecclesiastical ranks. He soon made his mark in the papal curia and gained international experience by accompanying legates to both France and England. His intelligence, his firm grasp of canon law, and his practical skills won him attention and respect, which meant he was entrusted with more and more assignments. In Paris in 1290, for instance, he settled the conflict between the religious (Franciscan and Dominican) and the diocesan clergy with dispatch and skill, but his abrasive and arrogant manner made him unwelcome ever to return. Through the accumulation of benefices he became one of the wealthiest cardinals, a step along the way toward fulfilling his ambition of putting his family on the same footing with the old Roman nobility such as the Orsini and Colonna.

From the outset his pontificate was bedeviled with questions about the legitimacy of Celestine's abdication. Was it legal for a pope to resign? In Celestine's favor it must be said that he consulted canonists before taking the step, but in Boniface's disfavor it must be said that he was among those consulted. This was a fact that would be thrown up against him and then distorted into a nefarious intrigue, as if he deceived the pope into taking the fateful step. Although there is no evidence that Boniface with malice aforethought misled Celestine, the allegation was plausible and spread among the pope's many enemies. Dante, who did not question the legality of Celestine's action, put him in hell for cowardice, for ducking the responsibility to which he was called (*Inferno*, 3.58–3.61).

One of Boniface's first acts was to rescind or suspend many of the decrees of his predecessor and to dismiss many of the officials he installed. For obvious reasons, Boniface kept a careful eye on Celestine, who at first moved around with perfect liberty. He became more concerned about him as an unwitting tool of his enemies and within a year had him locked up in the Castel of Fumone about forty miles south of Rome, where the aged pope soon died of natural causes. Rumors spread that Boniface had him murdered. Among Boniface's enemies the Spiritual Franciscans had an international network of monasteries that transmitted the rumors and allegations. Not only were they dismayed at Celestine's resignation, but they saw in Boniface the epitome of all they hated. Boniface meanwhile annulled most of the privileges Celestine had granted them.

The two cardinals from the Colonna family had voted for Boniface in the conclave, but they became increasingly critical of his high-handed behavior. They soon clashed with him over aspects of his international policy and, more specifically, over the expansion of the estates of the Caetani family in territory they considered their own outside of Rome. They joined in the campaign of rumors against him, which included the murder of Celestine. In May, 1297, Stefano Colonna, a brother of Cardinal Pietro Colonna and nephew of Cardinal Giacomo Colonna, highjacked a convoy of treasure on its way from Anagni to Rome. That action set off a series of confrontations between the pope and the family.

The cardinals agreed to return the money but refused to deliver up their relative to justice. They meanwhile intensified the campaign questioning Celestine's resignation and called for a council to adjudicate the matter. Things went from bad to worse, with Boniface first stripping all ecclesiastics in the family of their honors and benefices and then finally sending a military force against the Colonna that razed their fortresses and seized their stronghold in Palestrina. The cardinals fled to France, to the court of King Philip IV, known as Philip the Fair, who was himself in conflict with Boniface and not inclined to yield him an inch. The king was the grandson of Saint Louis IX but was as calculating and ruthless as his grandfather had been temperate and generous. All the pieces were now in motion for a collision of momentous proportions.

The dispute between the pope and the king arose over a clear-cut issue—the right of the king to tax the clergy. Lateran Council IV had decreed that such taxation imposed unilaterally was illegal. Boniface tried to enforce the legislation. In the first instance of his clash with Philip, 1296, he had to back down when Philip retaliated by forbidding the export of revenues of the French church to the papal treasury, upon which Boniface relied heavily. As a sign of his good will, in 1297 Boniface canonized Philip's grandfather, Louis IX.

In 1300 Boniface declared a year of jubilee to celebrate the anniversary of the Savior's birth, the first such jubilee in the history of the church. This event, highly successful, established a pattern for many other Holy Years to follow. Even as the pilgrims flocked to Rome, Boniface heard news of further encroachments of Philip on "the liberty of the church," which climaxed two years later when the king arrested a French bishop, put him on trial in his own presence on the usual charges of blasphemy, heresy, and treason, and then had him thrown into prison. The king's action was a flagrant violation of canon law, which stipulated that a bishop could be tried only by the pope. Angry exchanges between the two parties ensued. Boniface ordered the French bishops to come to Rome for consultation and, though Philip refused them permission to leave the kingdom, almost half of them appeared.

With that, in November 1302, Boniface issued the bull *Unam Sanctam*, one of the most famous documents in the history of the papacy. Without naming Philip, it was of course directed against him and his policies and especially against the French bishops who obeyed the king's command rather than the pope's. In essence the document was an assertion of the traditional doctrine of the superiority of the spiritual authority over the temporal. But its language was particularly strong and its famous final assertion categorical: "Therefore, we declare, state, define, and pronounce that it is absolutely necessary to salvation for every human creature to be subject to the Roman Pontiff."

Canonists and theologians have debated the interpretation of that assertion ever since, but Philip had no doubt what it was—a declaration of war. The king had no interest in replying except by force. In June 1303 he called together an assembly to hear charges against the pope that went on for pages. For instance:

> He does not believe in an eternal life to come . . . . and he was not ashamed to declare that he would rather be a dog or an ass or any brute animal than a Frenchman. . . . He is reported to say that fornication is not a sin any more than rubbing the hands together is. . . . He has had silver images of himself erected in churches to perpetuate his damnable memory, so leading men into idolatry. . . . He has a private demon whose advice he takes in all matters. . . . He is guilty of the crime of sodomy. . . . He has caused many clerics to be murdered in his presence, rejoicing in their deaths. . . . He is openly accused of the crime of simony. . . . He is publicly accused of treating inhumanly his predecessor, Celestine, a man of holy memory and holy life who perhaps did not know that he could not resign . . . and of imprisoning him in a dungeon and causing him to die there swiftly and secretly.

Meanwhile the king had dispatched to Italy two agents to gather a force to seize the pope and bring him to Paris to stand trial for his crimes. One of the agents was Guillaume de Nogaret, the king's chief minister, and the second was Sciarra Colonna, another brother of Cardinal Pietro Colonna. Boniface had meanwhile left Rome for his family home at Anagni where he prepared a bull excommunicating the king. While he was there a band of several hundred mercenaries under the leadership of de Nogaret and Colonna arrived at Anagni. It broke into the palace and into Boniface's quarters. The pope was awaiting them in full pontifical robes and challenged them to lay a hand on him, shouting, "Here is my head! Here is my neck!" Colonna wanted to kill the pope on the spot, but de Nogaret disagreed. As the leaders quarreled through the following day about the fate of their prisoner, the whole district was aroused against the invaders. The locals were finally able to rescue the pope and put his enemies to flight. Dante, no friend of Boniface, was horrified at what became known as the outrage at Anagni (*Purgatorio*, 20.85–20.90). Boniface returned to Rome a broken man and died there a short while later. Although Philip was deprived of the satisfaction of putting the pope on trial, he had otherwise triumphed over him and shown for all the world to see the practical limits of Boniface's claims. The papacy was again in full crisis, this time not because of an emperor but because of a king of France, whose mischief-making had by no means ended.

AVIGNON:
THE BABYLONIAN CAPTIVITY

Seven popes reigned between 1305 and 1378. All of them were French. Of the 134 cardinals they created during this period 112 were French. For those seventy-two years they resided not in Rome or even in Italy but in Avignon, a papal enclave in southeast France. Avignon is situated on the left bank of the Rhône about fifty-three miles northwest of Marseille. Contemporaries called this phenomenon the Babylonian Captivity of the papacy and saw it as incompatible with the popes' responsibilities as bishop of Rome. The allusion was of course to the deportation to Babylon of the Jews of the ancient Kingdom of Judah by Nebuchadrezzar II.

Popes had been absent from Rome before. In fact, for the century and a half before Avignon, popes resided in Rome for less than half that time. They had lived in cities of the Papal States—Viterbo, Anagni, Orvieto—and occasionally in France. Special about the Avignonese residency, however, was its length and its continuous character. Also special about it was at least the appearance that the popes were under the sway, ongoing, of the French monarchy. That monarchy was the mortal enemy of the English monarchy, and during the Avignonese period the Hundred Years War broke out between the two kingdoms. The popes had an image problem, therefore, with the English, but also with just about everybody else. Unfortunately, the splendid lifestyle of the papal curia at Avignon did nothing to improve the image.

Avignon was surrounded by the lands of the papal fief of Comtat Venaissin. It was, technically, independent of the French monarchy. Nonetheless, though contemporaries exaggerated the control the monarchy exercised during these seven decades, the kings did more than hover in the background. This was particularly true of Philip the Fair. The papacy's long sojourn in French territory seemed like Philip's ultimate victory over Boniface and all that he stood for, but Philip was not satisfied. Until his death in 1314 he pursued an aggressive policy of control, driven by his obsession to bring the dead Boniface to trial to answer for his many crimes.

The Avignonese residency of the popes was, however, not the result of a clever plot masterminded by Philip. It came about almost by accident. When Boniface died in Rome in 1303, the cardinals knew they had to act quickly and decisively, and they unanimously elected Niccolò Boccasino, cardinal-bishop of Ostia and former master general of the Dominican order, who took the name Benedict XI. The new pope had vigorously upheld the legitimacy of Celestine's resignation and, though he was not anti-French, stood by Boniface in the final denouement of his conflict with Philip. Once elected, however, he immediately had to face the question of how to deal with those involved in the attack on his predecessor. The situation was delicate in the extreme. He did not want further to provoke Philip, yet he needed to defend the rights of the church.

Reconciliation was Benedict's goal, but he went about it by caving in to most of the demands of the king and by lifting the sanctions levied against those involved in the plot against Boniface, with the exception of the ringleader, Guillaume de Nogaret. Most important, he absolved Philip and his family of any censures they might have incurred, a measure that did not quell Philip's determination to wreak vengeance on the dead Boniface. In Rome Benedict's concessions, which seemed to compromise the justice of Boniface's actions, outraged more people than they mollified. Factional strife broke out, and Benedict had to withdraw to Perugia, where, after a short pontificate of less than nine months, he died on July 7, 1304.

For almost a year the cardinals wrangled in Perugia over a successor to Benedict, bitterly divided between those who wanted a pope who would uncompromisingly vindicate Boniface's policies and those who were more inclined to compromise. When they finally realized that they could never agree on a candidate from their own number, they looked elsewhere. Their eyes lighted on Bertrand de Got, archbishop of Bordeaux, who was elected in absentia and took the name Clement V. His election was a victory for the pro-French faction but, though the new pope was known personally to only a few of them, the cardinals were led to believe he would respect Boniface's memory.

Clement, who had studied canon law in Bologna but lived almost his entire life in France, was at Bordeaux when he received the totally unexpected news of his election. Although he at first intended to set out for Rome, he never left southern France during his nine-year pontificate. Intelligent but vacillating, he suffered from a debilitating illness, probably cancer, which was a factor dissuading him from undertaking the journey to a city known for its unhealthy climate and unruly population. As a trained canonist, he knew what his duties were in safeguarding the church's position against a rapacious king, but he was unequal to the task of dealing with Philip. He capitulated to the king in the first instance by agreeing to be crowned not in Vienne, the city of his choice, but in Lyons, where the king had just enjoyed a triumph.

In 1309 he settled in Avignon, yielding again to Philip's wishes, and he seems at that point to have given up any idea of going to Rome. The king kept up the pressure to put Boniface on trial, while the pope played for time by making more and more concessions to Philip, which included the absolution of de Nogaret of all guilt and the canonization of Celestine V. Philip, who was also intent on suppressing the Order of Knights Templar, whose wealth he coveted, prevailed upon Clement to call a council at Vienne, 1311–1312. The council ratified Clement's acquiescence in the king's design to suppress the Knights. The sordid story of the confessions of their crimes that Philip had extracted from the Knights under torture has been often told. On only one issue did

Clement resist the king at every turn: the demand to put Boniface on trial.

Why this abject submission? Clement seems, not unreasonably, to have considered himself almost Philip's prisoner. He also was intent on launching another crusade, and for that enterprise he absolutely had to have the support of the king of France. Philip was astute enough to pay lip-service to a crusade but had no intention of doing anything about it. The unhealthy relationship between these two men ended only when they both died in 1314, which enabled a new phase of papal residency in Avignon to begin.

Clement had been pope for hardly a year when he created ten cardinals, nine of whom were French and four of whom were his nephews. In 1310 and 1312 he created more French cardinals, including another nephew, thus ensuring French domination for the foreseeable future. Lavish in his expenditures and deprived of income from the Papal States, he left the papal treasury exhausted. It comes as no surprise, therefore, that the process to elect his successor lasted twenty-seven months and concluded only when the Count of Poitiers, soon to be King Philip V, locked the cardinals in the Dominican convent at Lyons. The count's action finally forced a decision. The cardinals elected Jacques Duèse, cardinal and bishop of Avignon, age seventy-two, in ill health. He took the name John XXII.

The electors obviously envisaged a short pontificate, but Pope John XXII reigned vigorously—all too vigorously, thought his critics—for eighteen years. This wisp-like figure abounded in energy. In character he was a great contrast with Clement. Practical, experienced, morally upright, authoritarian, he met problems head-on and brooked no opposition. His was an unusually proactive pontificate. Personally austere, he showered benefices and other favors on his relatives.

He divided dioceses that had grown too large and redrew the boundaries of others. He confronted the Spiritual Franciscans and condemned their view that Christ and the apostles owned nothing of their own. His actions confirmed the Spirituals' belief that the pope was a heretic. Since John believed Thomas Aquinas held an orthodox view on the poverty question, he canonized him in 1323, the first Scholastic theologian to be so honored. He condemned the twenty-eight theses of the German theologian-mystic Meister Eckhart, and he excommunicated the Franciscan theologian William Ockham for siding with the Spirituals. He intervened in a disputed imperial election and won the enmity of the candidate who prevailed, Louis IV, whom he later excommunicated.

Perhaps most important, he put the papacy on a sound financial basis by initiating a practically new fiscal system. Besides the tithes bishops were supposed to pay annually, he imposed on bishops in all countries the payment to the Apostolic See of the annate, the total revenue of the benefice for the first year of the bishop's incumbency. By other taxes, new or more efficiently collected, he greatly increased the flow of revenues into the papal treasury. He also implemented a new method for fixing fees for official documents issued by the papal curia. As to be expected, measures like these increased resentment of the papacy among both clergy and laity throughout Europe and further damaged the image of the Avignon papacy. The papacy looked like an efficiently functioning and money-hungry secular court. Contemporaries complained it fleeced rather than fed the flock of Christ.

John and his successors used the funds for the operating expenses of an ever-expanding curia, for preparations for launching a crusade, for mobilizing resources for a possible return to Rome and, not least, for supporting the entourage and the high lifestyle of the cardinals and other curial officials. They also spent huge sums on warfare, including military expeditions to reduce the Papal States to obedience.

Also important at Avignon, however, was papal patronage of culture and the arts. Although previous popes funded and otherwise supported the building of churches and their adornment, the Avignon popes enjoyed after Philip's death a period of peaceful existence in a prosperous economy that allowed them to enlarge upon that tradition. They erected a magnificent palace for themselves (see fig. 14.1).

This prosperous and peaceful sojourn allowed them, as well, to become patrons of poets and scholars in a more consistent and almost programmatic way. The popes built up an impressive library, the nucleus for the future Vatican Library. Petrarch was only one of the important men of letters who profited from the situation.

14.1: Papal palace at Avignon

The Pope's Palace at Avignon.

© Jean-Pierre Lescourret/Corbis

Avignon, easy to govern, became after Paris the most exciting city culturally in Europe. Life was pleasant there, compared with the plague-ridden, flood-threatened, insurrection-prone city on the Tiber. Avignon suffered from the Black Death of 1347, true, but less so than many other cities. It enjoyed a central position for trade and commerce, more accessible than Rome. It had a good food supply and produced an excellent wine. Why ever go back to Rome?

Pressure to return mounted. The Romans, who could not live with the popes, also could not live without them. In the middle of the century Cola di Rienzo tried to found a Roman Republic, an independent city-state, but he failed and ended up murdered by a Roman mob. After his disappearance from the scene, Pope Innocent VI (1352–1362) dispatched the Spanish cardinal Gil de Albornoz with a military force to pacify the Papal States and restore order in them, a mission that was successful. The situation in Rome thus became more favorable, and more and more petitions arrived from the city begging for a return. Meanwhile, Innocent, an intelligent and committed reformer, set about eradicating abuses in the curia, simplifying the lifestyle in the papal household, obliging clergy to reside in their benefices, and making candidates for various offices provide proof of their fitness.

The popes at Avignon cannot be dismissed, therefore, as aesthetes without conscience. And their sense of responsibility to Blessed Peter weighed heavily upon at least some of them and was what ultimately motivated them to return to a place they feared would be hostile. As is well known, saints Bridget of Sweden and Catherine of Siena added their voices to the many urging the popes to make the journey, but by the middle of the century the popes did not need to be reminded of their duty. They needed, rather, to be assured that they could successfully fulfill it. In 1367 Pope Urban V, another austere reformer, not a cardinal when elected, who was beatified in the nineteenth century by Pope Pius IX, returned and, surrounded by heavy guard, was received with jubilation. He managed to remain for three years but in the face of a deteriorating political situation believed he could not safely stay on.

Urban died on December 19, 1370, a few months after arriving back in Avignon. In a swift election lasting only two days, the cardinals unanimously elected cardinal-deacon Pierre Roger de Beaufort (d'Égletons), age forty-two. Ordained a priest the day before his coronation, he took the name Gregory XI. Well educated and deeply religious, he from the beginning made it clear, over objections from the curia, that he would return to Rome. Like most of the Avignon popes, he wanted to promote reconciliation with the Greek Church, which entailed a crusade to help the Christians at Constantinople resist the Muslim advances. Rome was the appropriate center for such an initiative.

The difficulties facing him in returning were huge. Prodded by Florence, the Papal States broke into revolt, which forced the pope to send cardinal Robert of Geneva with a strong mercenary force to bring order. Other problems arose, but Gregory, resolute, set out on September 13, 1376. He of course took with him a heavy guard. His large entourage included all but six of the cardinals. Four months later, on January 17, 1377, Gregory made his solemn entry into Rome. Since the Lateran palace was in disrepair, he took up residence in the Vatican.

The pope was not back long before his troubles began. Hostilities with Florence dragged on, and Catherine of Siena bitterly blamed Innocent's intransigence for the stalemate. Meanwhile, the brutality of Robert of Geneva's tactics further aroused opposition to the pope, who for his own safety had to leave the city for Anagni. Never in robust health, the pope, now exhausted and depressed, brooded over evils he believed still to come. Fourteen months after his triumphal entry into Saint Peter's city, he died, in exile from both Avignon and Rome.

Ten days after Gregory's death, sixteen cardinals met in the Vatican for the first papal election in Rome in seventy-five years. Twelve were French, three Italian, and one Spanish. As they gathered, the city burst into an ugly frenzy. The Romans, fully realizing that most of the cardinals were French and that they themselves had all but driven Gregory from their city, feared the election of another French pope, who would take himself and his court back to Avignon. Their desperation sprang not out of piety but out of their realization, born from harsh experience, that the absence of the pope spelled the absence of revenue.

Excited crowds demonstrated in the streets, clamoring for "a Roman or at least an Italian" for pope. At one point they broke into the papal palace, and only with difficulty were they dispersed. That evening the heads of the various regions of the city visited the cardinals and warned them that the situation was explosive. One problem the cardinals faced in electing an Italian was that from their own number their choice was severely limited. But when rioting broke out again the next morning, the cardinals by barely the required two-thirds majority elected the archbishop of Bari, Bartolomeo Prignano, who of course was not present at the conclave. As Prignano's consent was being obtained, a mob again burst into the conclave and could only be got rid of by pretending that one of the few Italian cardinals, elderly and feeble, had been chosen. This desperate ruse distracted the mob sufficiently to allow the cardinals to escape from the bizarre scene.

They returned when Prignano accepted, and they duly enthroned him. The new pope took the name Urban VI. He was well known to the cardinals because he had served for twenty years in the curia in Avignon, where he was respected for his austerity and practical skills. He seemed like a good choice. Only after his election, it seems, did he reveal another side of his personality—obstinate, obsessive, paranoid, and prone to violent outbursts of temper. But for a few weeks the cardinals, as well as envoys of monarchs at the court, tried to excuse his tirades and insults. Urban announced a radical reform of the cardinals' lifestyle with vehement ranting, all the while accusing the cardinals of luxury and even misappropriation of funds from his treasury. His behavior became so eccentric that some wondered if they had elected a deranged man.

One by one the cardinals began to slip out of Rome to Anagni, there to decide the next step. Three Italians hesitantly stayed with Urban but eventually joined the others. The cardinals tried to reach an agreement with Urban, suggesting, for instance, a system of coadjutors but, not surprisingly, they got nowhere. Finally, on August 2, 1378, they called on him to abdicate, not helping their cause by labeling him "anti-Christ, demon, apostate, tyrant." Urban reacted with a fury, which further strengthened the cardinals' resolve. On September 20 they disavowed the April election as done under duress and therefore invalid, and they proceeded to elect a new pope, Robert of Geneva, cousin of the king of France, who took the name Clement VII. Urban responded in kind by creating twenty-five cardinals loyal to himself. The Great Western Schism had begun.

THREE POPES AT A TIME:
THE GREAT WESTERN SCHISM

Robert of Geneva, created cardinal by Gregory XI and leader of the military force that enabled Gregory to return to Rome, was present at the conclave that elected Urban. He was the first to do him homage but was also one of the first to react against him. He played a leading role in the drama that led up to his own unanimous election in September (the three Italian cardinals abstained but concurred). The new pope was neither the first nor the last churchman to be a skilled soldier and an accomplished politician. He was chosen as pope, however, most probably because he was related to both the German imperial family and the French royal family, and it was thought that with these and his other political connections he could rally support for the deposition of Urban and his own election. As it turned out, he was only partially successful in doing so. In the meantime, he tried by military force to establish himself in Rome and central Italy but was repulsed. On May 22, 1379, Clement, accompanied by the cardinals, bade goodbye to Italy for good and established himself and his curia in Avignon.

The two popes excommunicated each other. The schism that ensued was certainly not the first papal schism, nor would it be the last.
But it was important in ways the others were not. It dragged on for
almost forty years, two generations. It seemed then and now almost
impossible to resolve on juridical or historical grounds. Never before,
for instance, had the same cardinals elected the two contending popes.
For every reason favoring the validity of Urban, a reason could be
found favoring Clement. In the Vatican Archives there is a hefty port-
folio called the *Libri de Schismate* (*Documents on the Schism*), a collection
of testimonies and arguments from contemporaries, the examination of
which has consistently proved inconclusive for deciding who was the
rightful pope.

Saint Catherine of Siena stuck by Urban and called the cardinals
who deserted him "devils in human form," but Saint Vincent Ferrer, a
Dominican like Catherine, sided with Clement. The Catholic church
has never made a formal pronouncement on the claimants, but especially in the past hundred years the Holy See has in the lists of popes it
regularly publishes always sided with the Roman over the Avignonese
line.

Here are the issues. The election of Urban was irregular, done
under duress. That is clear. After the election, however, when the
danger dissipated, the cardinals did Urban homage, participated in his
enthronement, and performed other actions that indicated they themselves accepted the election as valid. Then Urban began to act strangely.
All canonists agreed that an incapacitated person could not validly act
as the head of a corporation. But was Urban truly deranged or at least
incompetent to such a degree that he could not validly function? His
subsequent actions as pope point in such directions. He went to war
with partisans of Clement in Italy, which helped plunge the peninsula
into violence and anarchy. At one point he had cardinals whom he accused of plotting against him tortured and put to death. The pontificate
was an almost unmitigated disaster, but it was not the first.

No matter who was right and who was wrong, the damage had
been done. What especially made this schism such a calamity was that
it became a truly international affair, not just a squabble between baronial factions in Rome. It divided nation against nation. The French of

course supported Clement, which meant the English supported Urban, which meant the Scots supported Clement. And so it went. Hungary, Poland, Scandinavia, Flanders, the Empire, and the northern Italian states rallied to Urban. Aragon, Castile, León, Burgundy, Savoy, and Naples went with Clement. This listing does not, however, do justice to the complexity of the situation because allegiances shifted and because princes, counts, and other magnates did not necessarily follow the lead of their sovereigns. The Hundred Years War between England and France continued its dreary course, further exacerbating the problem. Confusion reached down to the grass roots as the rival popes supported different bishops for a given town or city—and tried to exact taxes from them.

The rulers of Europe, despite their rivalries and their occasional attempts to draw advantage from the situation, were increasingly scandalized by it and began seeking means as best they could to provide a solution. When Clement died at Avignon in 1394, the cardinals took oaths stipulating that if they were elected they would do everything in their power to end the schism. With that they quickly and unanimously elected Pedro de Luna, who took the name Benedict XIII. He had been the sole Spanish cardinal at the election of Urban and the last cardinal to desert him. But he deserted because he finally became convinced that Urban was so incapable of governing that his election was voided. From that point forward he was utterly committed to the rightness of Clement's cause and therefore of his own.

Shortly after his election King Charles VI of France sent a delegation to Avignon led by his uncle and brother urging the new pope to abdicate, but with Benedict the delegation had not the slightest chance of success. The rebuff marked the beginning of a weakening French support for Avignon. Charles then went to work with other princes. Two years later, 1397, an Anglo-French delegation got nowhere with him, and a German delegation the following year met with the same result.

Clement and Benedict were the only two popes of the Avignon line throughout the schism. In the Roman line there were four. When Urban died in Rome in 1380, Boniface IX, a compromise candidate, succeeded him. During his fifteen year reign, he made no effort to end the schism and, unlike Benedict in Avignon, was under no serious pressure to do so. His successor Innocent VII, pope for two years, swore before his election to do everything possible to end the schism but did nothing. When Gregory XII was elected in 1406, he took a similar oath, seems sincerely to have meant it but, elderly, vacillating, and easily swayed, he was incapable of pursuing a solution with the persistence and conviction it required.

The situation seemed beyond redemption. Pressure from on high had been tried and did not work. What about a military solution? This possibility, called the *via actionis* ("the action solution"), was discussed in the universities as well as the royal courts but got nowhere for a variety of reasons. The easiest solution was to persuade one of the popes to resign in favor of the other, the *via cessionis* ("conceding"). It had been tried and failed, and prospects for future success with it seemed dim. How about both resigning to clear the way for a new election, or at least meeting together to work out a solution *via compromessi* ("compromise")?

After Gregory's election in Rome in 1406, pressure built from within both colleges of cardinals to force the two popes to meet. After stormy discussions and negotiations the popes agreed to do so. They were to meet at the latest by November 1, 1407, in Savona, a city on the Ligurian coast near Genoa that, though Italian in culture, was Avignonese in its allegiance. The popes set out, but Benedict stalled at Portovenere and Gregory at Lucca, within a day's journey of each other. They negotiated for months. The French monarchy was so disgusted with the farce that in May 1408, it officially withdrew its support from Benedict and declared itself neutral, a heavy blow. Benedict excommunicated the king.

Gregory's cardinals grew ever more exasperated with his delaying tactics, and in the same month of May they practically all deserted him, fled to nearby Pisa, joined forces with four of Benedict's cardinals, and in early July felt they had sufficient support to send out a summons to a general council to be held at Pisa the next year, in March 1409. They received an encouragingly positive response from most rulers and bishops. The council opened as planned. In attendance were twenty-two cardinals, eighty bishops plus one hundred proxies, forty-one priors or heads of religious orders, eighty-seven abbots, and three hundred canonists and theologians. Both popes were summoned but did not respond. In their absence they were deposed, and in their place a joint conclave of both Benedict's and Gregory's cardinals elected Pietro Philarghi as Alexander V.

In his *Dictatus Papae* three and a half centuries earlier, Pope Gregory VII had declared, "The pope is judged by no one." Even before the *Dictatus* this was an accepted principle of canon law, but the original formulation, which continued to be accepted and discussed by canonists throughout the period, was longer, "The pope is judged by no one unless he should be found to deviate from the faith" (*Papa a nemine judicatur nisi deprehendatur a fide devius*). Canonists and theologians serenely discussed, therefore, the possibility that a pope might fall into heresy and that, if he did, he could be "judged," that is, deposed. They came to define heresy broadly so as to include giving grave scandal, for such scandal led the faithful into heresy or schism.

But judged by whom? The traditional court of appeal in the church from the earliest times was a council, so it is not surprising that canonists proposed or assumed that a council was the body to which the task fell—the *via concilii*. Thus, in the decades leading up to Pisa, 1409, the idea that a council might be needed to end the Schism had gained strength and was ever more widely proposed as required by the desperate straits of the church. This was the situation in which Conciliarism was born, a theory about the superior authority of councils in relationship to the papacy.

Unfortunately, the term covers at least two understandings of that relationship, which has led to considerable confusion. The first, agreed to by most mainline canonists at the time, was that under certain circumstances a council might have to act against a pope. For the most part this seems to be the interpretation operative at Pisa and later at Constance. The second was more radical and, at least in the West, untraditional: that councils are the supreme authority, of whose decrees the popes are merely executors. This understanding gained ground in some circles after the Schism was resolved and provoked, of course, strong papal reaction. There were, besides, many variations on both these understandings.

Since both the *via cessionis* and the *via compromessi* had failed, and the *via actionis* was repugnant, the *via concilii* was the only alternative left. The cardinals who convoked Pisa were on solid, if not uncontested, canonical ground. When Pisa opened, therefore, the archbishop of Milan expounded sixteen reasons why under the circumstances a council could with full legitimacy proceed against the two popes. Much later in the century the next pope after Alexander V to take that name was at the time universally recognized as Alexander VI and has been thus known ever since. Moreover, until 1947, the Vatican itself in its official annual "catalog," the *Annuario Pontificio*, consistently listed both Alexander and his successor as the legitimate popes. The *Annuario* therefore terminated Gregory XII's pontificate in 1409, an implicit recognition of the legitimacy of Pisa's deposition of him.

However legitimate Pisa was, it did not work. France, England, Bohemia, Prussia, and northern Italy rallied to Alexander, and sentiment in favor of Alexander was otherwise widespread. But the two original popes, especially Gregory, managed to hold onto the loyalty, not very solid, of some constituencies. Then Alexander died suddenly after a pontificate of less than a year, which led to the hasty election of Baldassare Cossa, John XXIII. The new pope, who had been a driving force at Pisa, was probably elected because he was a soldier, somebody who could move against Gregory's allies to secure Rome and the environs. John was a poor choice made for a poor reason, and he soon alienated many who had supported Pisa. There were now three popes instead of two. The *via concilii* had made matters worse, not better.

The prospects for a solution seemed more distant than ever. At this point Emperor-elect Sigismund took the initiative, playing a role his predecessors had played at least since the time of Henry III. When after a three-party contest for the imperial throne he finally triumphed in 1410, he took the resolution of the Schism as a highest priority and went to work persuading John to convoke a council at Constance for that purpose. He obviously considered John the legitimate, or at least the most probably legitimate of the contending popes. John, wary and reluctant but hopeful the council would help him consolidate his position, finally agreed and convoked the council to meet in 1414.

For lack of an alternative, the *via concilii* was going to be tried again. This time, however, the council would take its time, do its utmost to observe all the niceties of canon law, and try to win as widespread support for its decisions as possible. It did not want a repeat of the problems that ensued after Pisa. The response to John's convocation, though encouraging, was not overwhelming. But when on Christmas Day 1414, the emperor himself appeared at Constance, he gave the council a needed boost in prestige, and attendance began to grow. The Council of Constance, 1414–1418, eventually grew to be one of the largest assemblies of clergy and laity in the Middle Ages. At its peak it could probably boast close to nine hundred participants. It immediately set for itself a three-fold agenda: (1) end the schism, (2) reform the church "in head and members, in faith and discipline," and (3) eradicate heresy.

John came to the council optimistic about his future, but he soon became aware of the growing sentiment for wiping the slate clean and also of displeasure at his behavior both before and after he became pope. After four months of council he became convinced the council would move against him. In mid-March 1415, therefore, he fled in disguise, thinking his action would either force the council to disband or call into question its legitimacy. He underestimated the determination of the participants to see the matter through, and he badly miscalculated the effect his flight had on them. His disruptive action only strengthened their resolve.

Two weeks later, March 30, the council issued its most famous decree, *Haec Sancta*, in which it asserted its authority over anybody who tried to frustrate its goal:

This holy synod of Constance, which is a general council . . . legitimately assembled in the Holy Spirit . . . has power immediately from Christ, and everyone of whatever state or dignity, even papal, is bound to obey it in those matters that pertain to the faith and to the eradication of the schism. Our most holy lord pope John XXIII may not move or transfer the Roman curia and its public office, or its or their officials from this city to another place.

Meanwhile, John had the misfortune to be caught and brought back to Constance under guard. He was tried for the usual crimes—simony, scandal, malfeasance, to which was added his perfidy in fleeing the council and trying to disrupt it. On May 29 the council deposed him and held him prisoner until a year after the council ended. After he was released, John was restored as a cardinal and treated graciously. When he died he was entombed with honor in a beautiful Renaissance monument in the baptistery of the cathedral of Florence, where it can be seen today.

The council then had to deal with Benedict and Gregory. While that long process was going on, it took up the business of heresy, which meant the Englishman John Wyclif, long dead, and a follower of his teachings in Bohemia, Jan Huss, very much alive. Wyclif (1330–1384), philosopher and theologian, had already been condemned by English bishops and by the papacy. He did not propose any great Trinitarian or Christological heresies but held that authority in both secular and ecclesiastical society was legitimate only if those who exercised it were in the state of grace. Influenced by the radical Franciscan movement, he used this teaching to denounce ecclesiastical wealth and the bishops and popes of his day, and he held doctrines on the Eucharist and other matters that clashed with orthodox positions. The council condemned, first, eighty-five and then another forty-five propositions attributed to this "pseudo-Christian."

Jan Huss was summoned to the council to answer for his teachings and was granted a safe-conduct by the emperor. When he arrived, he was tried, found guilty of heresy, and saw thirty teachings attributed to him condemned. He refused to recant. The council handed him over to the secular authorities and, despite the safe-conduct, he was burned at the stake at Constance. This action of the council left scars in Bohemia that have never healed. In 1999 Pope John Paul II expressed "deep regret for the cruel death inflicted upon Jan Huss."

Meanwhile the council's negotiations with Gregory, now ninety years old, were moving swiftly ahead. He finally agreed to resign on condition that he could formally convoke the council in his own name, which the council agreed to allow him. On July 4, 1415, Gregory abdicated, and the two colleges of cardinals, his and John's, were officially united into one.

The council had no such success with Benedict. No matter what stratagem it pursued, he refused to follow suite. The emperor himself went to see him at Perpignan to persuade him to abdicate honorably, but Benedict scoffed at the very idea. He was, however, now almost bereft of support. Finally, with no alternative left to it, on July 26, 1417, two years after Gregory's resignation, the council deposed Benedict. With that measure Benedict's support dwindled virtually to nothing, but he continued to breathe defiance until his death in 1423.

After Benedict's deposition the council could now, after almost three years since its opening, move to the election of a new pope. Badly disillusioned, however, by the behavior of the popes, it issued the decree *Frequens* ("frequent'), which required that henceforth councils were to be held regularly: the first one five years after Constance, the second after seven more years, and then every ten years thereafter in perpetuity. *Frequens* was a resounding vote of no-confidence in papal leadership.

For the election of a new pope at Constance it suspended "for this time only" the usual rules and expanded the electors to include besides the twenty-two cardinals thirty other members of the council. This expanded electorate took only three days in November 1417, to elect Oddo (Otto) Colonna, an excellent choice, who took the name Martin V. The council published the news of his election, which was received with jubilation and accepted practically everywhere as the long-awaited resolution of the schism.

PART

IV

Renaissance
and
Reformation

THE RESTORED PAPACY

Martin V, vigorous, able, and politically astute, lived relatively simply despite coming from one of the great baronial families of Rome. He nonetheless made ample, sometimes harsh use of his family's prestige and power when it served his purpose. He was determined to return the papacy to Rome, his family seat, but, more important, the see of Blessed Peter. To many people the decision to return there was not a foregone conclusion. Rome, never easy to govern or protect, had been neglected and allowed to drift for a century. The infrastructure had eroded, churches and public buildings fallen into disrepair, and the surrounding countryside become the home of brigands. Moreover, the Papal States, which provided the first line of defense for the city, were controlled by local lords or, sometimes, upstart men of fortune such as Braccio da Montone, who dominated much of the territory. Rome itself was held by Neapolitan troops, which required Martin to negotiate his entry with Queen Joanna II.

With Martin begins the slow evolution of the conviction on the part of the popes that they can no longer rely on foreign princes to protect them. They had tried that many times, and many times it had failed—their protectors turned into their masters. They would now try to rely on themselves, by establishing firm control over the States and increasing the strength of their army. They would begin ever more to consider themselves and be considered by others as monarchs in the full sense of the term. This was not exactly new, but it was now more obvious, deliberate, programmatic, and successful.

Martin slowly made his way from Constance to Rome, negotiating and threatening, until finally on September 28, 1420, two years after he had closed the council, he entered the city. Before he could do much else he had to bring Braccion under control, which he did when his forces defeated him in 1424. Five years later he had to put down a serious revolt in the States led by Bologna. Meanwhile he turned his attention to rebuilding the city, which marks the beginning of Rome's architectural renaissance. The restoration enterprise will be carried forward even more vigorously by Martin's successors to give us by the middle of the seventeenth century the Rome we know today. Although the papacy continued to suffer many vicissitudes, it and the city of Rome were on their way to a new stability.

Martin showed his organizational skills in his management of the curia and in his appointment of able and upright men as cardinals. He kept a tight rein on them. Like a number of his predecessors he wanted to better relations with the Greek-speaking church and, though nothing came of it, he even agreed in principle to the holding of a council in the East. He supported the charismatic Franciscan preacher, Saint Bernardino of Siena, against his detractors. He denounced violent anti-Jewish preaching and forbade under pain of automatic excommunication the forced baptism of Jewish children. He did most of the right things, but he ruled with an iron hand, which his family's wealth and connections enabled him to do. Martin in his turn favored his relatives with grants of land and other benefactions that fueled resentment against them and him.

Though elected by the council, he was as ardent a promoter of the traditional prerogatives of the papacy as any of his predecessors. He nevertheless considered himself bound by the decree *Frequens*. Precisely five years after the conclusion of Constance, he convoked a council for Pavia, near Milan, in April 1423. Plague forced the council to move to Siena. Martin, fearing antipapal sentiment, decided not to appear at it and, since attendance was poor, he was able to close it in February 1424, without its accomplishing much of anything. Bishops did not want to spend months away from home at meetings that had no urgency.

Before the Council of Pavia-Siena adjourned, however, it decreed that in conformity with *Frequens* another council was to meet in seven years, 1431, and it designated Basel as the site. Martin duly convoked the Council of Basel, but he died in February 1431, five months before the council opened. After his obsequies the cardinals gathered in the Dominican church of Santa Maria sopra Minerva in the center of Rome and chose cardinal Gabriele Condulmaro, a Venetian, nephew of Pope Gregory XII, who took the name Eugene IV.

The new pope was to have a long and stormy pontificate (1431–1447). A devout churchman, favored by his uncle with early promotions up the ecclesiastical ladder of honors, he lacked the finesse of his predecessor in dealing with the complicated problems facing him. He also lacked Martin's political base in Rome to back him in time of crisis. His pontificate ultimately ended well, but almost despite Eugene rather than because of him. Like Martin, he was extremely wary of councils, one of which had forced his uncle's resignation. His pontificate would be defined, however, first unhappily by the Council of Basel and then happily by the Council of Florence.

Even as he began to deal with the Council of Basel hundreds of miles away, he took on the Colonna family in Rome. He heavy-handedly forced members of the family to surrender vast territories Martin had granted them, and he similarly tried to move against Colonna partisans in other ways. Although what he tried to accomplish may have been praiseworthy, he acted too soon, too harshly, and in too unconsidered a manner. The Colonnas and their allies were not pleased. They were powerful. They stirred up as much trouble for Eugene as they could, which was considerable.

Within two years of his election, Eugene's position in Rome had become desperate. In May 1434, open rebellion against him broke out, and he tried to slip out of the city in such a clumsy disguise that he was recognized and pelted with stones and rotten fruit as he finally made a successful escape. He had already lost control of the Papal States, which were now overrun by the troops of Francesco Sforza working for Filippo Maria Visconti, duke of Milan. Eugene could not, therefore, take refuge in papal cities like Viterbo and Orvieto, so he threw himself on the mercy of Cosimo de' Medici in Florence and was taken in as an honored refugee. He would reside in Florence for the next nine years, until 1443.

While these dramatic events were unfolding, Eugene was also running into problems with the council, whose necessity he did not see and whose potential for trouble-making he feared. He was, meanwhile, continuing Martin's conversations with Constantinople, which again was looking to the West for aid against the Ottoman Turks threatening the city. When the council officially opened at Basel in July 1431, attendance was so poor that it could not do business. It was able to hold its first formal session only on December 14. The months of wheel-spinning had given Eugene the excuse he needed. On December 18 he dissolved the council and at the same time promised another in eighteen months in Bologna that the Greeks would attend and over which he would preside in person.

Eugene's precipitous action backfired badly. It stunned the council and set off a howl of protest, which won support for the council in the world at large—support that it had hitherto lacked. *Haec Sancta* and *Frequens* gave those present at Basel a strong sense of their authority. The council refused to disperse. On the contrary, attendance increased. Eugene by this time had lost even the support of his cardinals, with only six out of twenty-one siding with him. He backtracked but in stages, which further inflamed resentment. He eventually received an ultimatum from the council threatening to start proceedings against him unless he appeared.

For a short while it looked as if another schism was in the making, which was averted only through the intervention and mediation with the council of emperor Sigismund. Eugene, now with his hands full with the problems in Rome and the Papal States, had his back to the wall. In the most humiliating terms, he had to acknowledge the council's legitimacy and rescind his bull of dissolution. The council of Basel was moving rapidly into a radical Conciliarism: council supreme over pope.

Basel had won the first round, a victory that only increased its sense of power. Constance had taken reform of the church "in head and members, in faith and discipline" as one of its three major goals, but it had been able to address the reform only as the council was winding down in 1418. Basel now took it up with a vengeance. On June 9, 1435, it abolished throughout Christendom almost all papal taxes, including the annates, and forbade the exacting of fees for official documents issued by the curia—reform of "the head." Eugene immediately denounced the measures and sent a solemn protest to the Christian princes.

The council and the pope were on a collision course. What ultimately divided them was the possibility of reunion with the Greek church. Eugene was in contact with emperor John VIII Palaeologus, but so was the council. On September 7, 1434, the council issued a decree, making known that the emperor and the patriarch of Constantinople had received envoys from the council and that the Greeks had appointed three emissaries to it. The emissaries came to Basel and expressed their desire for reunion. The council offered several cities as possible sites for a council of reunion but excluded Florence and Modena, because Eugene had proposed them. The Greeks, however, favored the papal choices—they were of easier access for them. More important, the Greeks realized that for the reunion to work it had to be effected under the auspices of the bishop of Rome.

With that Eugene's moment had at last arrived. He transferred the council to Ferrara, an important city in the Papal States that was now under control, and the Greeks came. After six months, with pestilence spreading in the region and funds running out, Eugene transferred the council to Florence when Cosimo agreed to help fund it. He had struck a mortal blow to Basel. Although some bishops remained at Basel, it had lost its attractiveness. The prospect of a council of reunion, legitimately convoked by the pope, was appealing, and the prospect of another schism was horrifying. The still sizable remnant at Basel suspended Eugene in January 1438, declared him deposed the following year, and elected Felix V to succeed him. The French continued for a while to support Basel, but as Florence moved to its happy conclusion Basel sputtered almost into insignificance.

The Greeks arrived at Ferrara and then at Florence in full force, led by emperor John himself. He brought with him Joseph, the patriarch of Constantinople. The full delegation of bishops, theologians, notaries, and others numbered perhaps as many as seven hundred. Of those seven hundred "Greeks" about two hundred were not Greek. The delegation included, for instance, the metropolitan of Kiev and bishops from Georgia. With their exotic (to Western eyes) vestments and clothing and with their different liturgical forms and chant, they fascinated even the sophisticated Florentines.

In comparison the Latin representation seemed small and lackluster—only about two hundred bishops, supported of course by many theologians and hangers-on. But the pope was there, which gave the assembly its seal of authenticity. Both he and Joseph were present at the sessions, held in the cathedral, next to Giotto's magnificent *campanile*, bell tower. Florence was aglow with the first brilliance of its literary and artistic renaissance.

The council had a profound cultural impact on the West by sparking a new enthusiasm for Greek literature and philosophy. Except for a few pockets here and there, knowledge of the Greek language had practically died out in the West. What medieval scholars knew of Greek learning they knew through Latin translation. That now began to change rapidly. Cosimo de' Medici, for instance, commissioned the first translation into Latin of the works of Plato, a direct result of the impact the council had on him.

It was John, the emperor, who propelled the quest for reunion. As always, sincere piety was admixed with political exigencies. He desperately needed Western military assistance against the Turks. The Greek bishops felt the urgency less, but many of them, with the same mixed motives, wanted the council to succeed. Patriarch Joseph was old and in poor health. He died just as the council concluded and was buried in Florence. Although he provided weak leadership, the Greeks tried to hold their ground and were not ready for reunion at any price.

The council focused on four old issues: first, papal primacy—was it a primacy of honor or of jurisdiction; secondly, the *filioque*—did the Holy Spirit proceed from the Father and Son or from the Father through the Son; third, was there in the afterlife a state known as purgatory; fourth, in the Eucharist was leavened or unleavened bread to be used. On that last issue, which seems trivial but that carried centuries of symbolic weight, the council made the sensible and obvious compromise: the West could legitimately continue with unleavened, and the East with leavened. Purgatory was a teaching developed in the West in tandem with the development of indulgences and was undeveloped in the East. Nonetheless, the Greeks found sufficient basis in their own tradition to allow them to go along with it. The Greeks agreed with the teaching that the Spirit proceeded from both Father and Son according to the explanation of it provided in the decree.

The big sticking point of course was the authority of the papacy. Some of the Greeks were persuaded by arguments, some simply bowed to pressure. They in any case agreed to a remarkably strong statement: the pope had "full power of tending, ruling, and governing the whole church." A moment of supreme triumph for Eugene! Finally, on July 6, 1439, the bull of reunion was published, *Laetentur coeli*—"Let the heavens rejoice!" The Greeks departed, but further reunions were negotiated, with the Armenians in 1439, with the Copts in 1442, with the Syrians in 1444, with the Chaldeans and Maronites in 1445.

The reunion with the Greeks came to naught. Even in Florence many Greeks supported the decree only tepidly, reluctantly, and perhaps with fingers crossed. When the delegation returned home, it was greeted especially by the monks with cries of shame and betrayal. The expected financial, political, and military aid from the West never arrived. Constantinople fell to the Turks in 1453, less than fifteen years after the council ended.

The tragedy of the fall of Constantinople was in the future, however, when Eugene returned to Rome in 1443, enabled to do so by the great boost to his prestige from the council and to a favorable shift in the politics of the kingdom of Naples. The crusade he launched that year to help the Greeks ended disastrously, but otherwise his last years were tranquil and successful, a striking contrast with his first. He died in 1447. Only to his successor, Nicholas V, did the anti-pope of Basel, Felix V, submit his resignation in 1449. Nicholas received the resignation graciously, named Felix a cardinal, and incorporated several of Felix's cardinals into his college. He thus brought the schism to a quiet close.

Fortune smiled on Nicholas V. Elected as a compromise candidate, he proved to be just the adroit and conciliatory pontiff needed after stormy days. As a young man he acted as tutor to the children of some of the leading families of Florence, including the Medici, which gave him invaluable connections in that city. During the Council of Florence he made a favorable impression on Eugene, who created Nicholas a cardinal the year before he died. Nicholas owed the diplomatic and political success of his early years as pope partly to the fact that he had not been a cardinal long enough to get embroiled in the rivalries among them.

Nicholas declared 1450 a jubilee year. It was a great success, bringing thousands of pilgrims to the city, which pleased the merchants and helped fill depleted papal coffers. The single most celebrated event during the year was the canonization of Bernardine of Siena, which brought special jubilation to the Italian pilgrims who had heard him preach. The jubilee boosted the prestige of the papacy, which had been so badly damaged in the century leading up to the Council of Florence, and it also boosted the prestige of the city of Rome, now experienced by the pilgrims as something better than its reputation as a den of thieves and robbers. Funds from the jubilee provided the pope with money to repair an aqueduct. It brought water into Rome that later would flow into the famed Trevi Fountain. With Nicholas's pontificate the city's fortunes took a significant turn for the better, which would continue, not without setbacks, as the decades rolled on.

Nicholas is remembered most of all as a patron of culture. Deeply devout, he was also deeply and broadly learned. He had the papal library brought to Rome from Avignon. He invited scholars to his court to translate Christian and classical Greek authors into Latin. He was able therefore to add some 1,200 Greek and Latin manuscripts to the collection, which makes him the real founder of the Vatican Library. Elected on the feast of Thomas Aquinas, he initiated an annual liturgical celebration of the saint in the Church of the Minerva that grew to be the most solemn such event in Rome outside the precincts of the Vatican. At his behest Fra Angelico, the Florentine Dominican, frescoed a small chapel in the Vatican, an early sign that Rome would succeed Florence as a Renaissance city, par excellence.

Because the Lateran palace was in such a dreadful state of disrepair, Nicholas settled in the Vatican and set about restoring the Borgo, the area around it. His plans for that area for the most part remained plans, but he established a precedent. The Vatican displaced the Lateran as the popes' habitual residence, a tradition that has persisted to the present day.

In 1452 Nicholas crowned Frederick III emperor in Saint Peter's, the last imperial coronation ever to take place in Rome. It too was a triumph for the pope, but the next year he uncovered a plot to assassinate him, which revealed that underneath a surface calm in Rome unrest still seethed. The would-be assassin, Stefano Porcaro, dreamed of throwing off papal government of the city to establish a republic in its place. The fall of Constantinople that same year brought Nicholas further sadness. It ended for the papacy and the Christian church an era that began over a millennium earlier with the accession of Constantine the Great to the imperial throne and his transfer of the capital from Rome to the city on the Bosporus.

THE RENAISSANCE POPES

The expression Renaissance popes brings a wry smile to people's faces, as if to indicate they know what scoundrels they were. The name Borgia springs immediately to mind. Textbooks love to depict them as providing the goad that propelled Luther into denouncing the institution as a cesspool of vice and the popes as the very anti-Christ. But the expression brings another kind of smile to the faces of art historians, a smile of pleasure. From the middle of the fifteenth century into the middle of the seventeenth, the popes, their families, and others in their entourage were among the most enlightened and prodigal patrons of the arts of all times. They happened to have at hand towering geniuses—Raphael, Michelangelo, Bernini, and Caravaggio. As if these were not enough, they also had Botticelli, Signorelli, Perugino, Pinturicchio, Pietro da Cortona, Bramante, Borromini, and seemingly countless other artists, architects, engineers, and city planners of awe-inspiring, superlative talent. They turned Rome into a city of incomparable artistic treasure.

Although the lurid aspect of the papacy of the era has been exaggerated, it is almost impossible to exaggerate the achievement of the cultural aspect. Curiously enough, there is a connection between the two, which becomes clear only through an understanding of the problems the popes faced and the solutions they adopted to deal with them. The first and most pressing problem was the old one, their personal safety and the safety of the city. The problem extended to the Papal States, the first line of defense. That is not to deny that popes exploited the city and the States to enrich family and friends. But whatever the motives in play at any given moment, gaining effective military and political control of the States loomed large on the papal agenda during this period.

The popes were not, however, in a strong position to gain such control. Unlike most rulers in Europe by this time, they were elected to their throne. Every death, therefore, was a crisis for the institution. Popes were almost invariably elected when they were already in the final decade of their lives. They had short reigns. They were from now on rarely natives of the city or even the region. They had to establish their authority quickly, or they would not establish it at all.

Since they often did not know whom they could trust, they turned to their families. This was nothing new. Nepotism had for many centuries been almost endemic to the papacy. What was new about it in the Renaissance were a few spectacularly bad nephews and, as the papacy became more secure and prosperous, the prodigality with which the popes were able to lavish both the worthy and the unworthy with lucrative favors.

After the debacle of Basel, the popes became even more wary of councils than they had become of the purported friendship of princes. The Renaissance popes conveniently forgot *Frequens*. The oaths they were obliged to take before the actual balloting began in the conclave sometimes included a promise to call a council if they were elected, but no pope, once elected, felt obliged to observe it. Pius II, Sixtus IV, and Julius II, moreover, issued bulls prohibiting an appeal to a council over the head of the pope.

The popes wore both a crown and a miter. As they became more wary of princes, they became more professedly princes themselves—partly in self-defense, partly for less worthy motives. The prestige of the papal court took on a new importance, which meant the court needed a fitting setting for itself, a city that would be a credit to it. The defense, restoration, and adornment of Rome became a high priority for the Renaissance popes. Although this enterprise was driven by po-litical motives, it never could be divorced from the popes' zeal to honor God and the saints with the best that human talent could produce. Constantine had long ago set the standard. As the prior general of the Augustinian order, Giles of Viterbo, said of the new Saint Peter's as it was being built, "Let it soar to be a magnificent edifice that God might be more magnificently praised."

The three popes who succeeded Nicholas V did relatively little to promote the arts and in some ways hardly seem like "Renaissance popes." Callixtus III, pope for only three years, was another compro-mise candidate and, most surprising, a Spaniard. He burned with a determination, unrealistic in the extreme, to win back Constantinople and tried to launch a crusade to accomplish it. The first of the Borgia popes, he is remembered principally for creating his young nephew Rodrigo a cardinal, the first step toward putting the future and notori-ous Alexander VI on the road to the papacy.

Callixtus's successor, Pius II (1458–1464), was an altogether differ-ent type, the only pope who can genuinely claim to be a distinguished man of letters. He had had a checkered ecclesiastical career, which included being secretary to Felix V, the anti-pope at Basel. As pope he, like Callixtus, was consumed with the idea of a crusade to recover Con-stantinople but also like Callixtus was unable to rally kings and princes to undertake it. Despite his background, he did little to promote the cultural and artistic program Nicholas had set in motion.

Paul II (1464–1471), a nephew of Eugene IV, built as his residence while still a cardinal the Palazzo Venezia, even today one of the great monuments in the center of Rome. But as pope he too did relatively little for the cultural life of the city and was in fact unfairly accused of repressing it. The Turks were now pressing hard against Hungary. Paul was not able to do much more than supply some financial assistance against them. It was a pontificate of little import.

The same certainly cannot be said of Sixtus IV (1471–1484), Francesco della Rovere, one of the great enigmas in the history of the papacy. The values he seemed to espouse before he became pope con-trast so starkly with his actions as pope that he almost seems to be two different persons. Born of a moderately prosperous family in Savona, he as a teenager entered the Franciscan order, made a brilliant career for himself as a theologian and preacher, and rose to be elected in 1464 superior general of the order. Three years later he was cardinal, four years later pope.

He was elected as a compromise by the slimmest of the required two-thirds margin, twelve votes out of eighteen. New to the college, he was above factions, and he had among his peers a reputation for austerity, learning, and administrative skills. But something happened. The first signs of it appeared during the conclave itself with the machinations of his nephew, Pietro Riario, who acted as his attendant and who promised favors and preferments to the cardinals who voted for his uncle. During the early years of his papacy, the unscrupulous and ambitious Pietro became known as his "tutor," the man who educated his uncle in the ways of the world. Whether due to Pietro's influence or some other reason, the new pope, formed as a young man in the austerity and other-worldliness of the Rule of Saint Francis, soon displayed a this-worldliness and ruthlessness that shocked even jaded contemporaries.

The ballots were hardly counted before he made Pietro and another young nephew, Giuliano della Rovere (future Pope Julius II) cardinals and loaded them with benefices. He later made four more nephews cardinals, and through his appointments of thirty other men to the College of Cardinals launched a secularization of it that would not be reversed for a half-century. To pay for his soaring expenditures, he sold offices and privileges, while he meanwhile enriched a swarm of relatives and arranged for some of them, like his nephew Girolamo Riario, highly advantageous marriages.

When Pietro, whose luxurious lifestyle was itself a scandal, died in 1474, his brother, Count Girolamo, took his place at his uncle's side to involve him in some of the darkest political intrigues of the day. He was principally responsible for dragging Sixtus into the Pazzi Conspiracy in Florence, in which the murders of Lorenzo de' Medici, the ruler of the city, and of Giuliano, his brother, were planned for high mass in the cathedral of Florence on Easter Sunday, April 26, 1478. Lorenzo escaped from the assassins; Giuliano was not so lucky. It is not clear whether Sixtus was aware that assassination was the essential piece in the conspiracy, but Girolamo certainly did. In the aftermath the pope had to go to war with Florence, which led to further military involvements in the peninsula and other political machinations. Ten years after the conspiracy, 1488, Count Girolamo was himself brutally assassinated.

Sixtus was busy, however, about many other things. The Ottoman Turks continued their assaults—they occupied Otranto in southern Italy and continued elsewhere to press westward after Constantinople's fall. Sixtus spent lavishly on a fleet to oppose them, but with it he accomplished little. He granted many privileges to the religious orders, especially the Franciscans, that allowed them even more freedom than before from bishops' jurisdiction. He approved the feast of the Immaculate Conception, canonized Saint Bonaventure (the Franciscan rival theologian to Saint Thomas), and on November 1, 1478, he at the request of Ferdinand of Aragon and Isabella of Castile established the Spanish Inquisition and put its operation into their hands.

Sixtus was a prodigious and intelligent patron of art and letters. More than any of his predecessors he was responsible for the cultural and artistic renaissance in the city up to that point. He brought to Rome men of letters and gave them employment. Among such scholars was Bartolomeo Platina, whom Sixtus appointed as the first official Vatican librarian. Sixtus gave Platina funds and a free hand in expanding the collection and provided suitable space for it. If Nicholas V was the founder of the Vatican Library, Sixtus was the patron who made it into a functioning institution.

In the city itself he repaired bridges; restored the Aqua Vergine aqueduct; opened, aligned, and laid out streets; rebuilt the hospital of the Holy Spirit (*Santo Spirito*); and constructed and restored churches— John Lateran, Santa Maria della Pace, Santa Maria del Popolo, and Sant'Agostino. His most noteworthy achievement was the construction and decoration of the papal chapel. Although dedicated to Mary's Assumption, the edifice is known by the name of its builder, the Sistine Chapel (Sixtus in Italian is *Sisto*). To provide music for the liturgies appropriate to the setting, he founded the Sistine Choir.

For the painting of the chapel's side walls, Sixtus called to Rome, principally from Florence, the leading artists of the day—Perugino, Pinturicchio, Ghirlandaio, Botticelli, Signorelli, and Cosimo Roselli.

Along the left wall was depicted the life of Moses, and along the right a corresponding cycle of the life of Christ. Decades later his nephew, Julius II, would carry this stupendous monument to its full glory by engaging Michelangelo to paint the ceiling. A few decades after that Clement VII engaged him to paint the *Last Judgment*.

After a conclave filled with intrigue and promises of favors, Innocent VIII succeeded Sixtus in 1484. Irresolute and chronically ill, the new pope inherited immense debts from his predecessor, which he tried to pay off by creating useless offices in the curia that he sold to the highest bidder. Under him the moral caliber of the papal court sank even lower. Before he was ordained, Innocent had fathered two children. Perhaps his only claim to fame—or infamy—is that he is the first pope openly to acknowledge the fact. The great social event of his pontificate was the elaborate celebration in the Vatican of the marriage of his son Franceschetto to a daughter of Lorenzo the Magnificent of Florence. Innocent's eight-year reign, though troubled by heavy involvement in Italian politics, was an insignificant interlude.

In 1492 Alexander VI, Rodrigo de Borgia, almost a synonym for a degenerate Renaissance pope, succeeded Innocent for a pontificate of eleven years. Unworthy though he was of his office, he was not the moral monster depicted in fiction and fantasy. There were no orgies in the Vatican. Francesco Guicciardini, the great historian who was his contemporary, said Alexander "combined rare prudence and vigilance, mature reflection, marvelous powers of persuasion, skill and capacity for the conduct of the most difficult affairs." Nonetheless, his sensuality and his obsessive love for his children, which led him into a number of sinister political schemes, justify his bad reputation. He fathered nine children by different women and, most scandalous, two while he was pope. The cry of the Gregorian Reform of the eleventh century for a celibate clergy now went unheeded at the highest level of the church.

Alexander stirred up resentment on a broad scale because of his shifting political allegiances, his reckless promotion of his children, and his amorous affairs. No critic was more inflammatory than the apocalyptic Dominican preacher in Florence, Girolamo Savonarola. When King Charles VIII of France invaded Italy in 1494 to claim for himself the kingdom of Naples, he on his way south chased the Medici from Florence. Savonarola threw himself into the political gap, continued his preaching against ecclesiastical corruption, with explicit naming of Alexander, and proclaimed Florence as the New Jerusalem. In the summer of 1497 Alexander excommunicated him, which opened the way for Savonarola's political enemies to move against him. After the preacher confessed to falsifying his prophecies, recanted, and then confessed to them again, he was hanged in the public square of Florence and his body burned. The Dominican order has never entirely given up its hope of having him canonized.

Of all Alexander's children his son Cesare is the most notorious, the dark hero of Machiavelli's *The Prince*. Cesare, a brilliant soldier, with French aid successfully imposed his rule on the Romagna and the Marches, the largest provinces within the Papal States. Alexander deposed the papal vicars in those provinces, which he then conferred upon his son. Cesare continued his military exploits, planning to attack Bologna and move into Tuscany, but his plans were cut short by the death of Alexander on August 18, 1503, almost certainly not by poison, as so often alleged, but by a fever.

After the three-week pontificate of Pius III, nephew of Pius II, the cardinals upon receiving bribes and the promise of lavish benefactions unanimously elected, in a conclave of a single day, Alexander's mortal enemy, Giuliano della Rovere, nephew of Sixtus IV, who took the name Julius II. This was the *papa terribile*—not "the terrible pope" but the pope who by word, deed, and mere gaze struck fear and awe into those who knew him. This was the warrior pope, the antihero of Erasmus's satirical dialogue "Julius Excluded [from heaven]," in which after Julius's supposed death Saint Peter refuses to let him pass through the pearly gates because he cannot recognize as his successor this man clad in armor.

Julius was bigger than life. He mounted his horse, led his army, and ordered the cardinals to follow him as he began his military campaign to win back for the church the lands the Borgias had alienated. For the nine years of his papacy he used all his diplomatic and military skills to establish a strong papacy in Italy, free from foreign domination. This enterprise entailed almost endless warfare and won him foes from near and far. In 1511 at the instigation of King Louis XII of France and the emperor Maximilian I, a group of cardinals convoked a council at Pisa and summoned him there to answer to their charges. Never one to dodge a challenge, Julius responded by convoking the next year Lateran Council V, which easily carried the day against Pisa and went on to address problems of church reform.

Julius, despite owing his own rise to nepotism, broke the pattern set by his uncle and did practically nothing to enrich or advance his family. Despite being elected through bribery and other sordid means, he issued a bull declaring papal elections by simony nullified. He vigorously supported efforts to reform the religious orders. He spent great sums on his military campaigns and his art patronage, but he was a frugal administrator. He inherited an empty treasury but left a full one. Although he had earlier sired three daughters, he as pope behaved with the utmost decorum.

Like his uncle, his most lasting achievement was artistic and architectural. He followed Sixtus's lead in restoring churches, laying out new streets, and repairing bridges. But his greatest accomplishments were in the Vatican itself. Even since the days of Nicholas V, popes had worried about the dilapidated state of Saint Peter's. With characteristic decisiveness Julius engaged Bramante to replace the Constantinian church with a new basilica, a project that in its fullness was not completed for another century and a half.

He was a genius patron who had an eye for genius painters. Instead of more experienced artists he chose the young Raphael to decorate his apartments, which resulted in a series of great masterpieces like the *School of Athens* and the *Dispute on the Sacrament*. His stormy relationship with Michelangelo has been told again and again, as the genius patron jousted with the genius artist. Out of the sculptor Michelangelo he drew forth the painter. The result was the Sistine Ceiling. Julius was no saint, but for the Sistine Ceiling alone much must be forgiven him.

LUTHER, LEO, AND THE AFTERMATH

"Now that God has given us the papacy, let us enjoy it." Julius's successor, Leo X, never said those words. They miss the mark of the man, but there is just enough truth in them to have made them stick to him like glue. Leo was intelligent, devout, attentive to his duties as pope (as he saw them) and, in contrast to his recent predecessors, free of amorous liaisons. But he had about him an aristocratic languor that Raphael captured in his famous portrait. He gathered around himself a coterie of poets and musicians, in whose company he seemed to feel more comfortable than in any other. While pope he employed 683 servants, including a keeper of the papal elephant.

He was a Medici, second son of Lorenzo the Magnificent, the man who escaped assassination in the Pazzi Conspiracy. Emotionally detached though he might be from other pressing concerns, he certainly was not detached from the fate of Florence or his family. There was therefore no way he could or wanted to stay aloof from the vicious and ever shifting politics of Italy. Paolo Sarpi, the sharp-tongued historian of the seventeenth century, said of Leo, "He would have been an ideal pope if he had had the slightest interest in religion." Sarpi's assessment is as unfair as the enjoying-the-papacy attribution, but it hits the bull's eye if interpreted to suggest that Leo's core value was not the good of the church but the good of his native city and the Medici.

Giovanni de' Medici, made a cardinal at age thirteen, received a superb education in Florence in the household of his father. Driven out of Florence with the rest of his family in 1498, he two years later took up residence in Rome until the family was reestablished in their city in 1512. The next year he was elected pope—without money exchanging hands. Julius II's severe legislation against bribery had had its effect. He was only thirty-seven. His placid personality looked like an attractive change from the stormy and bellicose Julius.

Leo's first three years as pope were relatively uneventful. He had to bestir himself, however, in 1516 after the new French king, Francis I, won a crushing victory at Marignano and thereby was able not only to vindicate French claims to the Duchy of Milan but with his army posed a threat to Florence and the Papal States. Leo brokered with Francis the Concordat of Bologna, 1516. In it Francis agreed to rescind the royal decree of 1438, the Pragmatic Sanction, which, in support of the Council of Basel, asserted the authority of council over pope and suppressed papal annates throughout the kingdom. He also agreed, after Leo granted him Parma and Piacenza in the Papal States, not to move further into Italy. On the papal side, the Concordat dealt a serious blow to the idea that the pope's powers could be limited by a council, and it ensured the flow of revenues from France. But for these concessions Leo paid a terribly high price. Besides sacrificing Parma and Piacenza he granted the king the right of nomination of all the higher clergy in France.

The pope retained the right of veto of any candidate he deemed unworthy, and Leo's successors sometimes exercised that right. But the Concordat marked in France the definitive end of the elective principle for which the Gregorian reformers of the eleventh century had fought so passionately. It was the nuptial contract that legitimated the "marriage of throne and altar" that characterized the *ancien régime* in France. This aspect of the Concordat was congruent with the authority the popes were in this same era granting the Spanish and Portuguese monarchs in their overseas possessions, the *patronato* and the *padroado*. In France from this time forward the king could use church offices to reward his friends among the powerful aristocracy. The control the king now had over the French church made the Reformation not merely unattractive to Francis and his sons but a serious threat to their power.

The same year as the Concordat Leo undertook a war against the Duchy of Urbino in order to install a nephew there. The war was a financial and political disaster and was the spark that ignited an assassination plot against him among the cardinals. When Leo discovered it, he had the leader executed, other cardinals imprisoned, and then packed the college of cardinals with thirty-one new members, an unprecedented maneuver that raised membership from a traditional limit of twenty or twenty-five to more than double. Although a few of the new cardinals were men of genuine talent and piety, such as the Dominican theologian Tommaso De Vio (known as Cajetan) and the Augustinian Giles of Viterbo, most were political appointments.

Leo inherited from Julius the Fifth Lateran Council. Like all the cardinals, he vowed before his election that as pope he would continue it. The council wrestled with the problem of church reform, which had been a shrill cry in the church at large at least since the Council of Constance, and it did so more seriously than historians have given it credit for. Leo in principle backed the council's reform decrees, but he lacked the will to carry them forward.

From him the artists and architects patronized so intelligently and lavishly by Julius had every right to expect great things, given Leo's education and family tradition. They were disappointed. Leo loved Raphael, continued to sponsor his painting of the papal apartments, but failed to elicit from him the same genius that Julius had. Even in this area he behaved as the abstracted connoisseur who was more interested in sponsoring concerts and theatrical shows than big undertakings. His plans to continue the financing of the rebuilding of Saint Peter's through the issue of an indulgence backfired badly—much more badly than Leo ever seems to have realized.

Despite being a Medici, Leo X would probably rank among the more forgettable popes except for that indulgence, which led Luther to throw on him the spotlight of inglorious fame. The story is familiar. Luther, terrified by thoughts of what he believed God's justice demanded of him, found inner freedom and peace in the doctrine that we are saved not by our own efforts but by the grace (or favor or love) of God. We are not justified by our "works" (good deeds), as if we could force God to love us or save us simply by behaving properly. The idea that by contributing money toward the building of Saint Peter's, which was by definition a good deed, we could win God's grace or have an effect on souls in purgatory was utterly repugnant to him.

The indulgence, whose German intermediary was the archbishop of Mainz, was preached by a Dominican friar, Johann Tetzel, who seems to have preached it in crude terms. To counter Tetzel's preaching Luther posted his *Ninety-Five Theses*, a set of theological axioms, a few of which touched on papal authority or practice. Number 86, for instance, "Since the pope's income today is larger than that of the wealthiest of wealthy men, why does he not build this Church of St. Peter with his own money rather than with the money of indigent believers?" It hit a sore point that had been festering throughout Europe at least since the days of John XXII in Avignon.

Luther was a member of the Augustinian order. His attack incensed the Dominicans, who interpreted it as an attack from a rival religious order on one of their own number, and for a while in Rome the affair was viewed as just another squabble between two religious orders. Luther was soon presented in Rome, however, not as a theologian speaking about sin and grace but as one "speaking against the authority of the Holy See." The next year, prodded from several sources, Leo moved into action and ordered an investigation. Things moved quickly from bad to worse in a series of missteps and missed opportunities that led in 1520 to the drawing up of a bull of excommunication. Only at that point did Luther move into the role of a church reformer, and in his reform he took special aim at the papacy.

In 1520 he published his "Appeal to the German Nobility," in which he called upon the emperor and the German nobles to undertake a thorough reform of the church, which the popes not only had not done but had impeded. The "Appeal" is a long document, which for the most part is a summary of medieval grievances but now more rhetorically powerful for being marshaled into one list and articulated in highly inflammatory language. It called for a council and provided the reform agenda for it. Number 2 of the agenda was: "What Christian purpose is served by ecclesiastics called cardinals? Italy is now devastated by financial exactions, so that cardinals can have their revenues. Now that Italy is drained dry, they are coming to Germany. They think the drunken Germans will not understand what the game is." Another: "The pope has more than 3,000 secretaries alone. Who can count the staff of the pope and the cardinals? Even when the pope goes out riding, he is accompanied by 3,000 or 4,000 on mules much as any king or emperor. . . . Oh, my noble princes and lords, how long will you let these raving and ravaging wolves range over your land and people?" And another: "I urge that every prince and city should forbid their subjects to pay annates to Rome. The pope should exercise no authority over the emperor. No one should kiss the pope's feet. Pilgrimages to Rome should be disallowed."

Luther's message in all its hyperbole fell on willing ears—and on willing eyes, as the printing press sent it speeding through Germany. He was promised a safe-conduct to stand trial in Rome, but he refused, citing what had happened to Jan Huss, who also had a safe-conduct and ended up at the stake. Other attempts at reconciliation failed, and therefore on January 1, 1521, Leo's bull of excommunication, *Exsurge Domine*, took effect. That should have settled the matter. The new emperor, Charles V, was a devout Catholic, unfavorably impressed by what he heard about Luther. He considered Luther "a notorious heretic" and declared him an outlaw of the empire, but the political situation prevented him from seizing Luther and bringing him to justice.

In the ten years between 1509 and 1519 the politics of Europe, and therefore of the empire, had taken a decisive turn. In 1509 the young Henry VIII came to the throne of England, a country now recovered from the devastation and disruption of the War of the Roses and ready to take its rightful role in international intrigue. In France in 1515, the young Francis I ascended the throne of the most powerful monarchy and richest country in Europe, and that year he successfully invaded Italy to win Milan, traditionally claimed by the empire, as his prize and then, as mentioned, sign the Concordat of Bologna. In 1516 the young Charles of Habsburg inherited from his maternal grandparents, Ferdinand and Isabella, the thrones of Spain and all the Spanish possessions overseas. Three years later, he was elected emperor, defeating through bribery his chief rival, Francis I of France.

With the imperial election Charles, whose aunt was the queen of England, Catherine of Aragon, emerged as seemingly the strongest man in Europe, the first emperor since at least Frederick II in the thirteenth century to live up to the imperial claims of authority. But his very power was his weakness. His own German nobles, jealous of their independence, feared and resented him, and some of them saw in Luther a chance to reduce him to size. On his eastern frontier he faced a newly aggressive Turkish offensive by Sultan Suleiman the Magnificent. The fall of Constantinople in 1453 had opened the gates to Europe. The French king, sharing with Charles a claim to the rich Duchy of Milan, was surrounded by Habsburgs—Charles to his south in Spain, Charles all along his eastern borders, and Charles's aunt across the channel in England. He would do anything in his power to weaken his rival, even if it meant giving aid and comfort to the Lutheran princes in Germany.

Politics and religion could not have been more intricately intertwined. Charles needed his nobles' help against Francis and against Suleiman. As more and more of them took up Luther's cause, he had to pay heed, for they threatened civil war. Within less than a decade the Lutheran nobles formed the Schmalkaldic League, a military junta with the dual purpose of limiting Charles and promoting Luther's reform. Meanwhile they sought, sometimes with questionable sincerity, a peaceful solution to the religious situation by calling for a "free Christian council in German lands." Charles, who early emerged as the unwavering standard bearer for the Catholic cause, would for the next twenty years do his utmost to see the council become a reality.

But Leo X would live to see none of this. On December 1, 1521, the same year as the bull *Exsurge*, he died unexpectedly of malaria at the young age of forty-six. He had just a few months earlier bestowed on Henry VIII the title Defender of the Faith for his book on the sacraments against Luther. Even aside from the religious situation already exploding in Germany, this affable but ineffectual man left behind a heritage of bitterness and disappointed hopes. He also left behind an empty treasury.

A fifty-day, deeply divided conclave finally compromised by electing a cardinal absent in Spain, Hadrian Florensz who, contrary to what
was by now a long-standing custom, kept as pope his baptismal name.
Hadrian VI, an austere and dour Dutchman, had been professor and
rector at the University of Louvain and tutor to the young Charles of
Habsburg. His was a short pontificate of slightly more than a year.

Well intentioned, honest, and upright but rigid and gauche, "the
German barbarian," as he was known in Rome, probably would not
have accomplished much had he lived longer. His frugality and the
autocratic manner in which he imposed it on Rome and the court
alienated even many sympathetic to his aims. Through his legate at
the Diet of Nuremberg in December 1522, he frankly admitted to the
scandal of the curia, but he seems not to have grasped the complexity
of the situation in Germany. The story goes that when Hadrian died,
the Romans showed their gratitude to his attending physician for fail-
ing to keep Hadrian alive by posting on his door a placard, "Savior of
the Roman people." Hadrian was the last non-Italian pope until the
election of John Paul II in 1978.

After a conclave of almost two months, the cardinals on November
19, 1523, elected Giulio de' Medici, a first cousin of Leo X and the illegitimate son of Giuliano de' Medici, the young man assassinated in
the Pazzi conspiracy. He took the name Clement VII (not to be con-
fused with the Avignon Clement VII, Robert of Geneva). Handsome
and intelligent, he was raised by his uncle Lorenzo the Magnificent as
if he were his own child. One of Leo's first acts as pope had been to
brush aside the canonical impediment of Giulio's illegitimacy to make
his cousin and close friend a cardinal and archbishop of Florence. Despite Giulio's involvement in family politics, he was highly regarded
by contemporaries, who greeted his election with approval. He turned
out, however, to be the wrong man at the wrong time.

Disappointment with him set in almost immediately. He had a
knack for siding with the losing party each time in the back-and-forth
fortunes of the wars between Francis I and Charles V. Although Charles
had promoted him as his candidate in the conclave that elected him,
Clement made the huge mistake of supporting Francis when Charles
invaded Italy. Francis was badly defeated by Charles at Pavia in 1525

and taken prisoner. Charles's forces now had a free hand in Italy. They captured Florence, and then marched south to Rome.

On May 6, 1527, they broke into the city and subjected it to a terrible sack. Clement himself barely escaped capture when the invaders moved swiftly through the city and broke into the Vatican. He fled the few hundred yards from the papal palace to the stronghold of Castel Sant'Angelo, where he was safe but for eight days had to watch the burning and sacking of the city. After the sack came a devastating plague. Thousands of Romans died or were killed, and many more thousands fled the city. The population dropped precipitously from about ninety thousand to about thirty thousand in just a few months.

Clement eventually was able to make peace with the emperor, who was not personally responsible for the sack but in the courts of Europe was severely criticized for it. Only after a decade would the city return more or less to normal. In 1530 Clement crowned Charles, up to that point officially just emperor-elect, in the cathedral in Bologna, the last imperial crowning ever performed by a pope. Meanwhile Henry VIII's marital situation in England had reached a crisis point. Clement had characteristically evaded the problem, afraid of offending Henry whose aid he needed in his political maneuvering and afraid of offending Charles, whose aunt's honor was at stake. Finally his hand was forced by Henry's marriage to Anne Boleyn performed by the archbishop of Canterbury. He excommunicated Henry on July 11, 1533, and declared his divorce and his new marriage null and void.

Clement died a year later, a pontificate that was an almost unmitigated disaster. Besides everything else that went wrong, his precarious relationship with Charles meant that he never gave the emperor the support he desperately needed to halt the Ottoman advance into central Europe. The threat was dire. In 1529 the Turks were at the gates of Vienna. They were repulsed but would be back again.

Besides the Turks, by 1529 Charles faced the religious and military problem of the Lutherans at home. He sincerely believed that the only hope to resolve it was a council, and to that end he pressed Clement hard for one. Clement resisted, fearful the council would turn against him and even try to depose him. The councils of Constance and Basel had made popes wary of an institution they had earlier promoted.

But also, like practically all rulers in Europe except Charles, Clement feared Charles's might should he be able to solve his problems with the Turks, with the Lutherans, and with Francis I. With a victorious Charles Europe might at last have a master. A successful council would help Charles ascend to that pinnacle. Whatever his reasons, Clement remained evasive to the end. How different would the religious history of Europe be if early, 1525, for instance, or 1527, Clement had convoked a council? It is impossible to say.

PAUL III: A TURNING POINT

Clement VII died on September 25, 1534. It had taken a conclave fifty days to elect him but only two days to elect, unanimously and without bribery, his successor, Paul III, Alessandro Farnese. How to explain this rapid consensus in a body notorious for its contentiousness? The mood had changed. There was widespread disgust among cardinals of every faction with the shilly-shallying policies of Clement and with his bad political judgment. There was widespread concern, even panic about what the future might hold. The sack of Rome had been traumatic. The wonderful city that had seemed on the verge of a rebirth, the darling of the great artists of the time, had been mercilessly ravaged and its population scattered. Fortunately, none of the great works of art had been destroyed, but the effect was nonetheless devastating both materially and psychologically.

The Turks seemed unstoppable on the eastern frontier and raided southern Italian cities seemingly at will. The Schmalkaldic League of the Lutheran princes threatened a civil war in the empire that was a religious war as well. Luther was still at large, and his teachings had spread far and wide throughout Europe—and had penetrated even into Italy. Something had to change. In Farnese, who at sixty-seven was the oldest cardinal in the conclave, the others saw a man they thought could do it.

Alessandro Farnese had been a cardinal since 1492, for forty-two years. He knew the ropes, he knew how things worked, and he was widely respected for his diplomatic skills, his firmness of purpose, his intelligence, and good judgment. He had long and publicly proclaimed the necessity of a council and was not afraid of it. He had not hidden his disagreements with Clement's political policies or Clement's disregard for his advice. In his younger days as a cardinal, he had behaved like many of his peers and begot three sons and a daughter. But in 1513 he broke with his mistress, was ordained a priest six years later, and then undertook in his diocese of Parma an implementation of the reform decrees of the Fifth Lateran Council. From that point forward he became part of the small reform party in the curia.

Shortly after his election he announced the three goals of his pontificate. The first was to effect peace among Christian princes, by which he obviously meant peace between Francis and Charles, who had already gone to war against each other twice. The second was to convoke a council to resolve the religious problem. The third was to organize and promote a crusade to push back the Turks. These goals were interrelated, with the success of one being somewhat dependent upon the success of the other two. In that triad Paul's most palpable success was the Council of Trent, but his importance extends beyond the council.

There is no doubt that Paul's pontificate was a turning point, but he in two important regards still fits our image of a "Renaissance pope." The first is his patronage of arts and architecture in a city trying to recover from the sack. Among other geniuses he was able to employ was Michelangelo. Paul set him to work on the Last Judgment in the Sistine Chapel, a work first commissioned by Clement VII. The painting is more properly called "the resurrection," because the idea was to depict an article from the Creed, the resurrection of the dead on the last day. Despite the bright colors that the restoration of the painting uncovered, Michelangelo's depiction of the subject is dark, and hence the painting is often interpreted as emblematic of a change in mood in Rome (see fig. 19.1).

19.1: Paul III
Tarchiani, Filippo (1576–1645). Pope Paul III visiting Michelangelo's studio.
Casa Buonarroti, Florence, Italy.
© Scala / Art Resource, NY

Paul also commissioned Michelangelo to fresco a private papal chapel in the Vatican, the Pauline Chapel, which contains a magnificent painting of the conversion of Saint Paul and another of the crucifixion of Saint Peter. He also put the artist, now architect, in charge of the building of the new basilica of Saint Peter and in the city of Rome in charge of the redesign of the layout of the Capitoline Hill. Also in the city Paul razed a number of dilapidated buildings, laid out new streets, enlarged piazzas, and rebuilt the University of Rome. Finally, he engaged Michelangelo as architect for a palace for his family in the center of Rome, the famous Palazzo Farnese, best known around the world as the setting for the second act of Puccini's opera, *Tosca.*

The Palazzo Farnese brings us to the second way Paul fits our image of a Renaissance pope: his passion for his family, especially his children and grandchildren. This passion, sometimes blind, was not simply a scandal that dismayed reformers. It also led the pope into political maneuvers that badly hindered him from accomplishing the three goals he had set for his pontificate by involving him in intrigue and sometimes devious political maneuvers that especially damaged his relationship with Charles V. He tipped his hand almost immediately after his election when he nominated two of his teenage grandchildren as cardinals—Alessando Farnese (his namesake), and Guido Ascanio Sforza.

Although he provided for his relatives in other ways, nomination of them to the College of Cardinals turned out not to be the pattern he pursued. During this pontificate of fifteen years, he named a whopping seventy-one cardinals, most of them men of probity, some of them much more than that. They included John Fisher, the Englishman executed by Henry VIII the year after his nomination, and Reginald Pole, of the blood royal through his mother, Margaret, countess of Salisbury, niece of Edward IV. Pole and his fellow cardinal nominated by Paul, Giovanni Morone, were associated with a group of spiritually minded persons in Italy that included the poet, Vittoria Colonna, and even Michelangelo himself. Also nominated by Paul was Giampietro Carafa, one of the founders of a new, reforming religious order, the Theatines. By his nominations Paul did not drive out of the college all ambition or dissension, but he reversed the secularization that had characterized it since the days of Sixtus IV. This was a decisive step forward.

"Reform Rome, reform the world." This slogan caught a priority reformers had long been advocating, a priority all the more obvious after Luther launched his scathing attacks on the papacy and the curia. Paul, sensitive to the issue, established in 1536 a commission "on the reform of the church," headed by the devout and able Venetian, Cardinal Gasparo Contarini, and including Carafa and Pole. A year later the commission issued its secret report, in which the second paragraph contained the blunt lines:

The origin of all these evils in the church was that . . . teachers at once appeared who taught that the pope is the lord of all benefices and that therefore it necessarily follows that the pope cannot be guilty of simony. The will of the pope, of whatever kind it may be, is the rule governing his activities and deeds: whence it may be shown without doubt that whatever is pleasing to him is also permitted. From this source as from a Trojan horse so many abuses and such grave diseases have rushed upon the church of God that we now see her afflicted almost to the despair of salvation.

Unfortunately, the report was leaked and used by the Lutherans to confirm their accusations. Lutheran exploitation of the report may been a factor persuading Paul not to move vigorously on its specific recommendations, most of which had to do with the dispensations from canon law that the papacy granted in return for a consideration and with similar procedures that at least looked like simony and that had contributed so mightily to blackening the papacy's name.

In 1542, however, Paul moved decisively to try to stop the spread of Lutheranism in Italy when he established the Roman Inquisition, soon to be known as the Holy Office. The immediate context for its founding was the defection to Lutheranism of two prominent Italian reformers, the Augustinian preacher Pietro Vermigli (known in English as Peter Martyr) and Bernardino Ochino, the superior general of the newly founded reform branch of the Franciscans, the Capuchins.

The Roman Inquisition was a new institution, not directly related to the medieval inquisitions or even to the Spanish Inquisition founded by Ferdinand and Isabella a half-century earlier. It was, however, like them a tribunal, a judicial institution. Its remit was to investigate accusations of heresy and then, if the accusations were plausible, to put the accused on trial and then render a verdict. At first the Inquisition proceeded tentatively, but when Giampietro Carafa, one of its original members, became pope in 1555 it moved into high gear.

Paul's successful convocation of Trent of course had an immense impact on the future of Catholicism. Less dramatic than Trent but of similar impact was his support of new religious orders, the best known of which is the Jesuits—officially, the Society of Jesus. The original founders of the Jesuits, led by the Basque nobleman Ignatius of Loyola, were all graduates of the prestigious University of Paris, who originally saw themselves as a band of itinerant preachers and missionaries to foreign lands. They came to Rome in the late 1530s and won approval for their group from Paul on September 27, 1540. While still keeping their missionary purpose, they went on to found colleges and universities throughout Europe and in many other parts of the world. In northern Europe they were best known as in the vanguard of the Catholic Counter Reformation.

Paul also approved the Barnabites, the Theatines, and the Somaschans, which were much smaller than the Jesuits and during the sixteenth century located almost exclusively in Italy. Almost as large as the Jesuits, however, were the Capuchins, the reformed branch of the Franciscans mentioned earlier. They were zealous preachers and much respected for the austerity of their life. Although the defection of Ochino dealt them a severe blow, they quickly recovered.

Saint Angela Merici founded a group of laywomen known as the Ursulines, whose ministry was to teach catechism to young women and perform various works of social assistance. Approved by Paul III, the Ursulines spread through Italy and then especially in France, where in the seventeenth century they ran many more schools for young women than the Jesuits did for young men. They were the first in a notable outburst of similar women's orders in the seventeenth century.

These orders, and others like them that followed, did not come into existence because of papal initiative. Nor, for the most part, were they founded by clerics. They were the work of fervent lay men and lay women who saw a need and set about addressing it. Nonetheless, Paul III deserves credit for seeing them as helpmates and not as threats. His approval gave them security and legitimacy.

The burning question of the day, however, was a council to address the religious situation. Luther's teaching had been condemned in the bull *Exsurge*, but the demand swelled that it be reexamined in a council.

Besides the doctrinal questions, the call for "reform of the church in head and members" was even more shrill now than before, with the presumption being that only a council could effectively deal with it. Charles continued to press the necessity and the urgency of a council, and he now had an ally in Paul.

The problems of convoking the council were many, including the skepticism of bishops and others that it could ever be pulled off. Talked about for so long, yet a generation after the posting of the *Ninety-Five Theses* nothing had happened. Cynicism about it was almost universal. The most obvious obstacle, however, was the king of France, who repressed the Reformation in his own country but abetted it in Germany. As mentioned, Francis I saw the council as potentially easing Charles's situation in Germany, and hence the Most Christian King of France threw every obstacle in its path.

Paul acted decisively and convoked a council for Mantua in 1537, but the duke of Mantua insisted on such exorbitant conditions that Paul transferred it to Vicenza. Few bishops showed up, and he was forced to suspend it. Meanwhile, in Germany fear of civil war and a slight cooling of antagonisms resulted in a brief "era of good feeling" in which a religious colloquy was arranged between Catholic and Protestant leaders at Regensburg (Ratisbon). Paul chose for his legate Cardinal Contarini, widely regarded as the ideal candidate, respected even by the Lutherans who came to know him.

Luther, still officially an outlaw though he was teaching and preaching publicly in Wittenberg, could not attend. His place was taken by Philip Melanchthon, a convinced Lutheran but less polemical than Luther. Charles V pinned high hopes on the meeting. He, and others, felt that, if the meeting succeeded and Lutherans and Catholics could make progress toward resolving their differences, a council would not be necessary. At first things went well, with a fragile agreement arrived at even on the crucial question of justification, but then the meeting broke down over other issues. Contarini came back to Rome, accused by some Catholics of having betrayed the truth on justification.

Now a council was the only possible solution, which Charles, despite the experience at Regensburg, still hoped the Lutherans would attend. Paul convoked it to meet at Trent in 1542, but shortly after the bull of convocation was published Francis I once again opened hostilities against Charles. Paul was therefore forced to suspend the council. Finally, in 1544 Charles defeated Francis for the fourth time and made him agree to send his bishops to a council to meet soon at Trent. With that Paul again convoked the council, to open on March 25, 1545, *Laetare* Sunday (fourth Sunday of Lent). Only a half dozen or so bishops showed up, so great was the persuasion that the council would never be a reality. This pitiful showing meant the council had to be postponed—until December 13, *Gaudete* Sunday (third Sunday of Advent) that same year.

The active participants at the council on the day it opened consisted in four cardinals (three of whom were the papal legates, the fourth was the bishop of Trent); four archbishops representing Aix, Palermo, Upsala, and Armagh; and twenty-one bishops—sixteen from Italy plus two Spaniards, one Frenchman, one Englishman, and one German. Besides these prelates there were five superiors general of religious orders. A grand total of thirty-four! During this first period of the council, 1545–1547, the number climbed to about seventy bishops, and by the end of the council, 1563, to about two hundred, which was still a depressingly small representation. All through the council the vast majority of participants were from Italy and Spain. Despite Francis I's promises the French were notably absent until a small but important contingent arrived during the council's last year, 1563.

Charles V and Paul III had to act as allies to get the council going, but theirs was a fragile partnership. Even before the council opened they found it difficult to agree on two points. The first was the agenda. Charles wanted the council to deal principally, or even exclusively, with reform, because he believed abuses had caused the Reformation and eliminating them would go a long way toward solving the problem. He feared that doctrinal definitions would only exacerbate the situation. Paul wanted to reserve reform to himself. He wanted the council to answer the doctrinal challenge Luther, as well as Zwingli and the Anabaptists, posed. (Calvin was not yet in the picture.) This conflict was not resolved until the council itself decided it had to deal with both.

The second sensitive point was where the council should meet. Charles was adamant that it should meet "in German lands," while

Paul wanted it in Italy and, if possible, at some city in the Papal States such as Bologna. They were finally able to agree on Trent, which was part of the empire yet on the Italian side of the Alps. Neither party was fully satisfied with the choice, but it was the best they could do. Trent had about 1,500 houses, plenty to accommodate the thirty-four participants who opened the council. But the number of participants grew; the great rulers sent their envoys, and cardinals might have fifty or more secretaries and servants in their entourage. Lodging and provisioning were immense problems all during the council.

Neither Paul nor Charles ever set foot in Trent. The pope appointed three legates to chair the council in his name, and he chose an excellent trio—Marcello Cervini (future Pope Marcellus II), Giammaria Del Monte (future Pope Julius III), and Reginald Pole. A relatively fast courier service between Trent and Rome enabled the pope and the legates to keep in touch, but Paul, hundreds of miles away, obviously could not control the day-to-day flow of business on the council floor.

Paul appointed the legates only a few weeks before the council was supposed to open in March. When the legates arrived at Trent they realized, if they did not realize it before, that they had no procedures to guide them in chairing the council and would have to construct them themselves. They also realized that, despite the years that had elapsed since Paul first tried to convoke the council; no preparation had been made for it. There were no documents on hand to use as base texts to begin the discussion. Under these circumstances, it is not surprising that it took Trent a long time to be able to turn its attention to substantive business. Even so, at this point Paul and many others believed the council would last just a few months. Nobody dreamed that it would stretch out over eighteen years.

FIVE POPES AND A COUNCIL

The eighteen years of the Council of Trent, 1545–1563, extended across five pontificates—Paul III, Julius III, Marcellus II, Paul IV, and Pius IV. During those years the council was actually in session a total of only about four, which were divided into three distinct periods, with a ten-year hiatus between the second and the third, 1545–1547, 1551–1552, 1562–1563. Different sets of legates presided over each of the periods. So much time elapsed between the latter two periods and so few participants returned who had been at the first (death and old age had taken their toll) that many people demanded the third declare itself a new council. Other things were happening in Catholicism besides the council. Two crucially important developments for the Catholic Church during this period occurred altogether independently of the council—the founding of the new religious orders and the sending of missionaries to the Spanish and Portuguese overseas dominions. The popes themselves had other concerns besides Trent, with defense against the Turks weighing as much on their minds as did the council.

Contrary to the impression textbooks generally give, the Council of Trent did not try to address all aspects of Catholicism. It almost immediately decided that it had to handle both doctrine and reform, thus satisfying and making anxious both Paul and Charles. On those two broad categories the council adopted a specific and limited focus. Under doctrine the council meant to treat only Protestant teachings that were in conflict with Catholic teachings. Thus Trent made no pronouncements on the Trinity or Incarnation or other Christian truths over which there was no disagreement. In this regard Trent had Luther principally in mind, with some scant attention to Zwingli, the Anabaptists and, only in the third period, Calvin. This focus meant dealing principally with two issues—justification and the sacraments.

Reform had a similarly precise focus. For the bishops at Trent "reform of the clergy and the Christian people," as the council put it or, as it was more commonly expressed, "the reform of the church," meant essentially the reform of three precisely defined and traditional *offices* in the church—the papacy, the episcopacy, and the pastorate. That last office meant those who had the "care of souls," in the strict canonical sense of pastors of parishes and certain chaplaincies. The focus therefore was on local or diocesan clergy, the clergy under the jurisdiction of bishops, not on members of religious orders like the Dominicans and Franciscans.

As is to be expected from such a long, sprawling, and contentious meeting, these clear boundaries were not always observed, and the council spilled out occasionally into other areas. But it in principle set itself a limited agenda and did not try to deal, for instance, even with such a crucial issue as foreign missions. Moreover, it never quite got to the "reform of the Christian people" except indirectly through its assumption that reform of the clergy was the key to reform of the laity. As a legislative and judicial body, the council was concerned with external behavior and discipline. It was concerned, specifically, to assure that the office holders in the church do their jobs as set down in the canonical tradition.

The glaring abuse of which many bishops and pastors were guilty was absenteeism, bishops not residing in their dioceses and pastors not residing in their parishes. These absentees hired "vicars" to do their jobs for them. The principal reason they were absent was because they held several at a time (which was another glaring abuse) *and* collected revenues from them all, which gave them a generous income out of which they paid their vicars. Even in the first period, 1545–1547, the council tried to deal with these abuses, but by the third period, led by a few determined bishops from Iberia, it took on a new and uncompromising urgency.

Both of these abuses flagrantly violated canon law. How did they come about? The simple answer is through papal dispensations, which were granted, reformers alleged, as rewards for services rendered or for money exchanged. To reform the episcopacy and the pastorate necessarily entailed, it would seem, reform of the papacy. Reforming the papacy in that specific abuse led into the larger question of how the whole papal operation was financed. By the third period this aspect of reform put the council on a collision course with the pope.

For the first period, however, relations between Paul III and the council went relatively smoothly. The big achievement in this period was the decree on justification, over which the council labored for seven months. Practically everybody who has seriously studied the council without animus has assessed it as the council's masterpiece. Stung by Luther's accusation that Catholics were Pelagians who believed that their "works" rather than grace saved them, the council insisted that justification was accomplished always and everywhere under the inspiration of grace. "Good works" were no good for salvation and they could not of themselves win grace unless they were grace-inspired from the very beginning. Nonetheless, the council also insisted, human beings are not mere puppets but genuinely contribute, in some mysterious way, to the process.

When on January 13, 1547, the bishops at the council passed that decree, they felt that the council, already in operation for over a year, had accomplished its essential task and could soon wrap up its business. Things seemed to be going swimmingly even outside the council. Charles had finally gone to war with the Schmalkaldic League and in the early spring defeated it, which presumably meant the end of Lutheranism as an organized military force. He could now insist on Lutheran acceptance of the decrees of the council. At that moment, however, several bishops died at Trent, presumably of typhus, which raised the specter of plague. A few bishops slipped out of the city and headed for home. After contentious debates the remaining bishops voted 39 in favor of transferring the council to Bologna, fourteen against, and five noncommittal. The legates had authorization from Paul III to act in such an emergency.

Without any consultation with the emperor, Paul acquiesced in the transfer—to a city right under his eye in the Papal States. Charles was furious, accused the pope of bad faith and refused to let his bishops, mainly Spanish, leave Trent. Although most of the bishops went to Bologna, the council really could not function without Charles's support, so that in early 1549 Paul was forced to adjourn it.

The consequences of the move to Bologna were heavy. After it the relations between Charles and Paul, always fragile, continued to deteriorate. Charles, though now victorious over the Lutherans, felt he could no longer insist with them that the council was being held "in German lands" and therefore could not insist they go to it. He lost his momentum. Historians speculate that if the council had remained at Trent the German religious situation might have turned out altogether differently, but such speculations are speculations.

Paul III died the year he suspended the council. To elect his successor a conclave sharply divided between pro-French and pro-imperial factions took two and a half months. During it Reginald Pole failed by one vote to be elected. The successful candidate, Julius III, was Giammaria Del Monte, another legate with Pole at Trent, who was opposed by Charles because he had favored the transferral to Bologna. But the pressure was on both the emperor and pope to work together for the resumption of the council, which Julius successfully reconvened in May 1551.

In this period the council continued its work on the sacraments, begun at Trent and continued at Bologna. Charles, as a result of his victory over Schmalkalden, was able to insist that representatives from several Lutheran states attend, but their presence hindered rather than helped the council's progress. Meanwhile the new French king, Henry II, who refused to allow his bishops to go to the council, joined his forces to a resurgent Lutheran army and forced Charles to flee from Innsbruck, too near Trent for comfort. On April 28, 1552, Julius had to adjourn the council.

The pope was a typical career ecclesiastic, well-meaning but emotionally detached from the great moral and religious issues of the day.

Especially as his pontificate wound down he spent more and more time hunting, banqueting, attending the theater or simply passing his days in quiet luxury in the residence he had built for himself, today the Villa Giulia (which houses the world's most extensive collection of Etruscan artifacts). His relatives pursued him for favors, to which, despite his denunciation of the nepotism of his predecessors, he could muster only half-hearted resistance. His blind insistence on raising to the cardinalate a shifty street urchin, age fifteen, was the great scandal of his pontificate. After Julius's death, that cardinal's crimes caught up with him, and he ended his days in prison.

Nonetheless, Julius tried to be attentive to his duties. He set up a commission of six cardinals to make recommendations for reform of the curia. He was successful in reducing the size of his court and made some progress in curtailing the real and alleged venality of several papal bureaus. By 1555 he had a reform bull ready to issue, but his death prevented him from doing so. Although these measures did not go very far, they served as a basis for more extensive ones later. Julius continued to support Michelangelo as chief architect of Saint Peter's and defended him against his detractors.

The contentious conclave after Julius's death, divided again along political lines, allowed the reforming party to push forward its candidate, who in the end received a unanimous vote. Marcello Cervini, another legate to the first period of Trent, kept his baptismal name, which has been immortalized by Palestrina's *Mass of Pope Marcellus*. He was a striking contrast with Julius III, whose nepotism and luxury he had denounced in such outright fashion that he had to withdraw from Rome. The new pope, as learned as he was able and upright, set to work the very day after his election by cutting the expenses of his coronation almost to the bone. He gave half the money saved to the poor; the rest went to the depleted papal treasury. To forestall even the slightest suspicion of nepotism from touching him, he made it clear to his many relatives they were not welcome in Rome. One of his nephews, Robert Bellarmine (Roberto Bellarmino), later joined the Jesuits, won renown as a theologian, and was eventually canonized. The high hopes Marcellus's pontificate raised among reformers were dashed when he died suddenly of a stroke twenty-two days after his election.

At another divided conclave the reformers were once again able to get their candidate elected, Giampietro Carafa, who took the name Paul IV. Though seventy-nine years old, this stern, austere, and autocratic reformer was as vigorous as somebody half his age. He came from a wealthy and highly influential family of Naples. Although he owed his quick rise in rank to his uncle, Cardinal Oliviero Carafa, he was worthy of the trust his uncle placed in him. In the mid-1520s he, as mentioned, cofounded with Saint Cajetan the Theatines, had served on the commission on church reform, and helped head the Roman Inquisition.

It would be difficult to imagine anybody more zealous for the good of the church than Paul IV, but his intransigence and his unmitigated confidence in his own judgment destroyed the possibility of a constructive reign. The religious zeal of his early years had turned into fanaticism by the time he became pope. Ignatius of Loyola was said to tremble in every bone in his body when he heard of Carafa's election. For the Council of Trent Paul IV had a disdain bordering on contempt—it had accomplished nothing toward reform of the church and its doctrinal decisions, especially on justification, smacked of compromise with the Lutherans. He would undertake the reform of the church singlehandedly.

Paul saw heresy in the slightest deviation from his narrow orthodoxy, which meant he had Cardinal Giovanni Morone, the man who would later save the Council of Trent, put on trial for heresy and imprisoned in the Castel Sant'Angelo. He ordered Cardinal Pole, now archbishop of Canterbury and papal legate to Mary Tudor's England, back to Rome for the same fate, but Pole delayed and died in the meantime. He infused the Roman Inquisition with a new zealotry. In 1557 and then in a revised edition in 1559 he published the first papal *Index of Forbidden Books*, so extreme and categorical in its strictures that Saint Peter Canisius, a contemporary who was certainly not soft on heresy, called it intolerable and a scandal. Seeing the Jews as a source of disbelief, he erected for the first time in Rome a ghetto and had them herded into it.

Paul IV was scrupulously careful to make worthy appointments to the College of Cardinals, which bore good results in the future, but he made one colossal mistake. Reformer though he was, he two weeks after his election named his nephew Carlo to the college, an intelligent but devious and scheming young man, upon whom Paul unfortunately began more and more to rely for advice. *Papa Carafa*, a proud Neapolitan, hated the Spaniards for their domination of Naples for the past half-century. Carlo played on his uncle's prejudice to entice him into a military alliance with France against Philip II, Charles V's son, now king of Spain. The war ended in 1557 in a humiliating defeat for the pope, who did not become aware of his nephew's other machinations until the end of his pontificate. When he did, he took characteristically swift measures by stripping him, his brother Cardinal Alfonso Carafa, and the third brother, Giovanni, duke of Paliano, of all their offices. He forced them to leave Rome within twelve days.

Swift action, yes, but for most Romans the punishment was not severe enough to fit the crimes. When Paul IV died, roundly hated in Rome, his obsequies were interrupted by riots. At one point a mob broke into the prison of the Inquisition, destroyed records, freed the prisoners, and then threw a statue of Paul into the Tiber.

His successor, Pius IV, elected in 1559 as a compromise after a conclave deadlocked for four months, was as affable and seemingly as accommodating as Paul was the opposite. He was not known as a reformer. As a young man he had fathered three natural children, and even while he was pope there was speculation about his private life. Somewhat surprisingly, therefore, he turned out to be an effective pope. He at once began to reverse Paul's more repressive measures by freeing Cardinal Morone from prison, moderating the *Index*, and restricting the competence of the Inquisition. He abhorred Paul's anti-Spanish and anti-Habsburg obsession and immediately set about trying to improve relations with Philip II of Spain and Emperor Ferdinand, Charles V's successor. Although strongly urged to do so, he refrained from excommunicating Elizabeth I of England, who in 1558 came to the throne after the death of her half-sister Mary. His administration of the Papal States, in desperate condition after Paul's war with Spain, was masterly.

The pontificate opened with the sensational arrest and trial of Paul IV's three nephews, who were accused of theft, violence, assassination (including that of Giovanni's wife), abuse of power, and other crimes. Carlo and Giovanni were sentenced to death and their possessions confiscated. The trial, which seems to have been conducted fairly, won him favor with the Romans, who were convinced Paul IV, hard on everybody else, had let his nephews off far too lightly.

A year after his election, Pius IV named to the cardinalate one of his nephews. This appointment was as wise and successful as the appointment of Carlo Carafa had been disastrous. The nephew, age twenty-two, was the talented, deeply devout Charles (Carlo) Borromeo, who later as archbishop of Milan became the living exemplar of the reformed episcopacy for which the Council of Trent was striving. He would be canonized in 1610. Pius brought the young man to Rome, made him his closest confidant, and was increasingly influenced by him in the direction of church reform.

Pius IV won his respected place in church history, however, by successfully reconvening the Council of Trent and successfully bringing it to conclusion. Among the many things that had changed since the council's suspension in 1552, two were especially important. The French monarchy had in 1559 made its final peace with the Habsburgs, and French Catholicism was now seriously threatened by Calvinism. These two factors made the French more willing to cooperate. The monarch most strongly advocating the resumption of the council, however, was Philip II of Spain.

The council got under way in mid-January 1562, and concluded in early December the next year. It continued the discussion of the sacraments and brought it finally to conclusion, making use of the intense speculation on them by the Scholastic theologians of the Middle Ages. Important though those doctrinal decrees were, the drama of this period was over reform, and it centered on the obligation of the bishops to reside in their dioceses. Some bishops strongly and unflinchingly argued that the obligation was "of divine law," and therefore could not be dispensed even by the pope. Their object in so arguing was to make sure they had closed the biggest loophole beyond the possibility of its being reopened.

The issue brought the council to full crisis and to a grinding halt when the pope, insisting that he would himself handle the matter, instructed his legates to block the measure. Like all the popes Pius refused to allow any restriction on his freedom of action. But the bishops refused to back down. Just at that point Pius appointed the now fully rehabilitated Cardinal Morone as president of his legates to the council. Morone, dedicated as he was to the cause of reform, was able to engineer a compromise that saved the council from shipwreck. He then went on to mastermind a whole series of measures for the reform of the episcopacy and pastorate that in time transformed the pastoral functioning of those offices for the better. Once again, as in his nephew, Pius had in Morone made a brilliant choice.

When the council ended, Pius approved all of its decrees from the first to the last period, though some in the curia strongly advised him to be more selective. He then reserved to himself the interpretation of the council and for that purpose established in Rome a Congregation of the Council to advise him on the matter. In obedience to a decree of the council mandating bishops to create a seminary in their dioceses for the training of future priests, he in 1564 established the first such institution in Rome and put it under the direction of the Jesuits. After the hiatus of the pontificate of Paul IV, he resumed patronage of artists, architects, and civil engineers and laid the groundwork for even more extensive renovation of the city by later popes.

By the time he died in 1566 Catholicism, and with it the papacy, had entered a new era. Certainly, it would take a long time for the decrees of Trent to be implemented on a widespread scale, but many bishops returning from the council were changed men, determined on implementation. The bishops at Trent were unable to carry through on the reform of the papacy many of them fought for, but Pius and his successors set to the task, not always with the constancy, thoroughness, and determination desirable. Nonetheless, it was clear certain things would no longer be tolerated.

Along with this new moral and religious seriousness, the papacy was also the beneficiary of a newly stable political situation in Italy, due largely to the fact that Spain was firmly ensconced in both Milan and Naples. This meant that, along with everything that Julius II had been able to accomplish in bringing the Papal States under manageable rule, those States were no longer under military or political threat. The popes, who would still be deeply involved in European politics, now had a security at home that was new and that allowed them to pursue more consistent and constructive policies.

THE NEW ROME

New Rome? Of course, not altogether new, not Rome "the
eternal city," in which vestiges of era upon era of its long
history are visible to casual visitors even today. Yet certainly a new era had been in the making since the accession of Paul III
in 1534, and now, after the Council of Trent, the new papacy began
to take on more defined forms, which had an impact on the culture of
the city. The era marked the beginning of the formation of the modern
papacy, in which new functions, new responsibilities, new but characteristic institutions, and even new ideals emerged with prominence and
force.

A devout personal life was now the ideal that prelates, including
the popes, wanted to project. To have fathered illegitimate children
began to impede advancement in an ecclesiastical career and, surely,
if children had been fathered, they were not publicly acknowledged
and loaded with favors. As a young man, the future Gregory XIII had
a child, but his exemplary life after his ordination allowed his youthful
indiscretion to be tolerated.

For the popes implementation of Trent became an ongoing part
of their job description, for which they now had a Congregation to
help them. In this task they faced competition. Trent tried its best to

strengthen the authority of bishops, and in its wake a generation of strong bishops appeared, led by Charles Borromeo. Saint Charles, as well as others, saw the implementation of the council as being in the first place the responsibility of the local bishop, a view that sometimes brought them into conflict with Rome. The council, moreover, in one of its last acts reminded "princes" of their duties to observe the ordinances of the council and to see to it that their subjects did the same. This call was warrant for "the princes" to claim their traditional role as enforcers of council decrees. No one was more eager to undertake that role than Philip II. The interpretation and implementation of the council, therefore, often brought these three authorities into conflict with one another, and in those conflicts the popes did not always emerge the victor.

Implementation of the council meant for the popes more careful supervision of bishops, even though they had little to say in most cases about who became bishop. It meant being at least circumspect about handing out dispensations, especially if fees were attached to the transaction. It meant avoiding as far as possible even the appearance of any venality. It meant that Rome itself, the papal city, had to be a city of order, beauty and, most especially, a city of saints—a Catholic counterpart to the saints of Calvinist Geneva. Rome dipped back into its old heritage of sanctity to capitalize on it and then bring it up to date with saints of recent times.

Even as Rome and the Papal States enjoyed a new stability and security, parts of Europe were torn apart for a century by "wars of religion," which began with the war between Charles V and the Schmalkaldic League in 1546 and ended with the Treaty of Westphalia a century later, 1648, which concluded the Thirty Years' War. In between were the vicious Wars of Religion in France for almost three decades beginning in 1562, and the English Civil Wars, which also ended in 1648. The Turks continued to be a serious military and naval threat. Religion was the umbrella under which all these wars were ostensibly fought, but dynastic and political dominance were often the reality the umbrella covered. The popes did not stand aloof from these conflicts but threw vigorous support in men and money to the armies fighting for the Catholic cause.

With Pius V, successor to Pius IV, the papal pendulum swung again to the opposite extreme. The parents of Michele Ghislieri, the future Pius V, were well-to-do peasants. At an early age the talented boy entered the Dominican order and rose in its ranks. By 1551 he had come to the attention of Giampietro Carafa, who secured for him in 1551 the post of Commissary General in the Roman Inquisition, a post in which, ominously, Ghislieri felt comfortable. When Carafa became Paul IV he continued to look upon Ghislieri as his protégé. During the pontificate of the more tolerant Pius IV, Ghislieri kept a low profile, which made his election after a nineteen-day conclave all the more surprising. His zeal, earnestness, and unblemished reputation at least in part account for his election.

His major objective as pope was to put reform into effect in every sphere, beginning in Rome itself. He conducted official visitations of the great basilicas of the city, established a commission to do the same for the parishes of Rome and the Papal States, and made sure confessors and candidates for ordination were carefully scrutinized. He further cut down the size of the papal court and tried to reduce its expenses. Even as pope he lived as an austere Dominican friar and, as is sometimes said of him, was the first pope of the era to project an image of himself as priest rather than sovereign.

He fulfilled a mandate of the Council of Trent by publishing the *Roman Catechism*, which was intended as a handbook for pastors, much more extensive in its explanations than the smaller ones for the laity now circulating everywhere. Also in accordance with Trent, he revised the Roman Missal and the Breviary for the elimination of scribal errors, bad Latin, and redundancies that had crept into them, an operation that for the first time put liturgical reform firmly in the hands of the papacy.

He declared Thomas Aquinas a doctor of the church, which is the first such action in history. Until then only four doctors of the Western church were recognized—Ambrose, Jerome, Augustine, and Gregory the Great. A millennium after those four lived, Pius put Aquinas on the same level. His action boosted a revival of interest in Aquinas that had already been under way for a century. Aquinas's fortune faded in the eighteenth and early nineteenth century, only to be revived to become a hallmark of Catholicism.

His model as pope was his patron, Paul IV. Although Pius allowed some Jews to remain in the ghettos of Rome and Ancona, he banished others from the Papal States. He banned prostitutes from Rome. Like Paul, though not quite so obsessively, he ferreted out heresy with an almost reckless zeal and attended the meetings of the Roman Inquisition. Under him the number of persons accused and sentenced soared. Along with the Congregation of the Inquisition, he founded a Congregation of the Index, whose function was to examine authors and publishers to determine their orthodoxy. The Index now became an ongoing aspect of Catholic life. It was abolished only in 1966.

On the international scene his intransigence and aggressive insistence on the church's rights and privileges did not play well with monarchs. In 1570, though advised against it, he excommunicated and, presumably, deposed Elizabeth of England, the last such excommunication of a ruling monarch pronounced by a pope. The era of papal depositions, which began with Gregory VII, had passed. In this case, as in many others, the excommunication was counterproductive. It forced English Catholics to choose between their religion and their country and led to a bitter persecution.

His greatest, though ephemeral, triumph in European politics was his successful rallying of Spain and the Republic of Venice to join him in a Holy League against the Turks. On October 7, 1571, the League's fleet under Don Juan of Austria, Philip II's illegitimate half-brother, won a brilliant victory at Lepanto over the Turkish fleet, which for the time being ended its dominance in the Mediterranean. To celebrate the event Pius created the feast of Our Lady of Victory, which soon became Our Lady of the Rosary, October 7th. Although the rosary was a form of prayer long promoted by the Dominicans with considerable success, Pius's creation of the feast and the association of it with Lepanto gave impetus to the Rosary and increased its appeal, putting it fast on its way to becoming in the modern era the devotion most characteristic of Roman Catholics and most beloved by them. Pius died the next year, 1572, about six months after Lepanto. He was canonized in 1712, the only pope from the era thus honored.

His successor, Gregory XIII, somewhat more willing to compromise than Pius, nonetheless shared his predecessor's zeal for orthodoxy and for promotion of the decrees of Trent. He was more militant in a literal sense in that he even more actively supported and encouraged the use of force to restore or sustain Catholicism in various parts of Europe. He urged Philip II to invade England, supported Philip's military campaign in the Low Countries, subsidized in France the Catholic League in its military campaigns against the Huguenots, and engaged elsewhere in similar ventures. No single action betrays his priorities more tellingly than his ordering in 1572 the singing of a solemn *Te Deum* in thanksgiving for the Saint Barthomew's Day Massacre in which thousands of French Huguenots were butchered.

Until he was ordained at the age of forty, Ugo Boncompagni certainly did not lead an ascetical life. Born into a family of modest means in Bologna, he made his way in society through his talent and accomplishments, not by reason of birth. Even as a young man he was highly regarded for his legal expertise and his administrative skills. Already a bishop, he attended the last period of the Council of Trent. He played an important role in drafting some of the council's decrees, which intensified his concern while pope to see them properly implemented. After the council Pius IV entrusted him with an important diplomatic mission to Spain, where he won the confidence of Philip II.

Two weeks after the death of Pius V, Boncompagni was elected pope in a conclave that lasted less than twenty-four hours. The almost unprecedented brevity of the conclave testifies to the respect and confidence he enjoyed among his peers, but having the firm support of Philip II did not hurt him. His ventures into international politics were no more successful than were those of Pius, but they were not marked by colossal blunders. His achievement lay in other areas, beginning with his reform of the calendar, 1582. The commission charged with the task dropped ten days (October 5–14, 1582) and came up with a new rule for leap years that corrected the deficiencies in the old Julian calendar. The new calendar, which is in use worldwide today, was adopted almost immediately by Catholic states but resisted elsewhere. It was not adopted by Britain and the American colonies until 1752, by Russia until 1918, and by Greece until 1923.

He consolidated and strengthened the apostolic nunciatures to make them another characteristic of modern Catholicism. Papal nuncios (from the Latin *nuntius*, "messenger"), though they had precedents, date as quasi-ambassadors of the pope from earlier in the sixteenth century, and they would be more fully developed in the seventeenth. Nonetheless, Gregory rightly gets credit for establishing them in more places and for using them as agents for the implementation of Trent as well as for negotiations with Catholic monarchs. The development of the nuncio system during this era is another instance of the general centralization of authority in Rome characteristic of modern Catholicism.

Gregory continued the architectural transformation of the city under way now for a century, which included beginning to build on the Quirinal hill a magnificent new papal palace, which today is the residence of the President of the Italian Republic. Much more important, however, was the role he played in helping turn Rome into an educational center, especially for clerics. In 1303 Boniface VIII founded the University of Rome, whose fortunes fluctuated in concert with the fortunes of the city, but even in good times it never attained the eminence of the great Italian universities like Bologna and Padua. In 1552 the Jesuits opened their Roman College, which swiftly developed into a full-fledged university and within a few decades outshone the University of Rome. It attracted students from far and wide, which included many from noble or aristocratic families.

Gregory became a great patron of the institution and built for it a magnificent new building near the Pantheon in city-center, still standing today. The Jesuits were just as concerned with the proper education of future priests as they were of young laymen, and from the beginning the Collegio Romano was also a training ground for them. Shortly after the opening of the Collegio Romano, the Jesuits opened the Collegio Germanico for the training for the priesthood of young men from the empire. Those students lived at the Germanico but took classes at the Romano. Then, as mentioned, Pius IV entrusted to the Jesuits the Roman Seminary, a residence for young Roman clerics studying at the Collegio Romano.

It was this educational enterprise that Gregory aided and abetted in a notable way. Besides his direct assistance to the Jesuits, he, for instance, issued in 1579 a bull of foundation for the Venerable English College, whose students, exiles from their mother country and candidates for the priesthood, attended the Romano. The pattern was developing that soon turned Rome into the center for the training of Catholic clerics that it is today, something that was entirely new.

After Gregory came the five-year explosion of energy that was Sixtus V, 1585–1590. Born a farmworker's son in 1520, Felice Peretti entered the Franciscans when he was twelve and quickly rose to become a respected preacher and theologian. Austere and severe, known as "the iron pope," he as a young man won the attention of Paul IV, who named him inquisitor to Venice, where he was so unbending that he had to be recalled. He was elected pope through the influence of Philip II, who managed to squash opposition to him. During his reign he continued to give moral and financial support to anti-Protestant armies.

Sixtus's vigorous pontificate is important in many ways, including his extremely harsh but effective measures against banditry in Rome and the States, which included hundreds upon hundreds of public executions. He regulated food prices, drained marshes, encouraged agriculture and the wool and silk industries—all of which contributed to the well-being of his subjects, though they were not always appreciative of his efforts for them. Franciscan though he was, he was able through good management and new taxes to fill the papal coffers, left empty by Gregory, to the point that he became one of the richest princes in Europe. None of the accumulated sums did he use on himself. The fiscal miracle is all the more remarkable because the first of his two most lasting achievements was his outstanding contribution to the physical remaking of the city, a contribution that did not come cheap.

Papa Peretti was singularly modern as one of the first persons in the era to go about city-planning in a systematic and programmatic way. He opened up new streets and even great avenues in Rome, such as the one between the Lateran to Saint Mary Major, to connect the seven traditional pilgrim churches. To enhance the natural focal points in the city, including the piazza in front of Saint Peter's, he raised Egyptian obelisks that had rested on the ground in Rome since the early Middle Ages. This was no easy task: it took eight hundred men and forty horses to raise the obelisk in Saint Peter's Square.

He saw to the final completion of Michelangelo's dome atop Saint Peter's and rebuilt the Lateran Palace. He contributed generously to the University of Rome—unlike his predecessor, this Franciscan was not well disposed toward the Jesuits. He repaired aqueducts and planned to urbanize the higher, less densely populated areas of Rome by laying out streets that connected them with the more densely populated areas and with the roads leading to the Roman countryside. He thus created a new relationship between the city and surrounding area. Sometimes his dreams for the city fortunately foundered, such as his plan to turn the Colosseum into a huge factory for treating wool. The population of Rome grew to about one hundred thousand.

Sixtus, who fancied himself a scholar, gave generously to the Vatican Library and expanded its quarters with the impressive Sistine Hall. He founded the Vatican Press, still functioning today and publishing important works of scholarship. His own venture into scholarship, however, was not happy. He was so impatient with how slowly the commission entrusted with the revision of the Vulgate, the traditional Latin Bible, was moving that he took the matter into his own hands and published his version in 1590. It was full of so many and such elementary mistakes that after his death it had to be withdrawn from circulation.

His second most lasting achievement was a complete overhaul of the curia by creating or confirming fifteen permanent bureaus or departments known as Congregations, headed by cardinals. This creation of a modern bureaucracy was one of the first in Europe. Although in subsequent centuries the Vatican bureaucracy underwent a number of modifications, it is still the system that under the pope administers the Catholic Church today. Three Congregations were in operation before Sixtus became pope—the Inquisition (Holy Office), the Index, and the Council. The other twelve were new.

Among them were some that looked exclusively to the administration of Rome and the Papal States, such as the Congregation of the Navy for the creation of a fleet of ten galleys to defend the coast; the Congregation for the University of Rome; the Congregation of Roads, Bridges, and Aqueducts; and the Congregation for the Vatican Press. The more important, of course, were those that looked to the church universal, such as the three that predated Sixtus. Especially important was the new Congregation of Rites and Ceremonies, the centralized regulator of all matters liturgical, a significant innovation. That Congregation also regulated the processes for canonization, another instance of the growing centralization of decision-making.

Whether intended or not, the establishment of the Congregations reduced the power of the cardinals as a body. Since the eleventh century the cardinals gathered with the pope as a group on a regular basis to take action on serious matters. These meetings were called consistories, and they were important in developing policy. They also acted as a restraint on the popes, who hesitated to go against a strong position adopted by a consistory. Popes especially of the twelfth century, moreover, entrusted to consistories judicial functions such as judging between bishops in cases of conflict. Now, with the cardinals divided up among the Congregations, the pope dealt with them on a more individual basis, as his ministers rather than as a council to which he in some measure had to answer.

When in 1585 Sixtus required bishops to come to Rome before they took up their responsibilities and to visit "the Apostles" on a regular basis thereafter, he created another important institution characteristic of modern Catholicism, the so-called *ad limina* visits that bishops must make to the Holy See at set intervals. On the eve of the Age of Absolutism the popes set the pace with their new institutions, their new throne rooms, and their new buildings, all of which displayed their coat of arms prominently on their facades.

The new Rome! By the end of the sixteenth century the city was a far cry from the shrunken and neglected place it was at the end of the Great Schism. The physical transformation began at that time with Martin V, was forwarded energetically and intelligently especially by Sixtus IV and his nephew, the intrepid Julius II, and then brought further along by Paul III and his successors. Meanwhile the new religious orders had begun to do their part. The Jesuits led with the Collegio Romano and then with their mother church, the Gesù, finished in 1599, which soon was followed by the churches of the other orders, such as the Theatines' Sant'Andrea della Valle and the Oratorians' Chiesa Nuova. The renovation of the city was far from over—Bernini and Borromini had yet to leave their mark. But the Rome we know today as the city of great piazzas, ample and graceful fountains, and great palaces of great families with their great art collections was well on its way.

The papacy too had changed. Sanctity was in, easy morals were out. Some of the old abuses remained—nepotism, for instance, and a continued slackness about certain dispensations—but expectations had changed. Popes were more focused on the public welfare of the church than they were at the beginning of the century. They had assumed new responsibilities for the church and created new institutions to fulfill them. Many of those institutions continue to define the papacy today.

PART

V

INTO THE
MODERN ERA

THE STORM BREAKS

Well beyond the middle of the seventeenth century the popes and their city seemed to be doing well. Problems as always abounded, but major crises were few and eventually resolved, at least on the surface. The anti-pope phenomenon, for instance, which had dogged the papacy since the second century, had disappeared. Rome continued to attract pilgrims in great numbers and continued as the first training ground for aspiring artists. The city was resplendent with Renaissance and Baroque masterpieces. The Papal States, under control to a degree not known before and secure from foreign aggression, produced a decent revenue. The Turkish threat had somewhat abated, and calls for crusades against the infidel diminished. The church at large had recovered confidence after the trauma of the Reformation and had even reclaimed some areas formerly Protestant or in danger of becoming Protestant. Missionaries in Spanish and Portuguese America and even in Asia seemed to be making progress.

Although the popes were more than attentive to their families, they were also attentive to their duties. They were at least conventionally devout, some of them much more so. Innocent XI (1676–1689), for instance, was declared a blessed by Pius XII in 1956. Yet he and perhaps Benedict XIV (1740–1758) were as close as any of them came to greatness. The popes and the institution over which they presided had settled into a comfortable mediocrity. Nonetheless, on the surface, all seemed well—at least to a superficial observer.

Under the surface, however, things did not look so pleasant. The papacy's political situation was weak to the point of powerlessness in the face of the strong monarchies and empires that had developed since the beginning of the sixteenth century—the Spanish, Portuguese, English, Austrian and, above all, the French. The monarchs all subscribed to the doctrine of the divine right of kings, and by the middle of the eighteenth century felt not much more than disdain for the claims to temporal authority of the papal monarch with his tiny and economically backward state.

Despite King Francis I's renunciation in 1516 in the Concordat of Bologna of the principle of councils' superiority over popes, his successors in the seventeenth and eighteenth century promoted a close equivalent known as Gallicanism, which crystallized in 1682 at an assembly of the French clergy convoked by Louis XIV and which included severe restrictions on the authority of the pope in the French church. These are the famous Gallican Articles. The occasion was a dispute between the king and Pope Innocent XI over the appointment of bishops and over the beneficiary for the revenue of vacant bishoprics. The Articles continued to be held in France until after the French Revolution, affected the monarchies of Spain and Portugal, and had later counterparts in Austria known as Febronianism and Josephism. Although the popes condemned these phenomena and railed against them, they were incapable of eradicating them.

The ancient right of the emperor to veto the results of a papal election began to take on a different form in the seventeenth century, as the kings of France and Spain, as well as the emperor (now with his capital in Vienna) claimed as an "immemorial right" that they could designate a cardinal who in conclave could veto the candidacy of one of the contenders and thus eliminate him from the running. The popes acquiesced in this principle. Not until 1903 did Pius X annul it.

Meanwhile a momentous cultural shift had occurred that was most notable and noticeable in the field of science. Copernicus and then Galileo set things in motion, of course, presaging a great turn toward experiment and mathematics from supposedly authoritative texts such as Aristotle's works on "natural philosophy." With faith in the ancients' analysis of the physical world shaken, faith in their metaphysical categories could not be far behind. Descartes's search for certitude was of a piece with this new situation. The language and many of the presuppositions of learned discourse changed.

The Aristotelian principles that underlay Scholasticism, the dominant genre of Catholic theology, coupled with the papal condemnation of Galileo, led the church and the papacy into fighting a rear-guard action. The reliability of results that experiment provided fed a growing confidence in the power of reason and a growing skepticism about the claims of authority. The stage was set for the Enlightenment, which on the continent would take a much more virulent turn against Christianity, specifically against Catholicism, than it would in England or Scotland. Let Reason reign supreme, let dogma disappear! Voltaire's wish for the church was shared by many of his peers, Écrasez l'infâme—"Obliterate the dreadful thing!"

Even as culture wars were being fought on the highest intellectual level, among rank-and-file Catholics religious observance seems to have declined seriously. The great religious fervor that energized the sixteenth and the first part of the seventeenth century had cooled, at least in certain areas of Europe. Although the Jesuits and some other religious orders maintained a high membership, the houses of many monastic communities, including the once proud and flourishing Cluny, were practically empty.

The lower clergy, now generally better educated than before Trent, often felt alienated from a culturally and emotionally distant episcopacy. Bishops, drawn almost exclusively from the aristocracy, claimed their see almost as a family right in some cities. While many were devout and diligent about their duties, others left much to be desired. King Louis XVI was supposed to have remarked about a candidate proposed to him for Paris that he thought a bishop for such an important see should at least believe in God.

Within the strictly ecclesiastical arena, the religious orders sometimes waged wars against one another that, in their vituperation, rivaled or surpassed the antagonism they directed toward Protestants.

The Franciscans made fun of the Dominicans' reverence for the teaching of Aquinas, and the Dominicans tried to find ways to respond in kind. No order was spared, but from the middle of the seventeenth century through the eighteenth the Jesuits were the epicenter of controversy. Their spectacular success in almost every field they seemed to touch sparked jealousy, especially as their schools grew in size, prestige, and number—they had over thirty in Sicily alone. In great cities and small the schools with their attached churches occupied large areas of prime real estate in city-center, where besides preaching and classroom instruction they in many places offered an elaborate program of theater.

But the other orders had more specific grievances, among them none more serious than their criticism of Jesuits' evangelizing strategies in the Far East—in Japan, India, Vietnam, and China. These strategies led to an ongoing crisis known as "the Chinese Rites Controversy," in which the Jesuits were accused of so accommodating Christianity to indigenous cultures that they betrayed the faith. Pope Clement XI in 1715 condemned the Jesuits' position, but his action did not dispel suspicion as to what the Jesuits were about. The Jesuits' defense of the Amerindians in their Reductions in Latin America won them the suspicion and enmity of royal ministers in Lisbon and Madrid. The financial strategies the Jesuits used to pay the expenses of their elaborate ventures in the foreign missions raised questions about their probity.

The great theological controversy of the era was over Jansenism, a Catholic version of the strict Augustinianism for which Calvin was the major spokesman in the sixteenth century. The Jansenists presented themselves as the true followers of Augustine, which meant they held a dour view of human nature along with an extremely strict moral code. Despite the careful decree of Trent on justification, which supposedly settled the matter for Catholics, the controversy over free will and grace, that is, over justification, had bounded to the surface once again.

By the middle of the seventeenth century Jansenism had taken hold of a small but well educated and well placed number of French notables, including Blaise Pascal. The Jansenists saw the Jesuits as their principal enemy because of the Jesuits' more optimistic views of human nature and their supposedly lax moral code resulting from their espousal of Probabilism as a form of ethical reasoning. They took the Jesuits' cultivation of theater and ballet as proof-positive of their corrupting influence. Pascal's clever and devastating satire, *The Provincial Letters*, was directed against the Jesuits and did them great harm.

King Louis XIV, passionately opposed the Jansenists because he saw them as divisive, and worked along with the Jesuits to secure a papal condemnation. He was successful with Pope Innocent X, who issued the first condemnation in 1653. The Jansenists found ways to argue around this and successive condemnations until Clement XI's bull *Unigenitus*, 1715. After *Unigenitus* the movement went more or less underground, where it nonetheless remained strong all through the century especially in France but also elsewhere, including Rome.

The philosophers of the French Enlightenment hated and despised the Jansenists, yet they also hated the Jesuits, who were some of their most able intellectual opponents. For the *philosophes* to strike at the Jesuits was to strike at the church. The Gallicans also hated the Jesuits because they saw them as papal agents, as representatives of a foreign power. In their view the Jesuits were unpatriotic. In Spain and Portugal these same forces were at work against the Jesuits, who had by about the middle of the eighteenth century become the lightning rod for attracting a coalition of forces antagonistic to one another yet united in opposition to them in a politico-ecclesiastical climate turned increasingly sour and ominous.

This informal and highly unlikely coalition of Jansenists, Gallicans, and *philosophes* agitated for the suppression of the Jesuit order and bit by bit was able to convince, hoodwink, or intimidate the monarchs of Portugal, Spain, Naples, France, and finally Austria into pressuring the papacy for it. Clement XIII, elected in 1758 after Louis XV had vetoed the conclave's first choice, immediately had to face an all-out offensive against the Jesuits, the issue that dominated his pontificate. The offensive first boiled over in Portugal, where Pombal, the king's all-powerful minister, stood for state absolutism and hated the Jesuits. In 1759 Pombal obtained a royal edict sequestering the Jesuits' assets in Portugal and in its extensive colonies. He evicted Jesuits from their communities and delivered many of them uninvited to the Papal States.

Clement protested the suppression, to no effect. In 1764, France followed suit, in 1767 Spain, and the next year Naples and Sicily.

When Clement died in 1769, it took 185 voting sessions and more than three months to elect his successor, who also wished to be called Clement. The Jesuits were the issue that tore the conclave apart, as the cardinals and ambassadors of the leading monarchs agitated for a pope who would suppress them entirely. Although Clement XIV does not seem explicitly to have promised to do so, he could hardly have been elected without communicating in some form the desired message.

Once elected, he resisted the pressure as best he could, but on August 16, 1773, he finally issued the bull, *Dominus ac Redemptor* that did the deed. After the bull listed the many abuses of the Jesuits and ordered the Society disbanded, it continued, "We divest them of their houses, schools, colleges, hospitals, farms and any other property in any province or dominion where they may exist." The papal police seized the superior general of the order and imprisoned him in Castel Sant'Angelo, where he was held without trial until he died two years later.

The suppression of the Jesuits was a colossal tragedy for Catholicism. Along with its other dire effects, it wiped out in a single blow a vast educational network of some eight hundred institutions not only in Europe but also in Latin America and even in Asia. More broadly, it threw a glaring spotlight on the antagonisms with which Catholic Europe seethed, and it ominously adumbrated more trouble for the church soon to come. It made the papacy's weakness even in the ecclesiastical sphere visible to all.

Clement died a year after the suppression of the Jesuits. By the time his successor was chosen, Catholic monarchs, convinced by the suppression of the Jesuits that they could work their will with the papacy, wanted to reduce the pope to a ceremonial figure, with perhaps some limited authority to settle doctrinal questions when they became an international and political problem. Meanwhile in France the political scene became ever more menacing and the crown ever less secure. Even the most skilled pope could not have done much in this situation to avert the humiliating tragedy waiting to happen.

Pius VI, Gianangelo Braschi, elected after another bitter conclave that lasted over four months because it was not clear whether he was in the pro-Jesuit or the anti-Jesuit camp, did not lack talent or determination. But he was vain and superficial. The intellectual problems of the day, to which he applied heavy-handed solutions, were beyond his grasp, and the political situation in France was spinning into chaos. He reigned for twenty-four years, the longest on record up to that point and one of the most turbulent in recent centuries. In choosing the name Pius, he initiated a trend in papal names that would last until the middle of the twentieth century. He did not make the choice capriciously for he meant to emulate by his firmness Pius V, the uncompromising zealot canonized in 1712. His aspiration was greater than his will to pursue it.

The very year Braschi was elected, 1775, he issued the first of his two encyclicals, *Inscrutabile Divinae Sapientiae*, which was a categorical denunciation of the ideas associated with the Enlightenment. Modern ideas, the work of the devil, spread atheism and destroyed the right order of society. The encyclical was an official declaration of war from on high for a conflict that had been raging in the trenches for decades. It solidified a mind-set for the papacy that for almost two centuries would be uncommonly resistant to revision or qualification.

Despite wanting to emulate Pius V, *Papa Braschi* summoned to Rome two nephews, named one a cardinal and the other Duke of Nemi. After the Duke's marriage, his uncle built him a splendid palace in Rome, the last such edifice erected by a pope. The Duke's rapid rise to wealth and prestige damaged Pius's reputation, but the pope's favors to his family did not extend much beyond the nephews. The pope spent lavishly, however, on a new sacristy in Saint Peter's and a new museum in the Vatican. Besides bankrupting the papacy, this style of spending and favor-dispensing was badly out of keeping with the reality of the pope's situation.

Pius had to deal with an aggressive Emperor Joseph II, brother of the queen of France, Marie Antoinette, who took upon himself the task of putting the church in order in his realm. In 1781 without consulting the pope he dissolved over four hundred convents and monasteries that housed priests or nuns who were not engaged in an active ministry. Devout Catholic though he was, he granted freedom of religion to all his subjects. The next year Pius took the almost unheard-of step of traveling in person to Vienna to negotiate a compromise but, though he was received with elaborate ceremony, he got nowhere. At the same time Grand Duke Leopold of Tuscany, a Jansenist, followed his brother Joseph's example in his dealings with the church. In 1786 he sponsored the Synod of Pistoia, which became a byword for radical reforms that included reduction of papal authority. When a few years later Pius tried to establish a nunciature in Munich, the archbishop told him frankly that bishops ran the German church and that his interventions were not needed. The papacy had begun to look like an anachronistic nuisance.

In 1789 the French Revolution broke out. It changed everything. Pius VI's other problems suddenly seemed trivial in comparison. Would the Revolution send out a spark to ignite similar conflagrations elsewhere? Pius, of course hostile to the Revolution from the first shot fired, dithered. He held off from a confrontation even after the promulgation the next year of the Civil Constitution of the Clergy that reorganized the French church. But when an oath of allegiance to the new regime was demanded of the clergy, he denounced the document, suspended all bishops and priests who took the oath, and condemned the Declaration of the Rights of Man.

Things were going from bad to worse. To save itself from bankruptcy the new government in France confiscated the entire property of the French church and began a massive sell-off of church property, not only sacred vessels, paintings, and furnishings but also real estate. Churches were sacked, some left in ruins, as was the abbey church at the monastery of Cluny, the largest church in Christendom after Saint Peter's. Religious orders were, like the Jesuits, suppressed. Many bishops and priests courageously refused to take the oath and, as the Revolution devolved into ever more radical excesses, recalcitrant clergy were guillotined or drowned in punishment for their treason. Thousands upon thousands of clergy fled the country. The number is sometimes put as high as thirty thousand. "Liberty, Equality, Fraternity," the battle-cry of the Revolution, became anathema to devout Catholics, and to no one more anathema than to the pope.

In 1796 French troops under the command of Napoleon Bonaparte invaded Italy, and when Pius refused to rescind his condemnation of the Civil Constitution, they marched on the Papal States, defeated the papal army, and occupied Ancona and Loreto, forcing Pius to sue for peace. By the terms of the Treaty of Tolentino, 1797, the pope had to agree to French occupation of Bologna and Ravenna, allow the French free access to all papal ports, and pay the huge indemnity. To help raise the money he had the life-size silver statue of Saint Ignatius of Loyola over the saint's tomb in the former Jesuit church of the Gesù melted down. Besides that he gave Napoleon a choice of a hundred works of art, of five hundred manuscripts in the Vatican Library and Archives, and free access to the records of the Roman Inquisition. He then issued a letter recognizing the legitimacy of the French Republic and telling Catholics to be loyal to it.

That was not the end. When the next year a riot broke out in Rome during which a French general was killed, the French occupied Rome and proclaimed the establishment of the Roman Republic. When Pius refused to renounce his headship of the Papal States, the French declared him deposed and forced him under French surveillance to withdraw to a monastery outside Florence. While there Pius issued a bull, *Quam Nos*, November 1798, in which he left instructions for how a conclave was to be conducted if things turned out as badly for him as he feared.

With a shift in the military situation in central Italy unfavorable to the invaders, the French hustled their distinguished and gravely ill prisoner across the Alps. By July 1799, they had installed him in a citadel in Valence in southeastern France, not far from Avignon, where he died, age eighty-two, six weeks after his arrival. The local clergy, all of whom had taken the oath to the Civil Constitution, refused to give his embalmed body a Christian burial. His death was recorded in the town hall of Valence simply as that of "Citizen Braschi. Occupation: pontiff."

Pius VII:
Bowed Down and Raised Up

The humiliation was complete. Had the end of the papacy, long predicted, finally arrived? Maybe the institution could survive in vestigial form as the bishopric of a beautiful but otherwise backward city. Its pretensions had certainly caught up with Citizen Braschi, who died in ignominious exile in a provincial town. At that very moment in Italy, however, the political and military situation looked a little better for the papacy. Anti-Revolutionary forces led especially by Austria and Naples had in large areas been able to drive the French back and force them to evacuate cities they had occupied, including Rome and others in the Papal States.

In France, however, the very year Pius VI died, Napoleon was named First Consul, a modest title for somebody who had just grabbed dictatorial power. Shortly afterward he was back in Italy where at Marengo he won a stunning victory over the Austrians that restored territory to the French that the Austrians had recently taken from them and gave Napoleon control of northern Italy. The new pope would have to deal with him. And indeed there was a new pope, Barnaba (or Gregorio) Chiaramonti, elected in March 1800. In honor of his abused predecessor, who was also a distant relative, he took the name Pius.

On December 1, 1799, thirty-four cardinals had gathered in Venice for the conclave. Although the French were out of Rome at this point, the cardinals honored Pius VI's wishes to meet in Venice because it was, months before Marengo, secure under the firm control of the new Austrian emperor, Francis II. Besides, the emperor agreed to cover the costs of the conclave, at which the death of Pius VI was formally announced in terms that linked the church and the princes against their common enemies: restore the church and the enemies of the crown will shake in terror. Under these circumstances the conclave was of course difficult, divided between those who favored at least some attempt at rapprochement with the French and those who objected to the slightest concessions. The result was a fourteen-week stalemate, during which candidate after candidate failed to get the two-thirds majority required.

Finally, a young prelate, Ercole Consalvi, secretary to the conclave, suggested Chiaramonti as a compromise. His suggestion carried the day. The emperor, furious at the choice, since he feared Chiaramonti was soft on the French situation, forbade the use of the basilica of San Marco for the coronation ceremony, which therefore had to be held in the cramped quarters of the monastery of San Giorgio Maggiore. Despite snubbing the new pope in that way, he tried to dissuade him from going to Rome and invited him, instead, to reside in Vienna. Pius declined the invitation and entered Rome on July 3, 1800. One of his first acts was to name Consalvi his secretary of state, a brilliant choice. The two men formed a remarkably effective team that lasted the twenty-three years of Pius VII's pontificate.

Chiaramonti, though born of an aristocratic family from Cesena in the Papal States, did not quite fit the pattern of his immediate predecessors. As a young man, for instance, he entered the Benedictine order, whose influence on his lifestyle remained strong even when he was pope—he liked to make his own bed. Deeply religious but also witty and affable, his charm combined with high principle. Probably from the Benedictines he imbibed a love of learning that was broader than was common among Italian clerics of the time. His library contained, for instance, the critical edition by the Maurists of the Fathers of the Church. More surprising, when he taught philosophy and theology at the Benedictine abbey in Parma, he read Locke and was one of only twenty-seven inhabitants of the city who bought Diderot's *Encyclopédie*, that signature work of Enlightenment thinkers.

He of course did not subscribe to everything he read, but neither did he have his head buried in the sand. When he later taught at the Benedictine abbey of Sant'Anselmo in Rome, he aroused such suspicion and hostility among his fellow monks because of his openness to ideas they believed dangerous that he was transferred to the Benedictine abbey in his home town of Cesena. In 1785 Pius VI named him cardinal and bishop of nearby Imola, where he remained until elected pope. He thus had first-hand knowledge of the many problems in the cities of the Papal States.

After the French invasion and the Treaty of Tolentino, 1796, which ceded Imola to the French, he tried to keep down the violence between the occupying forces and those who resisted them by exhorting his flock to accept the situation. On Christmas Day 1797, he published a homily that caused a mild sensation. In it he said:

> The form of democratic government adopted among you, dearly beloved, in no way contradicts the maxims I have previously stated, nor is it repugnant to the Gospel; it demands all the sublime virtues that are learned only at the school of Jesus Christ and that, practiced religiously among you, will make for your happiness and contribute to the glory and renown of our Republic. . . . Yes! My dear sisters and brothers, be good Christians, and you will be excellent democrats.

Such a statement was unprecedented in papal territory, and especially as coming from a cardinal. In it he quoted not only from Scripture, the Fathers of the Church, and the ancient Roman historian Sallust, but from Rousseau's *Émile*. It was especially this homily that made Emperor Francis II wary of him when he was elected pope three years later.

His long pontificate falls into two clearly distinct phases: 1800–1814, dominated by Napoleon; and 1814–1823, given to rebuilding the church after the decades of devastation. Pius VII was a realist who knew he had to negotiate with Napoleon. The First Consul was also a realist, and he knew that most of the inhabitants of France were Catholic, some of them more fervent than ever in reaction to the excesses of the Republic. He needed the church as badly as the church needed him. As an indication of his goodwill and magnanimity, he allowed the body of Pius VI to be taken back to Rome for proper burial. He made his first overtures by saying that, if the pope were reasonable and understood the present situation, France and the church could be reconciled and "the Gallican church swept away"!

Negotiations ensued, over the objections of many cardinals. The goal was a concordat. For over thirteen months and through twenty-six different drafts the negotiations dragged on. Pius and Consalvi stalled for time, intent on getting out of Napoleon every concession they could. The delay drove Napoleon crazy. He threw tantrums. He threatened to become a Protestant. He threatened to have his troops march on Rome. But finally, on July 15, 1801, the concordat was signed.

It stated that Catholicism was the religion of the great majority of French citizens (not that it was the state religion), and that Catholics were guaranteed public exercise of it "in conformity to such police regulation as deemed necessary for public tranquility." Citizens who were not Catholics could also freely and openly practice. The buildings and real estate seized from the church during the Revolution were to remain in the hands of the new owners, but cathedrals and churches needed for worship were put at the disposal of the clergy as needed. The clergy, who must swear to uphold the government, were paid by the state, which is the first time in history for such a provision. As was earlier provided in the Concordat of Bologna, 1516, the state had the right to nominate bishops, subject to the approval of the papacy.

Finally, the Gallican church was in effect abolished through two articles: (1) the episcopacy would be reorganized according to new dioceses that corresponded to the new *départments* into which the Republic had divided the country, which meant sixty bishops and archbishops instead of the pre-Revolutionary 133; and (2) the pope asked eighty-five bishops actually in place to resign—forty-eight did so, thirty-seven resisted for a while but were gradually replaced. A clean slate! Pius's efforts to persuade and cajole the bishops to cooperate got better results than anybody expected. From this point forward Gallican sentiment in France gradually declined and was replaced by a vigorous "Ultramontane" or pro-papal sentiment (*ultramontane*, "other side of the mountains," or Alps, meaning Italy and Rome). Within a generation the pendulum swung from Gallicanism to its opposite extreme.

Count Joseph de Maistre gave a powerful impetus to Ultramontanism with his book, *Du pape* (*On the Pope*), 1819. Like many French aristocrats de Maistre as a young man was influenced by Enlightenment ideas, but after the Revolution, which for him had spelled nothing but chaos, he utterly renounced them to become a strong advocate for monarchy and for the supreme authority of the papacy. His argument was simple: there can be no order in society without religion, no religion without Catholicism, no Catholicism without the papacy, no effective papacy without its having sovereign and absolute authority. De Maistre was riding the wave of the future.

Pius and Consalvi were of course not happy with many provisions of the Concordat. The surrender of all the assets of the French church, the wealthiest in Christendom, was an especially bitter pill to swallow. But they had done their best to arrive at a settlement that was workable. In its main lines it was the settlement that would endure for a century through the many vicissitudes of French politics. Devout Catholics in France, especially in the upper classes, remained royalists and did not reconcile with the Republic until World War I. But the French church managed to negotiate its way through many tribulations, to come out in the end playing a major leadership role in the church at large during the nineteenth and well into the twentieth century.

Napoleon, not altogether happy with the Concordat, appended to it a document known as the Organic Articles which, even though Pius objected, regulated religious affairs in France beyond what the Concordat provided. And Napoleon became increasingly testy. In 1804 the French Senate declared him Emperor of the French. To solemnize the ceremony Napoleon invited Pius VII to Paris. Would "Napoleon's chaplain," as Pius was derisively called, accept? Cardinals objected, but Pius accepted. If Napoleon wanted to use the occasion to humiliate the pope, he failed miserably. Pius's slow journey from Rome to Paris turned, without any planning or orchestration, into a triumphant procession. Enthusiastic crowds greeted the pope as he moved along his way, to Napoleon's great chagrin. In Paris, though Pius anointed Napoleon and the Empress Josephine, the emperor-elect placed the crown on his own head. Despite that attempt to put the pope in his place, Pius emerged victorious. Napoleon complained, "Nobody thought of the pope when he was in Rome. Nobody cared what he did. But my coronation and his appearance in Paris made him important."

Napoleon had his revenge. The next year he decided he was King of Italy and set about making the claim a reality. His relationship with Pius rapidly deteriorated until he boasted that he would "strip that foreign prince of all his pretensions." On February 2, 1808, French troops occupied Rome again and held Pius under virtual house arrest in the Quirinal Palace. The French annexed the rest of the Papal States. Finally, on June 10, 1809, Pius excommunicated Napoleon. When Napoleon heard the news he ordered that the "raving lunatic" be locked up. During the night of July 6 the French broke into the Quirinal Palace, seized the pope, padlocked him into a carriage with Consalvi, transported him to Savona in northern Italy, and there sequestered him from the rest of the world. Then, after almost three years, they brought him to Fontainebleau, southeast of Paris, where he remained for another two years, until January 1814. It was here, ironically, that Napoleon would sign his first abdication.

Indeed, by the time Pius arrived at Fontainebleau Napoleon's fortunes had already begun to decline with his ill-fated invasion of Russia. In 1814 the emperor finally had to allow Pius to return to Rome. The second phase of Pius's pontificate began at that moment, even though it was temporarily threatened by Napoleon's brief comeback. The Congress of Vienna met for nine months, 1814–1815, to set things back to where they ought to be. All European states, great and small, that legally existed before the Revolution were invited to participate. Consalvi went to represent Rome and conducted himself admirably from every point of view. The major powers (Great Britain, Russia, Prussia, and Austria) set the pace, and they restored "the legitimate monarchs" everywhere—including the Papal States and even in France. The ideals of the French Revolution were now officially suppressed.

Pius had nine years left in his reign, during which he, assisted always by the faithful Consalvi, could expend his energies more directly on promoting the well-being of the church. He was respected even in Protestant lands because of the way he had borne himself in the face of Napoleon but also for the obviously priestly view he took of his office. Typical of him was the graciousness with which he received the disgraced members of the Bonaparte family and gave them refuge in Rome.

Within a few months of returning to Rome in 1814 Pius VII reinstated the Society of Jesus worldwide. He had years earlier, in 1801 and 1804, regularized the existence of small pockets of Jesuits who managed to survive because of technicalities in the bull of suppression. The Jesuits bit by bit attracted recruits in most countries of Europe and, although they never recovered their old buildings and real estate, they began to build new edifices for their many ministries. Their recovery helped stimulate the recovery of other orders, which had in some instances experienced almost total extinction in the turmoil of the times. "Restored" in an era of restoration, the Jesuits, and other orders as well, embraced a conservative, sometimes a full-blown reactionary approach to politics and church life not characteristic of them earlier.

Through Consalvi Pius negotiated a number of concordats with both Catholic and Protestant states that at least for the time being served the church well, even though in most cases the monarchs had the right of nomination of bishops. He totally opposed the South American republics in their revolts against Spain, but he prudently maintained an official neutrality. In France King Louis XVIII's efforts to negotiate a concordat more favorable to the church met with resistance, and the king had to abandon it, which revealed that the restoration the Congress of Vienna mandated was not going to sink deep roots. Any return to the *ancien régime* was going to be partial, superficial and, above all, temporary.

Consalvi's efforts to modernize the administration and economic management of the Papal States met at first with partial success, but it also managed to antagonize both conservative and liberal factions. It was not his fault. The States bore the burden of centuries of set ways of doing things, so that the process of what has been called "sacral rigidification" continued to take its toll. Moreover, young men in the States were well aware of the new liberal political ideas and, practically disenfranchised, grew restless under the "government of priests." The restoration to the papacy of the Papal States in 1815, which seemed at the time to be a great triumph of papal diplomacy, in fact put the institution on a collision course with Italian nationalism.

After a reign almost as long as his predecessor's, Pius VII died peacefully on August 20, 1823. During his lifetime the Holy See had been insulted, brought low, and declared ill beyond hope of recovery. But by the time he died its authority and prestige had been restored and were now as high as they had been in a century. As he lay dying his attendants kept from him the dreadful news that the basilica of Saint Paul outside the Walls, the last of the great basilicas still essentially the same as when built by Constantine in the fourth century, had burned almost to the ground.

BELEAGUERED, INFALLIBLE, AND PRISONER AGAIN

Afte Pius VII came the short pontificate of Leo XII (1823–1829) and the even shorter one of Pius VIII (1829–1830). Leo, pious but narrow-minded, was elected as the candidate of the most reactionary faction in the college, which wanted a break with the liberal policies of Consalvi. Immediately upon his election, the new pope dismissed Consalvi as secretary of state and set about dismantling some of his recent reforms in the States. He adopted an intransigent attitude toward heads of other nations that backfired so badly that he reinstated Consalvi and tried to regain lost ground. When Consalvi died in 1824, Leo lost an experienced and adroit counselor, who might have been able to hold him back from imposing on the city and the States a harsh police regime whose puritanical extremes would have been ludicrous had they not been so fanatically enforced. He put Jews back in the ghettos, whose gates were now fitted with locks, and made it illegal for them to own real estate. Such measures only increased the resentment against "the priests" that had long been smoldering. The short reign of Pius VIII did nothing to quell the unrest in the kingdom he called his own.

Only with the next pope, Gregory XVI, did the situation explode. The conclave lasted almost two months and was divided, as before, between the *zelanti* (zealots), who stood for uncompromising opposition to modern ideas, and others more moderate. The *zelanti* carried the day with the election of Bartolomeo Alberto Cappellari, who began his ecclesiastical career as a monk in the strict Camaldolese order. The new pope never compromised the austere lifestyle he learned as a young man and was exemplarily devout. But his vision was small and in some regards obscurantist. As pope, for instance, he banned railroads in the Papal States as "hellish" (in a play on words, *chemins d'enfer* instead of *chemins de fer*, French for railroads).

Long before he was elected he published *The Triumph of the Holy See and the Church against the Attacks of Innovators*, 1799, a resounding proclamation of papal authority in both the spiritual and temporal spheres. The book did not attract much attention until the author became pope, after which it was frequently republished in the original Italian and also translated into other languages. By that time it played well with the Ultramontanist drumbeat sounded by de Maistre and others that became louder and more insistent as the century progressed.

Gregory was completely dedicated to the good of the church as he saw it. To his credit, he condemned the slave trade (but not slavery) in 1839. His most notable achievement, however, was his encouragement of missionary activity among the religious orders that were now fairly well on the road to recovery after the great downturn in vocations during the Revolution. During his pontificate he appointed some two hundred missionary bishops.

As the nineteenth century unfolded it became after the sixteenth the century of the greatest Catholic missionary activity. But the nineteenth was different from the sixteenth in two regards. First, Catholic missionaries now had to compete with their Protestant peers, a phenomenon practically unknown earlier. Second, both sets of missionaries carried with them a more sharply articulated sense of the superiority of Western culture and of "the white man's burden" to impose it. The first was an ongoing problem for both Catholic and Protestant missionaries. The second would not backfire until the middle of the twentieth century after World War II.

But on the domestic front Gregory faced forces that he did not understand and could not control. Even before he was crowned a rebellion broke out in Bologna and spread through the States, threatening even Rome. The papal army could not put it down. With the Papal States on the verge of collapse, Gregory saved the situation only by the desperate measure of calling upon Austria to send troops to put down the rebels—and to stay thereafter to maintain order. France then sent troops to do the same, and the two armies did not withdraw until eight years later. The pope's own subjects had revolted against him, and on his own he did not have the resources to contain them—an ominous situation.

For the pope the culprit responsible for this evil as well as the general depravity of the times was "the terrible conspiracy of impious men," as he said in his first encyclical, *Mirari Vos*, issued in 1832 shortly after the rebellion was quelled. Among the false ideas that the "shameless lovers of liberty" spread were freedom of conscience, freedom of speech, freedom of the press, and separation of church and state. The solution to these evils was the inculcation of obedience to legitimate princes.

The silent target of the encyclical was the French priest Felicité de Lamennais, who proposed a form of Ultramontanism different from that of the royalist de Maistre. Lamennais believe the church, led by the pope, should ally itself with the people and baptize the Revolution. No more marriage of throne and altar. On the masthead of *L'Avenir* ("The Future"), the newspaper he founded, ran the inflammatory words "God and Freedom." His position won him the enmity of the French Catholic elite and, no surprise, it infuriated Gregory XVI.

The long stay of the Austrians and French gave Gregory time to shore up his position, so that he did not have to face another full-fledged insurrection. But in 1845, the year before he died, there was an uprising in Rimini and the next year another in Ancona. Conspiratorial societies operated almost openly. The papal police were impotent to disband them, partly because the police were themselves often in sympathy with their cause.

Gregory's successor would face formidable political challenges. Besides the unrest in the Papal States, the Risorgimento (resurgence, renaissance), the movement for Italian unification, had after the Congress of Vienna gained increasing momentum especially among intellectuals and the bourgeoisie. For the movement to be successful it of course had to persuade or force the smaller units like the Grand Duchy of Tuscany to join and surrender sovereignty, but it especially had to deal with the two greatest obstacles: Austria, which occupied much of northeastern Italy, and the papacy, which controlled the extensive States right in the middle of the peninsula and held the city that had to be the capital, Rome.

Pius IX was elected on the fourth ballot of a remarkably brisk conclave and elected as a moderate liberal, as somebody who would modulate the rigid policies of Gregory. He came from a noble, fairly well-off family that, surprising for its class, showed a sympathy, much qualified, for the new political and social ideals. He did not decide to become a priest until he was twenty-four, the result of a spiritual retreat, and he wanted nothing more than to be a pastor. Handsome, witty, and usually a pleasure to be with, he had sudden and severe mood swings that left his closest associates wary. Odo Russell, the British ambassador to the Holy See, was genuinely fond of Pius but remarked that he was intellectually limited.

Immediately upon his election Pius declared an amnesty, freed from prison everybody Gregory had put there on political grounds, and made some practical reforms in the States. He instituted broader consultation in the affairs of state and included laymen in it. He made gestures that suggested, or were interpreted as suggesting, that he favored Italian unification. He was certainly unhappy with the Austrian occupation in the north. He dismantled the ghetto in Rome, installed gas lighting in the streets, and set up a commission to introduce railroads into the Papal States.

For two years probably no one in Italy was more popular. Even the "Liberals," the generic name for those who held modern ideas about politics and economics and who were also ardent Italian nationalists, felt they had in him somebody they could work with. Conservatives in Europe, like Metternich, the Austrian statesman and a chief architect of the reactionary Congress of Vienna, were horrified at the pope's election and at his behavior in the early days of his pontificate.

When in 1848 Pius, as "father of all the faithful," as he reminded
the Italians, refused to join in a war to expel Austria, sentiment turned
rapidly against him. In Rome and the States an economic downturn occurred just as a wave of liberal revolutions swept Europe. On November 13, his prime minister Count Pellegrino Rossi was assassinated in
broad daylight. Matters went quickly from bad to worse. A week later,
in disguise, the pope fled the city for Gaeta about eighty miles south of
Rome. When a few months later the Romans declared a Republic, Pius
appealed to the Catholic powers to restore him to his capital. In July
1849, the French sent troops, which enabled Pius to return to Rome a
year and a half later, in mid-April 1850.

The first phase of Pius's pontificate was over, the second begun.
For the next ten years he was politically secure because he was able to
rely on foreign support, which enabled him to act with considerable
freedom. Whatever sympathy he may have felt for liberal ideas had
now completely evanesced. Although somewhat more restrained than
Gregory had been, he reverted to Gregory's repressive policies. One of
his chief confidants was the emotionally unbalanced Anglican convert,
Monsignor George Talbot, whose unmitigatedly reactionary advice
fanned Pius's suspicions of John Henry Newman. In Italy Pius became
the symbol of the intransigent churchman throwing obstacles against
the unification of the country. He was seen perfectly to exemplify what
the ultraconservative Cardinal Henry Edward Manning, archbishop of
Westminster, called "the beauty of inflexibility."

In Pius's favor it must be said that the Liberals were notoriously
anticlerical and many even anti-Christian, and the policies of the governments they installed were radically secularist, designed to eliminate
the influence of the church. Pius's fears of what they would do once
they triumphed were well grounded. But his own views swung to the
opposite extreme. He was scandalized, for instance, when the Grand
Duke of Tuscany, yielding to pressure, allowed Jews to attend the university.

The Virgin Mary played a strong role in Pius's spiritual life as she
did in most Catholics in the nineteenth century. Devotion to her dates
back at least to the Council of Ephesus, 431, which vindicated her title
as Mother of God, and it was strong in the West through the Middle

Ages, as the many images of her testify. It became even more popular in the sixteenth and seventeenth centuries and reached a new peak in the nineteenth. Mary began appearing to her devotees in France—to Catherine Labouré in Paris in 1830, to two shepherd children at La Salette in 1846, and to Bernadette Soubirous at Lourdes in 1858.

The Franciscans in the fourteenth century promoted the idea that Mary was immaculately conceived in that her soul never bore "the stain" of Original Sin, that is, the sin passed onto the human race by Adam. A feast of the Immaculate Conception was subsequently instituted, with its own mass prayers and readings. The idea took popular root and was promoted by the cult of the Miraculous Medal, inspired by Labouré's visions, on one side of which was an image of Mary with the inscription, "O Mary, conceived without sin, pray for us who have recourse to thee." The first medal was struck in 1832 and devout Catholics, male and female, soon began wearing copies.

In 1854 Pius IX on his own authority proclaimed the Immaculate Conception as dogma, to be believed by all Catholics as part of the apostolic faith. He had consulted the bishops of the world beforehand. Nonetheless, this was an innovation of the first order, something no pope had ever done before. The proclamation was greeted by most Catholics with jubilation and sparked an even further upsurge in devotion to Mary, now marked by a saccharin sentimentality typical of the century. Although the pope's authority in the temporal area was shaky, he was fully capable of asserting his absolute authority in the spiritual, thus vindicating the thesis of the Ultramontanists.

But the proclamation also points up a new development in the papal job description. For the previous few decades the popes had moved more and more into the role of teacher, while of course still retaining their more traditional role as judge and dispenser of favors. The popes' search for a mode in which to respond to the intellectual and cultural challenges of the day led to the development of the encyclical. They used that medium to propose, expound, and elaborate theological or doctrinal positions. By definition an encyclical is simply a circular letter and as such was used occasionally by popes and others from ancient times. But beginning in the eighteenth century with Benedict XIV's *Ubi Primum*, 1744, it took on a new significance. Whereas earlier encyclicals were simply a mode of communication, they now became, at least in large part, a mode of authoritative teaching.

The premise for earlier genres like bulls and briefs was that the pope was a judge in matters of controversy or a dispenser of favors. Insofar as popes "taught," they did so principally by condemning wrong teachings, as with Leo X's bull *Exsurge Domine* anathematizing forty-one errors of Luther. In the modern encyclicals, however, popes elaborated on ideas as would a teacher in a classroom. They took over a function reserved since the Middle Ages to professional theologians in the universities. The pope's increasing use of the genre is indicative of its growing importance. In twenty-four years Pius VI issued two, in twenty-three years Pius VII issued one, but Pius IX issued thirty-eight and his successor, Leo XIII, issued seventy-five. Today pontificates are largely defined by the encyclicals the popes produce, and their publication is eagerly awaited. The papal job description has shifted once again.

The development of the encyclical did not, however, spell the end of other genres. When on December 2, 1864, Pius IX issued his encyclical *Quanta Cura* he simultaneously issued one of the most famous papal documents of modern times, the *Syllabus of Errors*. In the *Syllabus* he condemned eighty errors of modern times. Condemned were rationalism, religious indifferentism, atheism, socialism, communism, Protestant Bible societies, secret societies, divorce, separation of church and state, the idea that the church ought not have temporal power, and many other aberrations. The final condemnation of the *Syllabus* brought it to a resounding and famous conclusion: "That the Roman Pontiff can and should reconcile himself and make peace with progress, with Liberalism, and with modern culture."

The world at large greeted the *Syllabus* with derision and most governments with a storm of indignation because of its categorical denunciation of many of the principles on which they had been operating for half a century. The French government, whose troops were at that moment the pope's only defense against the seizure of Rome by the forces of the new Italian monarchy, banned the *Syllabus* in France.

But in fact "modernity" in the nineteenth century was an ideology that bore with it many ideas inimical to Catholicism. It espoused progress, which meant progress beyond revealed religion; it believed that reason and science could and would answer every question regarding human existence. Extreme though the *Syllabus* sounds, it was not entirely off the point. If Pius seems out of touch with the times, his enemies were out of touch with the deep religious sentiments of most of the people.

At about the time he issued the *Syllabus*, he began entertaining the idea of convoking an ecumenical council, which would be the first since the Council of Trent three hundred years earlier. In June 1868, he announced that a council would open in Saint Peter's on December 8, 1869. Precisely what he originally hoped the council would accomplish is not clear, though some people speculated he wanted it solemnly to confirm the *Syllabus*. He may have wanted it as a show of Catholic strength worldwide against the church's enemies, especially in Italy, where his political and military situation seemed fatally jeopardized.

As plans for the council developed a broad agenda opened up—the council would deal with canon law, with the missions, with religious orders, and so forth, but the idea that the council should define that the pope was infallible in matters of faith began to be broached more and more often. At a certain point Pius seized upon it as the essential item on the agenda.

The idea of holding a council in Rome was bold, given the pope's precarious military situation. In 1860 the forces of the Risorgimento had captured the Papal States and incorporated them into the new kingdom. They were poised to move on Rome itself and to proclaim the city the capital of the new nation. Once again it was only the troops of Emperor Napoleon III that protected Rome and held the pope's enemies at bay. Should the French ever withdraw, the city would certainly fall. The papal army was far too small to defend it.

To the end, however, Pius could never bring himself to believe that God would allow such a catastrophe to happen. He went ahead with the council, the first ever to meet in Saint Peter's. To it came about seven hundred bishops from around the world, about a hundred of whom were from Asia and Africa, even though they were of European birth. About forty percent of the total assembly was from Italy. English-speaking bishops were, however, the third largest language group. The heads of state of Catholic countries were informed of the council and invited to pray for its success but, unlike previous councils, they were not invited to participate.

Despite the broad agenda that was anticipated, the council dealt with only two items. The first was the relationship between revealed truth and the powers of human reason, in which the council affirmed, principally against two German Catholic theologians, the distinction between the two spheres along with their compatibility. With that out of the way the council was to move to issues concerning the church, such as church-state relations and the role of bishops, but with the encouragement of Pius it bypassed them and moved directly to consideration of the papacy, under the two headings of primacy and infallibility (see fig. 24.1).

24.1: Pius IX
Pope Pius IX opens First Vatican Council, 1869. Photo: G. Dagli Orti. Palazzo Mastai, Senigallia, Italy.
© DeA Picture Library / Art Resource, NY

The popes had been proclaiming by word and deed their primacy over other bishops and their supreme jurisdiction in the church for at least fifteen hundred years. The purported reason for a solemn reaffirmation of it now was to lay to rest the already defunct Gallicanism, Febronianism, and Josephism that had recently challenged it, but Ultramontanist fervor is what really lay behind it. The terms in which the document proposed it could hardly be more absolute. "The Roman Pontiff has . . . full and supreme power of jurisdiction over the whole church, and this not only in matters of faith and morals but in everything that concerns the discipline and government of the church dispersed throughout the whole world . . . and over all and each of the pastors and faithful."

Unlike the primacy, infallibility met with much more resistance from bishops for a variety of reasons, one of which was lack of clarity as to just what was meant by the term. Did it mean, for instance, that the pope was infallible in his person? Extremists like Cardinal Manning seemed to think that every word the popes uttered was infallible. Other bishops, convinced that the pope under certain circumstances could speak infallibly, opposed the definition on the grounds that, given the times, it was inopportune. Some simply did not believe it. Bit by bit in a debate that was long and sometimes bitter, the council arrived at sharper distinctions. There was no doubt how ardently Pius wanted the definition, and directly and indirectly he made his will known. Finally, on July 13, 1870, the vote was taken, which tallied at 451 in favor, eighty-eight opposed, and sixty-two in favor but with qualification. When the final, solemn vote was taken a few days later, about fifty-five bishops withdrew from the council rather than register a negative vote on an article that was sure to pass. The declarations on primacy and infallibility mark such a high point in papal claims that it is difficult to imagine any surpassing them.

On almost the very day the final vote was taken, the Franco-Prussian War broke out, and Napoleon III was forced to withdraw his troops from Rome. The bishops dispersed. When Napoleon III lost a decisive battle at Sedan on September 2 and was taken prisoner, it was clear French protection was over. Eighteen days later, on September 20, the Italian troops breached the walls of Rome after not much more than a token resistance by the papal army. On that day almost a millennium and a half of history came to an end. Rome was declared the capital of the new kingdom of Italy, and shortly thereafter King Victor Emmanuel II took up official residence in the Quirinal Palace.

Pius and his advisers clung to the belief that Rome could not possibly fall, and after it did they clung to the belief that it was only a temporary situation. Rome had been seized before. The popes had always got it back. The heroic resistance to Napoleon of Pius VII was fresh in the memory of Pius and his inner circle. On October 20 the pope formally adjourned, but did not close, the council. He declared himself a "prisoner of the Vatican," even though the Italians placed no restrictions on his movements. Since Pius would not deal with his enemies, they unilaterally through the Law of Guarantees tried to regularize the situation. The Law was generous in its provisions which, as compensation for seized properties, included an annual grant of three and a half million lire, which in those days was a lot of money.

Pius refused to accept the money, but he tacitly, and to some extent perforce, went along with other provisions of the Law. He hoped "the Catholic powers" would come to his rescue, but no help was ever forthcoming. Yet, for the last eight years of his life he was able to continue his work as supreme pastor without interference from the Italian government and to some extent because of benefits received from it.

In 1868, before the seizure of Rome but well after the seizure of the States, the Holy See had issued a *Non Expedit* ("It is not expedient") that forbade Catholics to play any role in the new political arrangement. They could be Catholics or Italians, but not both. The popular motto expressing the idea was "Neither elected nor electors"—no holding of office, no voting. The decree was meant to underscore the illegitimacy of the government. In 1874 Pius renewed it, and it stayed in effect, with increasing qualifications, into the twentieth century. It was, for obvious reasons, only imperfectly observed.

The definition of infallibility set off a wave of anticlerical sentiment in many parts of Europe. It sparked the schism of the "Old Catholics" in Holland and Germany, small in number of adherents but significant in that it attracted the intelligentsia. It provided Bismarck with another excuse to launch his persecution of Catholics in the newly unified Germany, the *Kulturkampf*. Yet, once again, the papacy gained strength by its very defeat. Sympathy for Pius's plight among rank-and-file Catholics throughout the world surged after he declared himself imprisoned. When he died, a cry arose for his canonization. His pontificate marked the beginning of an almost defining characteristic of Catholics today, a sense of personal relationship with the man occupying the see of Peter, which includes an obligation to be "loyal" to him as an individual and sometimes, it seems, loyal to his every word and gesture. This was new.

LEO XIII:
SEARCHING FOR SOLUTIONS

T he nineteenth century was not kind to the papacy. For Catholicism at large, however, it brought a remarkable resurgence of fervor, activity, and growth. This resurgence occurred despite obstacles placed in its way by anticlerical governments. In almost every Catholic country vocations to the priesthood climbed to pre-Revolutionary levels. The religious orders of men and women, some of which were virtually extinct in 1800, rebounded at an astounding rate, and a strikingly large number of new congregations of nuns were founded. Pilgrimages, which had almost disappeared in the eighteenth century, revived mightily, due in part to easier travel by railroads. As mentioned, missionary activity in Asia and Africa flourished, sometimes supported by governments that at home were anticlerical—missionaries were expected to carry and brandish the national flag.

Primary and secondary schools run by priests, nuns, and religious brothers sprang up wherever Catholics were present in sufficient numbers. Dioceses launched programs of catechetical instruction that by mid-twentieth century resulted in the best catechized Catholic population in the history of the church. Almost every diocese of any size published its own weekly newspaper. The religious orders began publishing an almost incalculable number of popular religious magazines as well as many learned journals. Although in Europe Catholics were opposed to the intellectual mainstream, some few among them were testing the new historical approaches to sacred subjects like the Bible and the liturgy that would bear fruit later.

Back in the Vatican, however, by 1870 the situation of the papacy looked bleak. Pius IX died on February 7, 1878, after the longest pontificate in history and certainly one of the most important. Just a month earlier King Victor Emmanuel II died in the Quirinal Palace a mile away from the Vatican, across the Tiber. The king and his family were devout Catholics yet committed to the cause of unification, caught as were so many Italian Catholics between conflicting loyalties. The royal family had more in common with the old papal nobility than with some of the king's ministers. Consorting with the papal families was, however, not only politically impossible but carried with it the risk of a public snub from them. Pius quietly allowed the king's chaplain to absolve him on his deathbed of the excommunication he incurred for his part in "the spoliation of the church," and Victor Emmanuel II, "the Father of his Country," died as a Catholic reconciled to the church.

The state funeral of the king was staged as a solemn public manifesto of the irreversible character of the new order of things. What would happen with the pope dying so soon afterward? Obviously, the Italian government would not allow any ceremony that suggested papal claims to the city. The Vatican officials did not want any ceremony that suggested acquiescence in the new order. Thus, though for diametrically opposed reasons, the obsequies for Pius were carried out in Saint Peter's, safely in the Vatican, in a way that was satisfactory, under the circumstances, to both parties.

The death of Pius and the election of his successor dramatized how curious the relationship between the Vatican and the government was—and would long remain. Italian troops helped keep order in Saint Peter's while Pius's body lay in state. They were badly needed when three years later Pius's corpse was transported by night from Saint Peter's to its final resting place across the city in Saint Lawrence outside the Walls. A mob broke into the cortege and tried to fling the coffin into the Tiber.

What about the conclave? The cardinals were understandably anxious, but the government made clear it would keep order in the city and guarantee the cardinals all the freedom of action they needed to carry out their duties. With that, speculation that the conclave might be held outside Rome and outside Italy evanesced. The conclave opened in the Sistine Chapel just a week after Pius's obsequies, it briskly, on the third ballot, elected the cardinal bishop of Perugia, Gioacchino Pecci, Leo XIII.

The new pope was sixty-eight years old and in seemingly fragile health, so it was assumed, and probably hoped, that his would be a short pontificate, a "breather," after the long pontificate of Pius. Leo lived, however, for twenty-five more years. He had more native intelligence than Pius and was even more photogenic. Especially with his pontificate did Catholic institutions as a matter of course begin prominently to display photos of the pope, and some Catholic homes did the same, which was another sign of the growing "devotion to the pope."

The coronation of Leo took place in the small space of the Sistine Chapel, not in Saint Peter's, and afterward he did not appear on the balcony of the basilica to receive the acclamation of the crowds and impart his blessing. Once again, for diametrically opposed reasons, the arrangement was agreeable to both parties. The government did not want any gesture that might ignite the pro-papal sentiments of many Romans, and the Vatican (now the term can be correctly used of the papacy) did not want to suggest it gave a blessing to what happened in 1870.

Pecci was not well known in the curia. Cardinal Antonelli, Pius's long-term secretary of state, suspected he held liberal views and had kept him at arm's length. Although Leo, like Pius, came from an old aristocratic family, he grew up in a world more industrialized and more comfortable with certain new ideas than had Pius, born a half-century earlier. Nonetheless, despite what Antonelli thought, Leo was no liberal. He was a firm supporter of the *Syllabus*. He was no more ready to accept the loss of the Papal States as final than was Pius, and his foreign policy was dominated by wildly unrealistic hopes of persuading foreign governments to intervene in Italy for recovery of the States. At certain points in his pontificate, fearful without grounds of what the next move of the Italian government might be, he considered transferring the Holy See to someplace outside Italy.

But he had a more flexible personality and broader experience of the world than his predecessor. Gregory XVI had sent him as nuncio to Belgium in 1838, which entailed visits to Cologne, London, and Paris. He performed badly as nuncio, but for the three years of his appointment he had firsthand experience of the industrialized and parliamentary world of the north. He acquired some awareness of both its problems and its achievements.

As pope, he presided over and forwarded a remarkable expansion of the church outside Europe. Over the course of his twenty-five years he created 248 new sees, established a regular hierarchy in Scotland, North Africa, India, and Japan, and in Europe negotiated with Bismarck, at some cost, the end of the *Kulturkampf*. In 1892 he appointed to the United States the first Apostolic Delegate (papal representative in countries without diplomatic relations with the Vatican).

One of the first acts of his pontificate was to name to the cardinalate the distinguished English convert and theologian, John Henry Newman, whom many in the Catholic world viewed with suspicion because of his book arguing that doctrine changed over time, *Essay on the Development of Christian Doctrine*, 1846. Cardinal Manning was known to regard Newman as a heretic. In 1881 Leo opened the Vatican Archives to all qualified scholars, no matter what their political or religious beliefs. Actions like these signaled that Leo was not Pius.

The most obvious aspect of Leo's pontificate is the large number of encyclicals he produced—seventy-five over a twenty-five year reign, an average of three per year. The range of issues they covered was wide. Nine in succession dealt with some aspect of devotion to the Virgin Mary, another sign of the further blossoming of that aspect of Catholic life. He issued two encyclicals dealing with Protestantism and with the "return" of Protestants to the Catholic fold, the true church. He referred to them, however, not as heretics but as "separated brethren," a term that did not take hold in Catholic circles until the Second Vatican Council in the middle of the next century.

The church-state issue continued to be troubling. Leo was of course opposed to separation of church and state on purely theological grounds, but he also realized that the term was often code for anticlerical and anti-Catholic ideology. Like almost all Catholics of his culture and class, he had an almost instinctual dislike and distrust of republican or democratic forms of government, yet he softened the strictures of his predecessors against them.

He directly and indirectly urged French Catholics to unite behind the Third Republic, an initiative known as the *Ralliement* (a rallying). Only in that way could its unjust anti-Catholic laws be undone. He allowed that in the abstract all three forms of government France had experienced in the nineteenth century—empire, monarchy, and republic—were good. In 1901, two years before his death Leo resolved a bitter dispute among Catholics by allowing the legitimacy of the term "Christian Democracy." Even though he insisted on a restrictive definition of the term, Leo allowed the possibility that democracy and Catholicism were compatible.

In 1899 in his Apostolic Letter *Testem Benevolentiae*, addressed to the archbishop of Baltimore, Leo condemned "Americanism," an ill-defined movement in the United States that is sometimes described as "the phantom heresy." By the second decade of Leo's pontificate the leaders of the American hierarchy were divided between those who believed strongly in the democratic process and the separation of church and state as practiced in the United States and those skeptical of the compatibility of the American experience and the church. The former favored a more open relationship with Protestants and, allegedly, exalted the "active" virtues over passives ones like obedience, and similarly exalted natural virtues like honesty over the supernatural virtues of faith, hope, and charity. The Apostolic Delegate sided with the latter. Leo's letter, moderate in tone, tried to set the record straight about aberrations. The supposed culprits inside and outside the hierarchy denied the aberrations existed as they were described in the letter.

Leo made two extremely important and lasting contributions to modern Catholicism through two landmark encyclicals—*Aeterni Patris*, prescribing and promoting the study of the philosophy of Thomas

Aquinas, 1879, and *Rerum Novarum*, the first encyclical ever published on social questions like just wage and the right of workers to organize, 1891. No documents from the era illustrate more clearly the new role of teacher the papacy had now assumed. They are symptomatic of the strong emergence of the papal Magisterium, so characteristic of the contemporary papacy. In them Leo was not content simply to condemn modern philosophies, in the first case, or communism and laissez-faire economics in the second. He proposed remedies and argued the case for them.

While he was still bishop of Perugia he promoted the study of Aquinas by founding there in 1859 an Academy of Saint Thomas Aquinas. With the encyclical he hoped to establish a common vocabulary and set of principles with which Catholics, especially priests, could address the problems of the day. After an upsurge of interest in Aquinas in the sixteenth and seventeenth centuries, Scholasticism had fallen by the wayside. Aristotle's "natural philosophy"—physics, astronomy, etc.—had been left behind by the new systems of the scientific revolution, and the whole philosophical enterprise had taken new turns, beginning with Descartes and culminating with Kant. The result had been even in Catholic schools and seminaries an eclectic approach.

Leo set out to remedy that. As he said about the situation as he found it, "A multiform system of this kind, which depends on the authority and choice of any professor, has a foundation open to change, and consequently gives us a philosophy not firm, stable, and robust like that of old but tottering and feeble." Leo extolled the many benefits that would accrue to the church and society from a study of Aquinas, who was "the special bulwark and glory of the Catholic faith." Among the benefits the political loomed large. Thomas provided guidance on the true meaning of liberty, for instance, and on the divine origin of all authority and "on the paternal and just rule of princes."

Few papal pronouncements have had the success of *Aeterni Patris* in securing a course of action. The encyclical rode the tide of the nineteenth-century Romantic enthusiasm for the Middle Ages that was by no means confined to Catholics. It provided a stimulus for Catholics to claim the Middle Ages, now "the Ages of Faith," as peculiarly their own. Thus the powerful Neo-Thomist movement in Catholicism got underway. Although it began as a conservative measure, it sparked research into the wide range of philosophies and theologies that characterized the Middle Ages and led to results unexpected by its originators, which included the discovery that those phenomena were much richer and more complex than originally envisaged. By the twentieth century the movement, now broadened far beyond Aquinas and sustained by a variety of disciplines, had produced outstanding scholars who could hold their own among the best of their peers. Through what at first seemed to outsiders like a cultural byway, Catholics tiptoed into the cultural highways.

When in 1881 Leo for the first time in history opened the Vatican Archives not only to Catholics but to all qualified scholars, a move not well received by many in his curia, he in the world at large got deserved credit for opening to scholarship an extraordinarily rich resource. The Archives, though understaffed, have continued down to the present to welcome scholars from around the world, and especially in the past forty years they on a daily basis have been filled with them to capacity. The Archives are less than a minute's walk away from the Vatican Library, a similarly rich resource and similarly open.

About a dozen years after *Aeterni Patris*, Leo issued *Rerum Novarum*, literally "about the new situation," but generally titled "On the Condition of the Working Class." Leo's papal predecessors knew only the agricultural economy of central Italy, which still operated largely on feudal models, and they treated socialism and communism more as abstract philosophies than as movements that held great attraction for the working classes. As is well known, the liberal philosophy and laissez-faire economics that held sway among industrialists and entrepreneurs had little sympathy with the plight of workers, whom they considered expendable. But Leo had seen, howsoever briefly, the reality and realized it had to be addressed. The church was in danger of losing the working classes to radically secularized socialist associations or to professedly atheistic communism.

Rerum Novarum is a long encyclical. It reaffirms previous papal condemnations of socialism and communism. But its tone throughout is serene, and free from rant. It insists that the church is solicitous not only for everyone's eternal salvation but also for their well-being in this world because these two aspects of human life cannot be separated. While it proclaimed private property as a natural right, it insisted that it had its limits. That right cannot be allowed to harm the common good. If private property was a natural right, so was the right of the worker to a just wage and to humane working conditions. Most remarkable, the encyclical endorsed the right of workers to organize in order to obtain and secure their rights. The recognition that such organizations were legitimate carried the implication that the social order was to be formed by movements ascending from below as well as by power and authority descending from above.

Some Catholics were outraged and denounced the encyclical as a betrayal by the church, which was supposed to stand with the establishment and never countenance something as dangerous as workers organizing themselves. According to them, Leo overstepped the bounds of his office by addressing questions outside the realm of faith and personal morality. The church's business, after all, was to get people to heaven, not to dictate rules about purely economic and social matters

Despite such criticism, Leo managed to make his voice heard, and he provided a model that subsequent popes—Pius XI, John XXIII, Paul VI, and John Paul II would follow, to good effect. All these popes addressed "modern" questions in ways that were something other than condemnations of the status quo and hankerings for the good old days. When Leo's encyclical was explained to workmen and used by them and their leaders to obtain their objectives, they felt reassured that they had a friend in the church.

In the final years of his pontificate Leo became more aware of the new developments taking place in scholarship and increasingly concerned about them. He reinvigorated the Congregation of the Index with new and stricter norms about what books were to be condemned, even though there was now no way of hindering access to them. Freedom of the press was here to stay. In 1893 he issued *Providentissimus Deus*, an encyclical on the study of the Bible in which he commended the time-honored methods and warned against the dangers of the new.

In this long document he never once commended the reading of the Bible by the laity.

In 1902, the year before he died, he established the Pontifical Biblical Commission, whose function was to promote a thorough study of the word of God and ensure that it be shielded from even the slightest error. The Commission began issuing responses, universally conservative, to questions about specific interpretations. In 1906, for instance, it rejected the opinion that Moses was not the author of the Pentateuch, the first five books of the Old Testament, a question that had become almost a litmus test of orthodoxy for exegetes.

Leo saw the papacy as having the answers to all questions, and he did all in his power to underscore its absolute authority. In the theological textbooks of the time, the church was routinely described as a monarchy. Leo of course accepted that by-now accepted idea without question and put it into practice in great ways and small. He saw to it that the nuncios took precedence in protocol over all members of the local hierarchy. On a more mundane level, he insisted that the Catholics he received in audience kneel during the whole time, and he never allowed his own ministers to sit in his presence.

In Leo's as in other pontificates there were lights and shadows. His was, moreover, the first pontificate in a millennium in which the problems of ruling the Papal States dropped out of the papal agenda, where it had often been number one on the list of concerns. His was in that extremely important regard the beginning of a new papacy. Neither he nor his immediate successors could bring themselves to admit that the new situation brought them any benefits. Yet of course it did.

Among them is one of extreme importance that is rarely mentioned. The new Italian government, secular in character, did not claim any rights in the nomination of bishops, which meant that the nominations to the 237 Italian sees slipped right into the pope's hands. From this point forward the popes appointed the Italian bishops, no questions asked. The phenomenon promoted the idea that such appointments were the prerogative of the papacy, which therefore should prevail everywhere.

Perhaps partly because of the new political situation in which the papacy found itself, Leo died highly respected by Catholics and by most world leaders. Photos of him, in which he invariably had a gentle smile on his face, projected the image of a kind and intelligent man. His twenty-five years as pope, though not without their trials and tribulations, mercifully lacked the high drama of Pius VI's, Pius VII's, and Pius IX's. They did not for that reason lack importance for the future of Catholicism.

PIUS X: CONFRONTING
MODERN CULTURE

Liberalism, socialism, communism—they were not the only aspects of modern society and culture the church had to face. Those three, though born in the scholar's study, were from the beginning meant to impact society directly in the political, social, and economic realms, and they did so. There were other developments that were more strictly intellectual, yet they posed problems that cut deeply into how the church thought of itself and of its tradition. Although they of course differed among themselves in many ways, they were the product of the new enthusiasm for the historical, genetic approach to almost all disciplines that was characteristic of the nineteenth century.

By that time historians were striving to be "scientific" like their colleagues in the harder disciplines. Instead of merely telling a story with a moral or political message they wanted to discover "what actually happened," to use Leopold von Ranke's famous expression. Let the chips fall where they may! In their methods they professed objectivity and freedom from the contamination of apologetic or polemical concerns. Most of them, however, subscribed in some form or other to the idea that things were evolving for the better—"progress," which entailed focusing on the discrepancies between past and present to the advantage of the present.

For many Catholics the present was not only not the ideal state of things but the enemy to be overcome. Nonetheless, Catholic scholars could not help but be affected by this methodological shift, and they began to approach even sacred subjects like the liturgy, the Bible, and theology itself more historically. If the discrepancy between past and present could be utilized to the advantage of the present, maybe it could be utilized to demonstrate the superiority of the past, which could then act as a corrective of the present. This was an old idea, the basis in fact for most reform movements in the church like the Gregorian, but it got energized again in the nineteenth and early twentieth centuries. The papacy's reaction to such developments was generally suspicious or fearful but sometimes, as in the case of liturgy, selectively positive.

Meanwhile philosophy's "turn to the subject" with Descartes and Kant took more account of the subjective element in philosophical speculation, which undermined the solid objectivity and timelessness of philosophical concepts. Without being able fully to articulate the problem he was addressing, Leo XIII promoted Aquinas as a remedy for it. Aquinas came to be advertised as embodying the "perennial philosophy," *philosophia perennis*—firm, stable, and not subject to change. This was a countercultural manifesto that not all Catholic thinkers were able to appropriate.

Whether he and his electors were aware of it or not, the new pope would have to deal with this cultural ferment. When the conclave opened, Cardinal Mariano Rampolla, who had been Leo's secretary of state, seemed to be the favorite, but on August 2nd, just as the meeting got underway, it was announced that Emperor Franz Joseph of the Austro-Hungarian Empire vetoed Rampolla's candidacy. The announcement, received with great anger, threw the conclave into consternation, but voting proceeded on schedule. When Pius was elected he almost immediately outlawed such interventions, the end of a tradition that originated in slightly different form within a few centuries of the founding of the church. Some scholars speculate that even without the veto Rampolla probably would not have been elected.

It soon became clear that after Leo's long pontificate, the cardinals wanted somebody different from him. As one of the cardinals declared, they wanted a pope not with political but with direct pastoral experience. The choice fell on Giuseppe Sarto, patriarch of Venice, who had in fact spent his whole priestly life in direct pastoral ministry.

Sarto was the second child in a large family of truly modest means in a small town in northeastern Italy. His father was the village postmaster, his mother a seamstress. He studied at the seminary in Padua, which was his only formal education. For nine years he was a pastor in a country parish, the only pope to have had such experience. His effectiveness led to his appointment as bishop of Mantua, a diocese that by all accounts he revitalized. In 1893 Leo named him cardinal and patriarch of Venice, where he remained for ten years until his election as pope.

Pius X had a rich pastoral background, which accounts for his positive achievements. But his formal education was meager, and he had never set foot outside Italy. He saw things in terms of black and white. While still patriarch of Venice, he wrote to a friend, "When we speak of the Vicar of Christ we must not quibble. We must obey. We must not evaluate his judgments or criticize his directions lest we do injury to Jesus Christ himself. Society is sick. The one hope, the one remedy, is the pope." The words ring like an Ultramontanist manifesto.

Even as a pastoral pope he could not of course avoid making political decisions. He recognized his inexperience in such matters, so chose as his secretary of state Cardinal Rafael Merry del Val, forceful almost beyond measure, before whom even some of the foreign dignitaries attached to the Holy See were said sometimes to tremble. Although Pius despised the Italian state, he, motivated by fear of socialism, took the first step in easing the tension by allowing bishops to relax the severity of the *Non Expedit* in individual cases. In his dealings with some of the anticlerical and anti-Catholic governments in Latin America, he showed a flexibility that was lacking in his head-on and uncompromising confrontation with France in 1905 when the anticlerical government unilaterally annulled the Concordat of 1801 and enforced other measures against the church. He took the same approach to Portugal the next year. In both cases he vindicated the church's independence but at great cost. In France Catholics' relationship to the Third Republic deteriorated even further. In contrast with Leo XIII, Pius's diplomacy in Europe was blunt and uncompromising.

The pope's policy met with much criticism from Catholics in France, including some of the bishops. His encyclical the next year to the French clergy and laity, *Vehementer Nos*, was in part a response to that situation. It reiterated in absolute terms the hierarchical structure of the church, "a society composed of two classes of people, the pastors and their flocks." The duty of the former is to direct "the multitude," the duty of the latter is to obey.

Pius, uneasy in the political realm, felt much at home in the pastoral. In 1904, the year after he was elected he set in motion a program to codify canon law, which by that time had become an unmanageable and sprawling corpus of documents. Although this project was not completed during his lifetime, he deserves credit for an undertaking that brought more order and even-handedness to the church's procedures.

In Italy he suppressed a number of seminaries in small and poor dioceses in favor of regional institutions, a measure that ensured a much higher level of instruction. He himself scrutinized the dossiers of candidates for the episcopacy to make sure they were worthy of their office. The bishops for their part had to prepare a detailed report of the status of their diocese by answering a series of stipulated questions and be prepared to discuss it with the pope when they appeared before him on their required visits.

His greatest achievement and pastoral impact was, however, in liturgy. He built on several generations of historical scholarship whose origins can be precisely traced. In 1833 Prosper Guéranger, Benedictine monk and zealous Ultramontanist, refounded the monastery of Solesmes in France with the idea of providing a model Christian community united around the liturgy of the church. Such a community would be the answer to the rampant individualism of modern society.

Guéranger made the official liturgy—the mass and the Liturgical Hours like vespers—the center of piety and wanted to move it away from where it was currently centered—on the many other services and devotions like novenas and the Stations of the Cross that had proliferated in Catholicism since the late Middle Ages. Guéranger reached an international audience with his immensely influential publications, especially *L'année liturgique* (1841–1866), a nine-volume historical and devotional commentary of the feasts and solemnities of the church year, translated into English as *The Liturgical Year* in 1867–1871.

Monasteries sprang up especially in France, Germany, Austria, and Belgium more or less modeled on Solesmes, in which study of the history and practice of liturgy played a big role. The monks (and then other scholars) began to see clearly how present practice did not accord with what they took as the more normative models and practices in the past. Nothing became clearer than that over the course of the centuries the active participation of the faithful in the celebration had diminished to practically nil. There were two areas where it seemed feasible and desirable to change that situation.

The first was participation through singing parts of the mass like the Creed and the Gloria. Pius looked upon this idea with great favor. The very year he was elected he issued a call for the use of Gregorian chant and sacred polyphony in ordinary parishes and for the singing of it by the congregation. Because very few people were familiar with those musical forms and because of the difficulty of learning them, the pope's call was not easily or widely implemented. But the principle of congregational participation had been established, and other forms of congregational singing developed in some places.

The second was participation through reception of the Eucharist. If Pius's promotion of chant and polyphony met with only modest success in influencing how Catholics worshiped, his success in promoting frequent, even daily Communion was, over time, close to spectacular. During his pontificate the Holy See issued a number of documents related to the Eucharist, the most important of which was *Sacra Tridentina Synodus* ("The Holy Council of Trent"), 1905, that made frequent communion the norm.

At the time the decree was promulgated, most Catholics received the Eucharist only once or twice a year, but by the middle of the twentieth century weekly reception had become standard for large numbers in a typical Sunday congregation. Daily reception was no longer uncommon or considered strange. The Jansenists had been the major opponents of frequent Communion, and Pius's decree is rightly seen as a final and determining countermeasure to their persistent influence on Catholic piety.

Pius thus gave encouragement to liturgical scholarship, which during his pontificate took off with new momentum. The Belgian Benedictine Lambert Beauduin stands out for many reasons but especially for translating the Latin Missal, the priest's book that contained all the prayers and readings for the mass, into French and Flemish. For the first time, therefore, the persons in the pew could participate in a new way by following the mass with the very same text the priest was reading. Beauduin's initiative sparked imitation in other languages. Pius meanwhile oversaw a much-needed revision and simplification of both the missal and the breviary.

Pius, like Leo, was fearful of the turn Biblical studies had taken. Certainly, some of the scholarship stripped the sacred text of all transcendent meaning, but much of it was measured and respectful. Among the outstanding Catholic exegetes was the French Dominican Marie-Joseph Lagrange, who almost singlehandedly founded a center of biblical studies in Jerusalem, *L'École Biblique*, still functioning today. It was the first school and research institute in the Catholic world that programmatically made use of the new historical methods.

In 1909 Pius founded in Rome the Pontifical Biblical Institute, which was modeled in a generic way on *L'École Biblique* but intended as a conservative counterweight to it. He entrusted it to the Jesuits. For some time the Biblical Institute more or less lived up to the conservative hopes Pius placed in it, but with the passing of the years the professors had to come to terms with the new methods and utilize them. It has trained generations of Catholic biblical scholars and ranks as one of Pius's lasting achievements.

Advocacy among Catholics of a sometimes undiscriminating adoption of new methods of exegesis and the more critical historical approach to other fields became part of an amorphous and much broader phenomenon known as Modernism. This broadly inclusive label helps explain why it is difficult to find a common thread linking the so-called Modernists beyond their desire to help the church reconcile with what they believed was the best in intellectual culture as it had evolved to the present.

A general but not universally accepted premise of the movement (if it can be called that) was the pervasiveness of change and the need to reckon with it. The Modernists tended to be skeptical about metaphysics and critical of the intellectualism of Thomism. Some saw democracy as the system to which society had evolved. Some saw Christian truth as founded on intuition and religious experience that were then articulated into symbols and rituals.

The storm broke on July 3, 1907. On that day the Holy Office issued a decree that condemned sixty-five propositions supposedly held by Modernists. Two months later Pius came out with his long encyclical *Pascendi* ("Feeding the Lord's Flock"). The pope presented a synthesis of the teachings of the Modernists in which he described the heresy as resting on two false principles: (1) the rejection of metaphysical reason, which led to skepticism regarding rational proofs for God's existence, and (2) rejection of the supernatural, which led to the idea that Christian doctrine derived solely from religious experience. He especially rejected the idea that "dogma is not only able but ought to evolve and to be changed, for at the head of what the Modernists teach is their doctrine of evolution." Modernism was not so much a heresy as "the synthesis of all heresies."

Given the amorphous and ill-defined character of what came to fall under the Modernist label, Pius's analysis was about the best achievable under the circumstance. But the most striking feature of the encyclical was the draconian remedies it demanded be applied to deal with the evil. First, greater insistence on the teaching of Saint Thomas; second, anybody found showing "a love of novelty in history, archeology, or biblical exegesis" was to be excluded from all teaching positions; third, bishops were to establish a "Vigilance Council" whose function was to inform the bishop of anybody possibly tainted with the heresy; fourth, every three years they were to submit to the Vatican a sworn report on how these provisions were being fulfilled.

The definition of Modernism was so general, virtually equated with "any novelty," that it could be applied to almost any work of any philosophical or historical school. A veritable purge followed, with excommunications, dismissals from office, and the banning of books reaching epidemic proportions. With more than a grain of truth it has been described as a reign of terror. No doubt, some of the tenets of the Modernists could not be reconciled with Christian belief no matter how broadly that belief was interpreted, but in the wake of the encyclical the innocent got stigmatized and in some cases their careers ruined. The papal actions dealt a heavy blow to Catholic theological life and to Catholic intellectual life more broadly, from which the church suffered for two generations. But they could not utterly stamp out methods that had struck such deep roots in culture at large and that scholars saw as yielding new truths about old texts and old beliefs.

Pius died on August 20, 1914, just a few days after World War I broke out. Even those who disagreed with him on his policies saw him as a man of sincere, even if simplistic, piety. While he was still alive, he was spoken of as a saint. Forty years after his death, 1954, Pope Pius XII confirmed that opinion by canonizing him.

The Papacy
as a Global
Institution

WAR, PEACE, FASCISM

When Giacomo della Chiesa succeeded Pius X on September 3, 1914, he had been a cardinal only three months. On one level, therefore, his election was a surprise, but on another not. If the cardinals who elected Pius wanted a pastoral pope, those who elected Benedict wanted somebody diplomatically astute, who could navigate the church's way during the bloody war that had just begun. They made an excellent choice. Benedict XV has been described as having "a first-rate political mind," but he had more than that. He was a wise and humane leader who made good decisions under difficult circumstances. Although he is often described as "the forgotten pope of the twentieth century," those who have studied him agree that his short pontificate of eight years was important and that he managed it well.

He came from an old and distinguished family of Genoa, won a degree in civil law at the University of Genoa, after which, at twenty-one, he entered the seminary. As a young priest he trained for the papal diplomatic corps, spent four years in the nunciature in Spain, returned to serve in the curia in the Secretariat of State. In 1906 Pius X named him archbishop of Bologna but because he distrusted him withheld for seven years elevating him to cardinal, which was usually automatic for the see of Bologna.

Immediately upon his election Benedict replaced as secretary of state the unbending Merry del Val with the skillful and more conciliatory Cardinal Pietro Gasparri. Although Benedict shared Pius's assessment of the dangers of Modernism and enforced the measures against it, he turned down the heat. In his first encyclical, *Ad Beatissimi*, he told Catholics to refrain from rashly accusing other Catholics of disloyalty and heresy.

World War I of course overshadowed everything else during his first four years in office. He maintained for the Vatican a strict neutrality, even after Italy entered the war on the side of the Allies. He publicly denounced the war as a "senseless massacre" and a "hideous butchery," which won him enemies everywhere. The Allies decried him as "the German pope," and the Central Powers as "the French pope." In 1917, as the war showed signs of drawing to an end, he proposed a seven-point peace plan, which certainly was more just than the actual settlement imposed at Versailles. His plan went nowhere. The Italian government was especially distrustful of him because it feared that through peace negotiations he would use his influence to try to regain the city of Rome. If Benedict's repeated pleas for a peace that was "just and lasting," that is, not vindictive, had been heeded, World War II might possibly have been avoided.

Although his efforts to reduce the war's horrors and to ensure a just peace failed, his efforts to aid the war's victims did not. What he did constitutes one of the most beautiful episodes in the history of the papacy. He opened a bureau in the Vatican for reuniting prisoners-of-war with their families. The bureau received 170,000 requests for information, assisted in 40,000 repatriations, and communicated with 50,000 families. The pope persuaded Switzerland to receive soldiers of whatever country suffering from tuberculosis. After the war he actually stepped up such relief efforts with other services—providing for the wounded, for refugees, for war orphans. The Vatican, which these efforts came close to bankrupting, became known as the Second Red Cross. Perhaps the most striking tribute to him in this regard is the monument erected to him shortly before his death in the Muslim city of Istanbul, where the tribute reads in part, "the great pope of the world tragedy . . . the benefactor of all people, irrespective of nationality or religion."

Benedict put his diplomatic skills to good use in the political problems involving the Holy See. He was particularly eager to mend relations with France. He encouraged Catholics to a more positive approach to the Third Republic. During the war some 25,000 priests or seminarians were conscripted into military service under the Republic's flag and were a credit to their calling. Catholics in large numbers died for the Republic they despised. This anomaly prompted at least some Catholics (and others) to rethink the situation. In 1920 Benedict canonized Joan of Arc, a symbolic gesture much appreciated after the complete rupture between church and state under Pius X. The government of France sent representatives to the canonization ceremony, a symbolic gesture much appreciated by the other side. From that point forward relations greatly improved.

The burning politico-diplomatic issue for Benedict was the so-called "Roman Question": how to repair the rupture that occurred in 1870. He laid the groundwork for the resolution that would come with his successor. As early as 1915 he insinuated to the Italian government through Gasparri that the Vatican was willing to enter into conversations on the matter. In 1919 he gave his blessing to the Popular Party founded by the priest, Luigi Sturzo, which meant Catholics could participate in the political process of their country. That blessing marked the end of the *Non Expedit*. It also suggested approval of democratic government. In the elections that year the Party won 103 seats, a remarkable victory for such a new organization. The next year Benedict lifted the ban that forbade the heads of Catholic states from paying official visits to the Quirinal, which was a soft way of recognizing the legitimacy of the Italian state.

In 1917 he promulgated the new Code of Canon Law, finally completed under the leadership of Gasparri. The Code was important in many regards but especially important in settling at least in principle an issue that recurred again and again in the history of the church, the method of selecting bishops. Canons 329 and 330 set down that the pope has the right to establish criteria for their selection and freely to appoint them. Although for many centuries the popes effectively claimed the right to name persons to certain bishoprics especially in Italy, they never had or claimed the right to do so for the whole church.

Even after the promulgation of the Code, the Holy See continued to honor the provisions of concordats and long-standing local traditions that qualified the bald assertion of the canons, but 1917 marked the definitive abandonment of the principle of free election for which the reforming popes of the eleventh century had fought so bitterly. It also added a new and extremely important item to the job description of the modern papacy. Never before had the popes such firm control over the episcopacy, a development that for the church was not an unmixed good. Canons 329 and 330, untraditional though they were, defined the inner polity of the Catholic Church from this point forward.

With Benedict's encyclical, *Maximum Illud*, 1919, he initiated a crucially important new phase in Catholic missionary activity by insisting with bishops that they cultivate vocations among the indigenous population and that they separate themselves from their image as representatives of Western governments. He rebuked the "indiscreet zeal" of bishops guilty of promoting the political and economic interests of their homelands. Calls for the training of an indigenous clergy were not new, but Benedict's marked the great turning point. He made himself heard. Twenty years after the encyclical native bishops headed some fifty mission territories. Within another twenty years the face of Catholicism had changed to represent the international and supranational character the church claimed for itself.

On January 22, 1922, Benedict died unexpectedly of influenza that turned into pneumonia. His successor, Achille Ratti, archbishop of Milan, was a surprise. Not elected until the fourteenth ballot and on the first receiving only four votes, he was a compromise. His first act was dramatic and an indication of the decisiveness that would mark the pontificate: he appeared on the balcony of Saint Peter's to give his blessing to the crowd gathered there, the first pope to do so since Pius IX in 1846.

Pius came from a financially comfortable family. He earned advanced degrees at the Gregorian University in Rome, which helped this bright young man develop into the first scholar-pope since Benedict XIV in the eighteenth century. Although his most important publications were in church history, he was keenly interested in science and technology and was abreast of changes in culture. His publications led to his appointment early in his career as prefect of the Vatican Library. In 1918 Benedict XV sent him as nuncio to Poland where he witnessed first-hand a Bolshevik attack on Warsaw, an experience that helps explain his fierce anti-Communism. In Warsaw he conducted himself well in an extremely difficult situation. In 1921 Benedict made him a cardinal and archbishop of Milan. The next year he was pope.

More than any pope in a hundred years Pius tried to make the papacy once again the patron of art and learning. He erected the Vatican *Pinacoteca*, the painting gallery, enlarged the reading room at the Vatican Library and reorganized the cataloging system, founded the Pontifical Institute of Christian Archeology and the Pontifical Academy of Science, reequipped the Vatican Astronomical Observatory and moved it to Castel Gandolfo, and founded the Ethnological Museum at the Lateran. Perhaps most important, he quietly rehabilitated some scholars censured during the Modernist crisis.

While many French Catholics rethought their relationship to the Republic after the war, many, including many bishops, were just as opposed to it as before. They thought they had an ally in Charles Maurras and the movement he sponsored, *Action Française*. Maurras, baptized as an infant, was an unbeliever but presented himself as the banner-carrier for Catholic values and French civilization. He was rabidly anti-Semitic, an ardent monarchist, and otherwise altogether reactionary. He was, as well, a darling of the anti-Modernists and a favorite of Pius X.

Pius XI was convinced, correctly, that Maurras was exploiting religion for political ends, and he began pressuring the French episcopacy to move against him. Finally, in 1926 the pope issued a condemnation of Maurras's movement. The condemnation shocked large segments of the French Catholic elite and was not received well even in certain segments of the Vatican. Angry voices denounced Pius for taking such unwarranted action against the church's best champion. The papal condemnation weakened but did not crush the *Action*, which continued to function until World War II. Royalist sentiments persisted among French Catholics but in ever diminishing numbers and intensity.

In 1931 Pius installed in the Vatican under the supervision of Guglielmo Marconi himself a radio station. He was the first pope ever to speak over the radio. (Today Vatican Radio has some four hundred employees representing sixty-one nationalities.) The next year Marconi opened for him the world's first microwave radio-telephone link between the Vatican and the pope's summer residence at Castel Gandolfo. Pius could hardly be more different from Gregory XVI, for whom railroads were an instrument of the devil.

Pius's broad vision caused him to influence many aspects of church life. Like Benedict he insisted on the necessity of raising up indigenous clergy in mission lands. In 1926 he created great fanfare by consecrating in Saint Peter's six Chinese bishops. Shortly afterward he consecrated three Japanese. Under him the number of indigenous clergy rose from about three thousand to seven thousand. He was the first pope to take serious steps toward internationalizing the College of Cardinals. By the time he died there were twenty-seven non-Italians out of sixty-two, still not a majority but moving toward it.

In comparison with his predecessors, he was a great saint-creator. During an average pontificate a pope might canonize three or four, often fewer. Pius canonized about thirty-five, which included Thomas More, John Fisher, Bernadette Soubirous, Theresa of the Child Jesus (the "Little Flower"), Jean Vianney (the "Curé d'Ars"), Isaac Jogues and Jean de Brébeuf (the martyrs from New France, that is, Canada and the United States), Peter Canisius, Robert Bellarmine, and Albert the Great. The first he canonized was Theresa, to whom he was particularly devoted. His devotion to her is noteworthy for a pope highly regarded for his coolness of judgment and hard-headed decision-making. He created several new Doctors of the Church, among whom was another mystic, the Carmelite poet John of the Cross.

There was, then, a soft side to Pius XI. His subordinates never saw it. He was as authoritarian in his manner as any of his predecessors. He brooked no opposition and exploded into angry tirades. He got advice only when he asked for it, and brave were the souls who dared to volunteer it. His church was the church militant, and he was commander-in-chief. Yet the growing ease of modern travel brought flocks of pilgrims to Rome, whom he received graciously. He could be a witty conversationalist and enjoyed the company of scholars.

In a more explicit and insistent manner than any previous pope, Pius XI encouraged an active engagement of the laity in the mission of the church, a phenomenon known as Catholic Action. He described what he had in mind as the laity's participation in the apostolate of the hierarchy. This participation was not to be organized into political parties as such but in different ways to instill Christian values in the marketplace. It was assumed this engagement would take different forms in different countries. In the United States the idea found expression, for instance, in the National Council of Catholic Men and the National Council of Catholic Women, the former of which began to sponsor on Sunday evenings a radio program, "The Catholic Hour."

Perhaps the most important of his many encyclicals was *Casti Connubii* ("On Chaste Marriage"), 1930. It was long and wide-ranging. While it spoke in positive terms about the beauty of the sacrament of matrimony, it was especially intent on condemning depraved morals to be found "even among the faithful." It insisted that a valid marriage could never be dissolved. What caused the encyclical to become one of the most cited even today is the relatively short but pointed and absolute condemnation of artificial birth control, that is, the use of any prophylactic method. Another encyclical, *Quadragesimo Anno*, celebrated the fortieth anniversary of the publication of Leo XIII's encyclical on social questions, *Rerum Novarum*. Pius took up Leo's themes and carried them a step further, which consolidated in most people's minds the right of the papacy to speak on such matters.

Pius settled "the Roman Question," following up on the tentative steps taken by Benedict XV. Mussolini took the hints that the two popes were making, and on January 4, 1925, gave a famous speech indicating his availability for discussion. Mussolini, like Napoleon, was a cynical politician who realized that it was in his interest to end this long standoff. Finally, on February 11, 1929, the two parties signed the so-called Lateran Agreements.

The most momentous aspect of the Agreements was the establishment of Vatican City as a fully independent and sovereign state, with its own postal service, police force, full diplomatic corps, and so forth. The Italian state agreed never to interfere in the free functioning of Vatican City and ensured full and safe access to it by anyone the papacy wanted to receive. The papacy agreed never to try directly or indirectly to reestablish the Papal States, and it relinquished in perpetuity all claim to the city of Rome. Another aspect of the Agreements was financial. The Italians paid the Vatican a huge indemnity for the properties seized between 1860 and 1870. The state would cover expenses for the repair, upkeep, and restoration of churches that were historical monuments. The year 1929 marked the formal and final ending of a period of papal history that had lasted for a millennium and a half.

Mussolini staged his march on Rome in 1922, the year Pius was elected, after which King Victor Emmanuel III asked him to form a cabinet. That gave Mussolini the opportunity to create a dictatorship. At first Pius saw in Mussolini a bulwark against socialism and communism and as somebody who could bring stability and organization to a state that badly needed it. His attitude toward him cooled and then after the settlements of 1929 became confrontational as Mussolini moved against Catholic organizations that he believed disloyal to him. As early as 1931 Pius, without in any way calling for a change of regime, denounced its actions in his encyclical *Non Abbiamo Bisogno* ("We have no need"). By 1938, after Mussolini allied himself with Hitler and published anti-Semitic racial laws, the situation grew tense. Pius gave an important address in which he proclaimed that Christians were "all spiritually Semites."

In 1933 Pius through Cardinal Eugenio Pacelli, the future Pius XII, negotiated a concordat with Hitler's government shortly after Hitler came to power. The concordat has often been denounced as giving Hitler prestige at a moment he badly needed it and as in the long run weakening Catholic resistance to him. The criticism enjoys the twenty-twenty vision of hindsight. At the time Pius was trying to ensure certain basic rights for the church, and Hitler had yet to reveal the full extent of his program and duplicity.

Disillusionment with him set in almost immediately. Between 1933 and 1937 Pius sent thirty-four formal notes of protest to the German government about violations of the concordat. Finally in 1937 he had smuggled into Germany his encyclical *Mit brennender Sorge* ("With Burning Concern") to be read on Sunday from every pulpit in the country and to be published in full in every Catholic newspaper. The letter listed the violations of the concordat and implicitly but unmistakably denounced the regime as anti-Christian and intolerable. It denounced "the myth of race and blood." The German ambassador to the Holy See delivered from his government an official protest. Pius did not back down.

The next year Hitler paid a state visit to Rome, for which the city was plastered with swastikas, the jagged-cross symbol of the Nazi party. Hitler, a great lover of Italian art, had made known his desire to visit the Vatican Museums and Sistine Chapel while in Rome. Pius closed the museums and access to the Chapel "for repairs." He seemed destined, however, to receive Hitler in formal audience. Since the signing of the Lateran Agreements, the protocol for state visits to Rome was for the dignitary to be received by the king in the morning at the Quirinal Palace and by the pope in the afternoon at the Vatican. Pius, determined not to show Hitler that respect, set off for Castel Gandolfo, where popes never went except during the extended summer vacation. While there he gave a short speech denouncing a cross that in his words was an enemy of the cross of Christ.

Toward the end of his pontificate, therefore, his denunciations of communism grew fewer, his denunciations of fascism in speeches and conversation more frequent. In early 1939 the pope determined to give a speech to the Italian bishops denouncing fascism, but he fell gravely ill. On February 10, 1939, Pius XI died, almost ten years to the day since the signing of the Lateran Agreements. Mussolini was not sorry to see him go: "At last that stubborn old man is dead." By that time war seemed almost inevitable. Almost within the same generation, Europe headed for another bloodbath. Pius's successor was caught in the middle of it.

PIUS XII: SAINT OR SINNER?

O n March 2, 1939, his sixty-third birthday, Eugenio Pacelli was elected by forty-eight votes out of fifty-three on the third ballot of the conclave. His election came as no surprise. Besides being well known even to the non-Italian cardinals, he had spent his whole life in Vatican service, and for the past nine years, after the death of the formidable Gasparri, he had been Pius XI's secretary of state. As was true for the election of Benedict XV, the cardinals wanted somebody with political experience and diplomatic skills to guide the church through the war inexorably rolling over the horizon.

If Pius XI was the first pope to speak over the radio, Pius XII was the first to appear on television. After World War II he encouraged pilgrimages to Rome, and in the two Holy Years he proclaimed, 1950 and 1954, vast crowds poured into the Eternal City where they had opportunities to see him in person in great public audiences. No pope until that time had been photographed as often and had his picture appear as often in as many publications around the world. No pope addressed so many people from so many different walks of life on so many occasions. He issued forty encyclicals. In published form his speeches, encyclicals, and similar documents fill twenty volumes, each of which runs to at least five hundred pages. No pope had ever produced such

28.1: Pius XII with crowd

Pope Pius XII gives the "Urbi et orbi" blessing to a crowd filling St. Peter's Square on Easter.

© /ANSA/Corbis

a mass of documentation, but Pius was simply setting the trend that would be followed by his successors (see fig. 28.1).

Rarely criticized in the public press, Pius XII evoked veneration from Catholics, many of whom considered him a saint, and he commanded respect from most others. Yet within fifteen years of his death, he had become an object of passionate debate about his conduct during World War II—the problem of "the silence of Pius XII." Although he possessed the moral authority effectively to decry the horrors of the Holocaust he, according to his critics, took the course of a tacit bystander. The controversy has continued to this day and shows no signs of abating.

Pius XII came from an old, aristocratic Roman family, which had for generations enjoyed special ties to the Holy See. This was true for both his mother's and his father's side. Filippo Pacelli, his father, was a lawyer for the Roman Rota, the Vatican tribunal. His brother Francesco played an important role in the negotiations leading up to the Lateran Agreements. An older cousin, Ernesto, helped manage Vatican finances under Leo XIII. Eugenio's ordination in 1899 attracted as guests many members of the old noble families as well as important ecclesiastics, including Cardinal Vincenzo Vannutelli. Two years later young Father Pacelli entered the service of the Holy See, which he was never to leave, and shortly thereafter began to work with Cardinal Gasparri on preparing the Code of Canon Law. During this time he received several offers to join university faculties to teach canon law, including one from The Catholic University of America, but he declined in every case.

This talented, discreet, well connected young Roman rose rapidly in the curia. In 1911 he was included in the official Vatican delegation attending the coronation in London of King George V. During World War I Benedict XV enlisted him to negotiate with the German government about the pope's peace plan. Then, at war's end, when he was only forty-one, Benedict appointed him nuncio to Munich and in 1920 to the new German Republic. He stayed in Germany until 1930 when Pius XI named him secretary of state to succeed Gasparri, a strong vote of confidence from a strong pontiff. During his years as secretary, Cardinal Pacelli, an accomplished linguist, paid official visits to Argentina, to France (twice), and to Hungary. Vatican watchers speculated that Pius XI was preparing Pacelli to succeed him.

In 1936 the cardinal secretary of state visited the United States. The visit was not official because the United States and the Vatican did not have formal diplomatic relations, but it was anything but a vacation. It gave Pacelli first-hand knowledge of the American church and its hierarchy. During the visit he met Franklin Roosevelt, which established a personal bond between the two men that during World War II was highly advantageous to both. During the war, in fact, the Vatican had probably its best relationship with the United States among the great powers. In his correspondence to Pius, Roosevelt raised eyebrows in the Vatican by signing his letters as "your friend," something unheard of in the formal protocol of the Vatican.

The war broke out six months after Pius XII's election. He had made every effort to forestall it, pleading in a famous speech that "nothing is lost with peace, everything is lost by war," but the inevitable happened. Then he turned his efforts to keeping Italy out of conflict, fearing what Italy's entrance into the war might mean for the new, vulnerable, and still fragile Vatican State. When King Victor Emmanuel III paid a state visit to the Vatican, Pius returned the courtesy with a visit to the king in the Quirinal Palace, the first time a pope had entered the former papal residence in seventy years. But such a gesture made no impact on Mussolini, now set on riding on the coattails of the victorious Nazis.

Pius proclaimed the Vatican's absolute neutrality. Catholics were fighting on both sides. Because of its very neutrality, the Vatican became an important listening post where in seemingly casual conversations in corridors indiscretions might be heard. The governments of all the major powers engaged in the conflict except the United States had their ambassadors accredited to the Vatican and used it for that purpose. Roosevelt, aware of the importance of the Vatican but realizing that at the time in the United States to suggest the establishment of an embassy there was political dynamite, got around the problem in 1939 by appointing his "personal representative," Myron Taylor. (Not until 1984, under President Ronald Reagan, did the United States establish formal diplomatic relations with the Holy See.)

Once Italy surrendered in 1943 and the Germans established themselves in Rome, the Vatican's situation became more dangerous. Nonetheless, Pius harbored refugees in the Vatican and intimated to the many convents and other ecclesiastical establishments in Rome that enjoyed a certain immunity according to the Lateran Agreements that they do the same—or at least, it seems, he turned an approving blind eye to it. By the time Rome was liberated by the Americans in the spring of 1944, these houses were filled with an estimated five thousand Jews. After the war was over the chief rabbi of Rome expressed his gratitude for what the Holy See had done.

Even during the last years of the conflict, Vatican Radio continued to function. Pius tried to use it to good effect. On Christmas Eve 1944, with war's end in sight, he delivered a surprise in a radio address transmitted around the world. He singled out and praised democracy as a form of government appropriate for the times: "Taught by bitter experience, people today more and more oppose monopolies of power that are dictatorial, accountable to no one, and impossible to reject. They want a system of government more compatible with the dignity and liberty due to citizens." He speculated that "the future belongs to democracy."

This was the first time in history that a pope had publicly and at length commended democracy. It acted as the official death sentence for the yearning, already virtually extinct, to reestablish monarchy, and it was rightly taken by young Catholics in Europe and Latin America as an encouragement to strike out in politics in ways that earlier the Vatican viewed with suspicion or hostility. Within a few years after the end of the war Catholics led the democratic governments in countries where for at least a century and a half they had been excluded or sidelined—in Italy Alcide De Gasperi, in Germany Konrad Adenauer, and in France Robert Schuman, who led such an exemplary life that he is now being considered for beatification.

Engaged though the pope was with the war, he did not allow it to distract him from specific church issues. In 1943 he published two important encyclicals. *Mystici Corporis* dealt with the church as the Mystical Body of Christ. Written primarily by Sebastian Tromp, a Dutch Jesuit, the encyclical built on the results of the revival of interest in the Fathers of the Church, especially Saint Augustine, a revival that had been going on since the nineteenth century. While the encyclical sometimes described the church in hierarchical and juridical terms, it softened the approach that had prevailed since the Reformation, in which the model for the church was the state. Now the model was organic, the Body of Christ. The encyclical insisted on the role of the Holy Spirit in the church and thus on the balance that needed to hold between hierarchical structures and the charismatic gifts of the Spirit. The encyclical was an implicit recognition that not all initiative in the church comes from officeholders, which was the top-down model favored by Gregory XVI, Pius IX, and Pius X.

Of more immediate and practical import was *Divino Afflante Spiritu* ("Inspired by the Holy Spirit"), written by another Jesuit, Augustin

Bea, and a Dominican, Jacques-Marie Vosté. The encyclical endorsed in almost enthusiastic terms the new literary, philological, archeological, and historical methods of exegesis that had been developing since the nineteenth century. It marked a significant departure from the hostility toward those methods that antedated Pius X's crusade against Modernism but that the crusade intensified. The encyclical's positive tone and its suggestion that contemporary scholars might carry understanding of the biblical text beyond levels achieved in the past were new and striking.

The encyclical did not convince everybody of the legitimacy of the new methods, and suspicion of Catholic exegetes who employed them continued to be strong in some circles. Nonetheless, the encyclical energized Catholic biblical scholarship, which within a decade flourished in Germany, France, and Belgium. Especially in the United States biblical scholars tried to show the relevance of the Bible for the spiritual life of Catholics, and Bible study groups sprang up in many parishes throughout the country. The encyclical thus had an impact on the men and women in the pews and on their devotional lives.

A third encyclical, *Mediator Dei* ("Mediator of God"), published after the war in 1947, had in its implications an even more palpable impact on the people in the pews. It was the first papal encyclical ever devoted entirely to the liturgy of the church. With this long document Pius gave his blessing to the results of the research that had been under way since Guéranger and Beauduin that sought not only to promote devotion to the liturgy but also looked to change it in ways that would make it more attractive, more effective in accomplishing its purposes, and more in accord with its true character.

The blessing was not unreserved. Pius condemned many abuses in the liturgy, but he took seriously the implications of what he had written. The next year he set up a commission to advise him on a general reform of the liturgy. Shortly thereafter he took action that included a modification of the fast required before receiving the Eucharist, which made it possible to celebrate mass in the afternoon and evening. In two decrees, 1951 and 1955, he modified the liturgies for the Sacred Triduum, that is, for the last three days of Holy Week. This reform entailed, among other things, moving the liturgy for Holy Thursday from early morning to evening, the liturgy of Good Friday from early morning to midday, and the liturgy for Holy Saturday from early morning until just before midnight so that it would be a true vigil of Easter. In the history of the papacy no pope had ever made interventions like these that in such dramatic fashion broke with centuries-long liturgical practice.

A later, fourth encyclical, *Humani Generis* ("Of the Human Race"), 1950, was a startling contrast to the three just mentioned. It was an unremitting condemnation of "false opinions" and "novelties" that threatened to undermine Catholic truth. It seemed inspired by the fear that Modernism had risen from the grave, and some passages in it seemed to step back from positions Pius earlier took—or at least they gave comfort to those who were opposed to the positions in the first place. The most recurring complaint of *Humani Generis* was that theologians were not giving due respect to the official teaching of the church, especially as expressed in encyclicals. Pius decried again and again criticisms of Thomistic/Scholastic theology and programs designed to replace or modify it.

The encyclical threw a glaring spotlight on encyclicals. What was the binding power of this relatively new genre? To what extent were theologians and others (including later popes) able to differ from their teachings? The generic and even official answer was "it depends." But then the circle began again—"depends upon what?" In any case, after the encyclical a number of French Dominicans and Jesuits were removed from office or forbidden to teach or write. Among them were the Dominican Yves Congar and the Jesuit Henri de Lubac, who would ten years later be leading figures at Vatican Council II. The crackdown was in no way as severe as what happened during the Modernist crisis earlier in the century, but it was serious and came as a shock. Meanwhile, during the last years of Pius's pontificate, the Holy Office under Cardinals Pizzardo and Ottaviani took action against more and more theologians.

For the church Pius did more than write encyclicals. He further internationalized the College of Cardinals, which broke the majority that Italians had held in it since the Great Schism. He established some five hundred new dioceses throughout the world, and he discreetly encouraged a limited theological dialogue with other Christian churches. In

1950 he defined the dogma of Mary's bodily Assumption into heaven, the second such papal definition in history. He declared 1954 a Holy Year in honor of Mary, which excited an enthusiastic response from Catholics around the world. With Pius Catholic devotion to the Virgin Mary that had been gaining momentum since the nineteenth century reached its climax.

The pressing public problem facing the church after the war was Communism. The Iron Curtain had descended, and Catholics behind it suffered greatly. The contact the Holy See had with bishops behind the Curtain differed from country to country, but in no case was it easy. The arrest and trial of the primate of Hungary, Cardinal József Mindszenty in 1948 opened the world's eyes to the brutal attitude of the Communist regime toward the church. In the West the strongest Communist political parties were in two of the most traditionally Catholic countries—Italy and France.

Pius loved German music and culture, but he despised the Nazis. He despised and feared Communism even more, partly because in Munich in 1919 he had been held by a band of Communists and threatened with pistols. He survived unscathed, but he never forgot the experience. Now, with the Fascists and Nazis gone, his beloved Italy seemed poised to drink the poison. With his blessing on July 1, 1949, the Holy Office issued a decree excommunicating any Catholic who was a member of the Communist Party and declaring Communism and Catholicism irreconcilable. In the Cold War the United States had no more staunch ally than Pius XII.

In 1953 he suffered a life-threatening illness. Within a few months, however, he was much better. Nonetheless, in his last years he became ever more withdrawn in the Vatican, though he continued to give speeches and make pronouncements on a wide variety of subjects. Rumors spread that he had been blessed with visions of Christ and Mary. Sister Pasqualina, his German housekeeper for many years, was ever more in charge of his appointments, to the great distress of cardinals and other Vatican officials.

By the time he died, after a long and eventful pontificate of almost twenty years, his reputation was much higher outside the curia than inside it. Today his reputation seems to hinge, unfortunately, on a single issue, his failure forcefully to condemn the Holocaust and other Nazi atrocities. The controversy broke in 1963 when Rolf Hochhuth's long-winded and rambling play *Der Stellvertreter* (usually translated "The Deputy" but more properly "The Vicar [of Christ]") opened in Berlin. It depicted the pope as self-absorbed, concerned only with the good of the church, and emotionally isolated from what was happening to the Jews. The work was immediately translated into other languages and aroused bitter controversy. It was both denounced as a vilification of a saint and welcomed as a much needed exposé—by somebody who finally had the courage to tell the truth.

The outcry prompted Paul VI the next year to open the Vatican Archives for the war period to a team of four Jesuit scholars, which resulted in the publication of eleven volumes of documents (1966–1981). These volumes did not end the controversy, which continues to resurface. In 1999 Pope John Paul II appointed a new commission of three Catholic and three Jewish historians to reexamine the issue, but the commission disbanded inconclusively in 2001.

Even if new information is turned up, which seems ever more unlikely, it will almost certainly not resolve the issue because what is at stake is not so much the facts as the criteria by which the pope is to be judged. His critics demand of him a heroically prophetic stance that takes little account of the historical reality of the situation and of the possible consequences of such a stance, whereas his defenders sometimes seem in principle unwilling to admit any serious missteps. Pius XI, many people believe, would have acted differently.

Pius XII seems to have been genuinely convinced that he had in 1942 and 1943 condemned the Holocaust. He did so, however, in the measured diplomatic language that since his youth he had made his own. It was, for better or worse, the only way he could talk or think. Today what he said sounds bland and hopelessly abstract, but at the time it was specific enough to enrage the Nazis. They at least got the point. Pius believed that more open criticism would lead to reprisals, as happened when the Dutch bishops spoke out. Does that adequately explain his actions? Could he, should he have done more? Such questions will probably never be answered to everyone's satisfaction.

JOHN XXIII:
PEACE AND RECONCILIATION

On October 9, 1958, Pius XII died at Castel Gandolfo, the papal summer residence a few miles outside Rome, whose status as Vatican territory the Lateran Agreements guaranteed. Bouts of serious illness had plagued the pope in recent years, but for the world at large his death came suddenly at the end. That world was spared some of the gruesome details of the next days. Badly embalmed by Riccardo Galeazzi-Lisi, who had been dismissed as official papal physician in 1956 but still managed to be present in the final days at Castel Gandolfo, the body had begun to ferment. Although hastily embalmed two more times, it still gave off a bad stench as it lay in state in Saint Peter's. The doctor then sold to the popular French weekly *Paris Match* photos he had taken of the pope in his nightclothes on his deathbed, gave a press conference in which he described in detail the embalming process, and tried to publish a diary he kept of the pope's last four days. Just before the cardinals entered into conclave they dismissed Galeazzi-Lisi on the spot and banned him from Vatican precincts for life.

This sordid and sensationalist ending to the life of a pope of such dignified bearing created a heavy atmosphere when the conclave met. Pius had allowed the number of cardinals to dwindle, and now nearly half were in their late seventies or early eighties. The person some cardinals wanted to support was Giovanni Battista Montini, archbishop of Milan, but since he was not a cardinal he was effectively out of the running. The precedent of electing somebody within the college had become an unwritten law. But among the cardinals there were no particularly strong candidates. *L'Osservatore Romano*, the Vatican newspaper, prepared biographies of twenty-five possible popes so that it would be sure to have copy ready when the name was announced. The field was open.

Angelo Giuseppe Roncalli, age 77, was among the twenty-five but was by no means considered the most likely. Nonetheless, after a conclave of three days he was elected on the twelfth ballot, October 28. When he appeared on the balcony of Saint Peter's, the contrast with his predecessor was striking. Pius was austere, slender, and never photographed smiling. John, in contrast, appeared smiling and was notably rotund. In fact none of the white cassocks prepared ahead of time for the new pope fit him. The one he wore had to be rapidly cut and stitched so that he could get into it and appear on the balcony in good time.

It soon became known that he liked to tell jokes and that, unlike Pius who was shy and ever more reclusive, he enjoyed being with people and was a good conversationalist. As these traits became known, some felt he was too undignified to be pope, but his spontaneous manner and warm humanity began to win a quiet affection for him that soon overrode reservations. People almost immediately realized that this "transitional" papacy, however long or short it might be, was going to have a style different from Pius XII's.

That he chose the name John was significant. It broke the Pius-pattern that had prevailed since the late eighteenth century. He chose it, he said, because it was his father's name and the name of "the humble church" in which he was baptized, and now it was the name of his cathedral, Saint John Lateran. He did not, as so many popes had done, choose it to honor some previous pontiff but took a name for more personal reasons that looked to pastoral service.

Papa Roncalli was born on November 25, 1881, into a large family of peasant origin in a village near Bergamo in northern Italy and grew up in a household where the ground floor was occupied by six cows. He entered the seminary when he was twelve, never seems to have looked back or have entertained any ecclesiastical ambitions. He wrote in his diary that he became a priest only to help the poor in as many ways as possible. But his superiors recognized the talent of this good-natured yet astute young man and in 1901 sent him to Rome for his theological studies.

The next year he was drafted into the Italian army. Although he hated army life and the interruption of his road to the priesthood, he rose to the rank of sergeant. Honorably discharged in December 1902, he returned to his studies and was ordained in Rome in 1904. No members of his family were present for the occasion because they were too poor to make the trip. He became secretary to Bishop Radini-Tedeschi of Bergamo, whom he much revered, and at the same time he taught church history at the local seminary. At the outbreak of World War I he was again conscripted and became first a medical orderly and then a chaplain. This experience once again thrust him into a life altogether different from the sheltered world of the seminary and the bishop's office.

In 1921 he was called to Rome to act as a fund-raiser in Italy for the Congregation for the Propagation of the Faith. In 1925 Pius XI made him an archbishop and sent him as apostolic delegate to Bulgaria, whose Christian population was predominantly Orthodox, and after nine years sent him in the same capacity to Muslim Istanbul for Greece and Turkey, where he remained until 1944. He thus spent almost twenty years outside the Roman Catholic sphere. Received coolly in both places when he first arrived, he had won esteem and affection by the time he departed. During World War II he worked quietly but effectively during the Nazi occupation of the Balkans to save Jews from deportation to concentration camps.

During his time in Istanbul he published the first volume of a five-volume edition of the records of Saint Charles Borromeo's pastoral visit to the diocese of Bergamo in 1575. He continued to work on this scholarly edition in his spare time for the next twenty-two years, until the final volume was published the year before he became pope. Roncalli was, therefore, a scholar in his own right, a fact often overlooked in assessments of him. His edition was published by a highly respected Florentine firm, Olschki, not by an ecclesiastical press.

It is plausible that Roncalli's fascination with Borromeo, who saw the bishop as the primary interpreter and implementer of the Council of Trent and who therefore convoked a number of diocesan and provincial councils to do so, played a role in John's "inspiration" to call a council. At any rate, John had through his almost lifelong study of Borromeo a perspective on the history of the church that was not exclusively Rome-centric.

In 1944 Pius XII named Roncalli nuncio to Paris, the Vatican's most prestigious diplomatic post, at an extremely difficult moment for the church there after the city had been liberated by the Allies. He replaced Bishop Valerio Valeri, whose removal General Charles de Gaulle demanded because of Valeri's compromising relationship with the Nazi puppet state in southern France, the hated Vichy regime. A relatively large number of French bishops had tarnished reputations because of allegedly similar sympathies, and de Gaulle, devout Catholic though he was, was on the warpath against them. The next year seven prelates quietly left office. Although Roncalli cannot get credit for the solution, he acquitted himself well in this potentially explosive situation. In 1953 Pius named him patriarch of Venice, which pleased him immensely because it meant that he could give himself to the direct pastoral service that he had wanted since his ordination.

He was faithful to his diary all his life, and it is now being published in Italy in a magnificent multivolume edition. Shortly after he died portions of it were published entitled, in the English-language edition, *The Journal of a Soul*. This is the first time in history, if we make a very qualified exception for the diary of Pius II in the fifteenth century, that a pope has left us such a record of his thoughts, reactions, and spiritual values. The diary is an incomparable help in understanding this complex yet also simple man.

Cardinal Roncalli made an important, typical, and prescient diary entry when he heard of the death of Pius XII: "One of my favorite phrases brings me great comfort. We are not on earth to be museum-keepers but to cultivate a flourishing garden of life and to prepare a glorious future. The pope is dead. Long live the pope!" Within a few weeks he found himself in a position where he could "cultivate a flourishing garden of life" with a new and greatly enhanced authority. No pope had ever had life-experiences in any way comparable to his before his election.

At his coronation ceremony he introduced himself by using an image dear to him, the one in which the youngest son of Jacob reveals himself to his brothers who have come begging to Egypt, "I am Joseph, your brother." Unlike his predecessors he made clear that his pastoral responsibilities to his diocese of Rome were a priority. He began to visit Roman parishes. Two months after his election, he revised the old custom of visiting the Roman jail, Regina Coeli, on Christmas Eve and on the next day Roman hospitals. After he celebrated mass at the jail, instead of immediately going back to the Vatican he stayed to chat with the prisoners (see fig. 29.1). His first words shocked and delighted them when he said he remembered when his uncle was in jail.

In the Vatican itself he reestablished regular work audiences for the offices of different sectors of the curia, a procedure that had completely disappeared under Pius. This greatly facilitated simple and direct communication between the pope and his coworkers. He almost immediately began to name new cardinals to rejuvenate the College of Cardinals and internationalize it even more. Giovanni Battista Montini, with whom he had had a warm working relationship when he was in Venice, was among the first named. By 1962, the eve of Vatican Council II, he had raised the number to eighty-seven, the largest ever.

In 1961 Italy celebrated the centenary of its unification, which had been accomplished though the seizure of the Papal States. John signaled that he looked upon the Lateran Agreements as something more than a grudging concession to a status quo that was not going to change. On the occasion he received the Italian prime minister Amintore Fanfani in audience and in his official greeting said to him, "The celebration this year of the hundredth anniversary of Italian unification is a cause of great joy for Italy, and both of us, on the two sides of the Tiber, share the same feeling of gratitude toward providence for it." The trauma of the Risorgimento had been fully overcome.

29.1: John XXIII with prisoners

Kneeling prisoners applaud as Pope John XXIII visits the Regina Coeli (Queen of Heaven) Prison, Rome's largest, Dec. 26th. The Pontiff spent an hour and ten minutes with the 11,300 male prisoners in the jail, as he personally carried the Christmas spirit into the bleak cells. The visit revived a custom of Pope Pius IX, who visited the prisoners every Christmas.

© Bettmann/CORBIS

John disappointed the Italian episcopacy because of his policy, clear from the beginning, of staying aloof from Italian politics, which meant not displaying overt support for the policies of the Christian Democratic Party. There were many political parties in Italy that held seats in parliament, but the great recurring contest in every election was between the Christian Democrats and the Communists. By his distancing himself John seemed to be giving aid and comfort to the enemy. When the Communists gained votes in the election in the spring of 1963, John was blamed. The brilliant and disreputable movie director, Pier Paolo Pasolini, a prominent Communist, in 1964 dedicated to John's memory his film, *The Gospel according to Saint Matthew*.

From the beginning John hoped to ease the tensions of the Cold War, and he believed he saw signs from Russia that looked promising. The Cuban Missile Crisis in 1962 gave him an opportunity, during which his speech calling on Russia and the United States to back off their confrontational stance helped in some measure to diffuse the situation. The pope and the Soviet premier Nikita Khrushchev exchanged Christmas greetings that year, something unheard of, and early the next year the Soviets released from prison Bishop Slipyj of the Ukraine, whose long imprisonment had been a major source of friction between the Vatican and Moscow. The next month John received in audience Khrushchev's son-in-law, Alexis Adzhubei. The event created a sensation. It could never have happened with Pius XII, and it sent a striking message of policy shift. The American theologian Joseph Clifford Fenton reflected a widespread assessment in conservative circles when in his diary he described John as "definitely a lefty."

A month later the pope published his last encyclical *Pacem in Terris* ("Peace on Earth"), addressed not just to Catholics but to all humanity, in which he developed the theme of collaboration among the peoples of the earth and calling for "reconciliations and meetings of a practical order" that now were needed more desperately than ever with the nuclear threat hanging over the world. The development of nuclear weapons, he maintained, made a just war no longer possible. If there was a single theme for John's pontificate, it was reconciliation.

He is best remembered for convoking on January 25, 1959, the Second Vatican Council, which in a number of ways transformed the church. When he announced it he said that the council would reaffirm doctrine and discipline, but he then went on to indicate two special purposes. The first was to promote "the enlightenment, edification, and joy of the entire Christian people," and the second was to extend "a renewed cordial invitation to the faithful of the separated communities to participate with us in this quest for unity and grace, for which so many souls long in all parts of the world." The reconciliation theme was up-front. The council was to be a word of friendship.

He made the word practical. In 1960 he received in audience Geoffrey Fisher, the Archbishop of Canterbury, the first Anglican archbishop ever to be received by a pope. In 1961 he sent special envoys to greet Athenagoras I, the Orthodox patriarch of Constantinople (now called Istanbul). Most important, he created for the council the Secretariat for Christian Unity under Cardinal Augustin Bea. The purpose of the Secretariat was to establish communication with other Christian bodies to facilitate their participation in the council. The result was the presence of anywhere from fifty to one hundred fifty or more "observers" or "guests" from other Christian churches or denominations, including the Orthodox, at every session of the council. Once the council opened, the observers/guests were almost overwhelmed by the warmth and courtesy with which they were received and the welcome with which their comments on issues before the council were heard.

The announcement of the council came as a total surprise and left some people stunned. After the definitions of primacy and infallibility at Vatican I, theologians had predicted there would never be another council because the pope could, and would, solve all problems. But would this council be a continuation of Vatican I, which, after all, had never been formally closed, only adjourned? On July 14 John laid all doubts to rest when he informed his secretary of state, Cardinal Domenico Tardini, that the council would be called Vatican II.

With that John set in motion a process that would lead to the holding of what was, when all features are taken into consideration, the biggest meeting in the history of the world. It was not the biggest gathering but biggest *meeting* in the sense of an assembly called together to make decisions. In the spring of 1959 Tardini sent letters to almost

2,600 cardinals, archbishops, bishops, and other prelates asking them to send in, "with complete freedom and honesty," items for the agenda. He received almost two thousand responses. He sent similar letters to others, such as the Congregations of the Curia and universities around the world that held papal charters. The materials received were then reviewed and reworked into draft documents to be considered by the council. The responses and the drafts, published after the council, fill nineteen large-format volumes, each of which runs to at least five hundred pages.

The council met in four ten-week periods from the fall of 1962 to the fall of 1965. On average about 2,300 bishops, coming from 116 countries, were present at the different periods. Only thirty-six percent were from Europe, a striking contrast with every council since Lateran I in the twelfth century. Besides the observers/guests, hundreds of theologians were present, plus a large staff to keep things moving smoothly. On a given day probably three thousand or more persons were present in Saint Peter's. The Communist governments of China, North Korea, and North Vietnam prohibited their entire episcopates from attending, and governments behind the Iron Curtain made participation difficult or impossible for their bishops.

As the council approached, a basic question surfaced. Would the council be a confirmation of the status quo and perhaps a tightening of it? Or was it intended to move beyond it in some way? Cardinal Giovanni Urbani, who had succeeded John in Venice, anticipated that the bishops had not come to the council merely "to sprinkle holy water," whereas others expected just that and did their best to ensure it. John's address opening the council on October 11, 1962, was therefore looked forward to with great anticipation. Its opening words were "Mother church rejoices" (*Gaudet Mater Ecclesia*), and hence that is the name the address bears. John wrote it himself, revising it many times. Although the words were carefully chosen, to those untrained in the language of papal discourse the speech sounded unexceptional.

In gentle but unmistakable terms, however, it answered the question. The council was to be "predominantly pastoral in character." It was to "make use of the medicine of mercy rather than of severity," so that the church "show herself to be the loving mother of all, benign, patient, full of mercy and goodness toward the children separated from her." The church must of course remain true to itself, but at the same time it must make "appropriate changes." Although the full import of Pope John's message was not grasped by everybody who heard it, it was properly taken as encouragement by those at the council who wanted to do something more than sprinkle holy water on the status quo.

Once the council settled down to business, John kept to a hands-off policy except when a stalemate occurred that required action. In November 1962, that is precisely what happened when the council rejected a document prepared for it by the Doctrinal Commission under the chairmanship of the conservative Cardinal Ottaviani. The vote fell slightly short, however, of the two-thirds required for such an action. John not only intervened to validate the majority vote but curtailed the authority of the Doctrinal Commission that was trying to dictate the course of the council.

By the end of the first period it was clear that drastic action was needed to speed the council along. John acted decisively by setting up a Coordinating Commission to which he entrusted almost plenipotentiary powers to expedite the work of the commissions entrusted with the preparation and revision of the documents. He chose as members of the Coordinating Commission cardinals who were leading the council beyond the status quo, members with whom he increasingly began to identify himself, as is clear from his diary. The diary also reveals how uncomfortable John felt in the company of Cardinal Ottaviani and how confident he grew of the leadership of the forward-looking Belgian, Cardinal Léon-Joseph Suenens. As things turned out, many of the most influential theologians at the council tended to be, as mentioned, those disciplined by the Holy Office during the last years of Pius XII, such as Congar and de Lubac.

John died of stomach cancer on June 3, 1963, after the council had met for just one of its four periods. His successor, Paul VI, presided over the remaining three. In many persons' minds, nonetheless, the council was and remained, as contemporaries termed it, "Pope John's council." He put his stamp on it as much by who he was as by what he said. His death evoked an outpouring of grief worldwide that had never occurred for any other pope. People saw in his death the loss of a great world leader, but many also felt the death almost as the loss of a personal friend, of somebody who understood them, who could tell jokes, and whose heart was warm. He was himself, as he said of the church, "benign, patient, full of mercy and goodness."

PAUL VI: IN A TIGHT SPOT

"M y bags are packed." That is how John XXIII expressed the state of his soul once he learned he was sick unto death. As the first period of the council drew to a close, concern about his health mounted, but no official announcement concerning it was forthcoming. By the spring of the next year it was apparent that the pope had only a short time to live. Yet his death came as a shock, as death almost always does. In this case, moreover, it raised the momentous question of what was to become of "Pope John's council."

With eighty cardinals present, the conclave to elect John's successor was the largest in the history of the church. Only twenty-nine were Italians. Although the non-European world was reasonably well represented, the leaders were from the continent. In the council prominent cardinals had openly clashed in a contest over the direction the council was to take, with some opposing any serious change and with others advocating the opposite. Cardinals of both persuasions (and everything in-between) entered the conclave looking for a pope sympathetic to them. Passions ran high.

The world press picked Giovanni Battista Montini, the archbishop of Milan, as almost surely the next pope. When after a conclave of less than three days Montini's election was announced, it came as no great surprise. Nonetheless, the conclave was difficult. Afterward Cardinal Gustavo Testa, known for his indiscreet outbursts, said, "Hair-raising things happened at this conclave. I will have to ask the pope's permission to speak about them." He either did not ask or did not receive permission because he said no more. Other indiscretions, however, confirm his assessment. Montini was elected only on the sixth ballot and with a vote-tally not much exceeding the minimum required

Working against him was a reputation for indecisiveness, which his supporters dismissed as a misleading impression stemming from the long years he spent in the curia in the shadow of Pius XII. Montini had kept a relatively low profile during the first period of the council until the very end, when he made an important speech seconding a powerful speech by Cardinal Suenens that the council take the church as its central theme. Although his speech implied a rejection of a conservative draft-document on the subject, the cardinal of Milan was still not clearly identified with either of the two parties that had emerged. The seeming neutrality, or ambivalence, raised hopes and fears in those who voted for him.

Pope Paul VI came from an old, distinguished, and prosperous family in Brescia in northern Italy, where his father, a lawyer, was a leader in Catholic circles. Frail as a boy, he was in part home-schooled and later, when he decided to be priest, had permission to do his seminary training as a day-student, living at home. Although he seriously considered becoming a monk, he was ordained as a diocesan priest at age twenty-two, furthered his education in Rome at the Gregorian University, and soon entered the service of the curia.

He devoted his free days and hours working with Catholic university students, whom he tried to help in their opposition to the Fascist party. From his family as well as from his experience during these years, he harbored a deep sympathy for the Christian Democratic movement, which had yet to receive strong papal support, and he forged bonds of friendship with the young men who after World War II would lead Italy. In 1933 his responsibilities in the curia at the Secretariat of State became full-time. He would remain in its service for twenty-one years, until Pius named him archbishop of Milan in 1954.

When he left for Milan he took ninety crates of books with him. Enamored of French culture, he had read widely in the theologians caught in the strictures of Pius's encyclical, *Humani Generis*. While in the curia, he was generally reputed as one of its more open-minded and approachable members. "Battista," as he was known in his family, was slow to judge or condemn. As Paul VI he felt his responsibilities heavily, sometimes giving the impression he felt the whole burden of the church on his shoulders.

He took the name Paul, which not only set him off from his two immediate predecessors but implied a commitment to a church on the move in imitation of the great Apostle of the Gentiles. A few days after his election he announced that the council would reconvene on September 29, a decisive act that showed he gave no ear to the voices urging that the council be suspended "for a while," to be resumed at some unspecified date in the future. He later announced modifications in council procedures and held an important meeting with all the members of the curia in which he gently but firmly told them to expect changes in their mode of operation.

Paul VI was in a difficult situation. The strong majority that had emerged in the council advocated positions that important cardinals in the curia like Ottaviani, head of the Holy Office (today called the Congregation for the Doctrine of the Faith), and Arcadio Larraona, a juridically minded Spaniard, head of the Congregation of Rites, opposed with might and main. Paul saw his role as mediating between the majority and the small but aggressive minority led by Ottaviani, Larraona, and a few others. While his sympathies were generally with positions advocated by the majority, he worked hard to move the council toward consensus.

At the end of the second period of the council, 1963, the first while he was pope, he electrified all those gathered in Saint Peter's for a solemn public closing ceremony with his surprise announcement that in January he would go on pilgrimage to the Holy Land. Prolonged applause! With only a few insignificant exceptions no pope had left Italy except as prisoner of a foreign power for four hundred years. No pope had left the precincts of Vatican territory since 1870 until in early October 1962, John XXIII made a pilgrimage to Assisi and Loreto, some hundred miles away, to pray for the success of the council. Accustomed as we are today to popes traveling the globe, it is difficult to recapture how startling and significant Paul's announcement was to those who heard it. The era of "the prisoner of the Vatican" was now really over. Paul was living up to the image of his biblical namesake. He was an apostle on the move.

For three days, from January 4 to January 6, the world through television witnessed the exciting and unprecedented event. Nothing like these vivid images of a world leader jostled by enthusiastic crowds had ever been seen before. The high point of the trip was Paul's encounters with Athenagoras, patriarch of Constantinople. Not in anybody's wildest dreams could such meetings have been imagined even a year earlier, and they gave the council a powerful impetus to press forward with its statement encouraging Catholic participation in the ecumenical movement. Hopes soared. For a few days everything seemed possible.

In the last period of the council, fall of 1965, the council entered the final stages of debate on the controversial document on religious liberty, which advocated separation of church and state. A principal architect of the document, which was solidly and effectively supported by the American hierarchy, was the American Jesuit, John Courtney Murray. Even at this late stage the document's fate seemed to hang in the balance. When it was finally put to a vote, however, it passed by an overwhelming majority, which set the stage for another spectacular journey by the pope, this time to the United Nations in New York City.

The dramatic occasion showed Paul VI at his very best. The trip had immense symbolic value. The pope addressed a completely secular institution on its own turf, and he did so not to proselytize for the Catholic Church but to promote the well-being of the human family. By his very presence at the United Nations on October 4, 1965, he gave needed support to an organization just when many had begun to belittle it. He spoke from his heart on a matter of greatest concern to him as world conditions seemed to be deteriorating and violence escalating.

Paul was determined to make his address to the United Nations the unquestionable focus of a visit to New York that lasted less than thirty-six hours, though his mass that evening in Yankee Stadium is what most people remembered. The address—direct, simple, delivered in elegant French and televised around the world—was powerful. Paul introduced himself as "a man like you, your brother." The point he drove home was how imperative it was for nations to cooperate for the common good of humanity. "What you proclaim here is the rights and fundamental duties of human beings—their dignity, their liberty, and above all their religious liberty." Just a few years earlier such a statement from a pope about religious liberty, even though John XXIII had paved the way, would have been almost unthinkable.

The most moving and emphatic moment came when Paul spoke of the horrors of war and the absolute necessity of world peace. He pleaded, with deep emotion in his voice, "No more war! War never again! It is peace, peace that must guide the destiny of the peoples of the world and all humanity." These words expressed the heart of his message and made a deep impression on all who heard him.

As the council wore on, his many interventions, no matter how well intentioned, generated among the bishops confusion and sometimes resentment. A typical but particularly difficult instance occurred in the last period of the council. A section in the document entitled "The Church in the Modern World" treated marriage, which seemed to require a statement on the sensitive subject of birth control. In 1963 just a few months before he died John XXIII had established a secret commission to study the question, a fact that Paul announced in 1964. Although Paul made it clear that the council was not to touch the issue, he in the final weeks of the council intervened to insist it repeat Pius XI's prohibition in *Casti Connubii*. When it was objected that the council could not honestly issue a statement as its own on an issue it had been forbidden to discuss, he continued to press the matter. Then, silently acknowledging the mixed signals he was giving, he after a few days essentially withdrew his demand.

Despite rough moments like this one in Paul's relationship to the bishops gathered in Saint Peter's, his great achievement was to bring the council to conclusion. On December 8, 1965, when the council officially ended, he could take satisfaction in the fact that the massive and cumbersome meeting of well over two thousand bishops had generated sixteen substantial documents as guidelines for the church in the future. An especially moving and important event had taken place in Saint Peter's the day before. Bishop Johannes Willebrands read from the pulpit a "Joint Declaration" of Paul VI and Patriarch Athanagoras regretting the excommunications of the Greeks by the Latins and of the Latins by the Greeks in 1054, acknowledging the responsibility of both sides for the tragedy, and promising to work toward a full communion between the churches. The "Declaration" was the fruit of the meetings between the two leaders two years earlier in the Holy Land.

The council was too momentous an event to summarize in a few words. Its major achievements were the result of the historical and philosophical scholarship of the previous hundred years, much of it done under an atmosphere of suspicion and repression. The decree on the liturgy especially recovered the principle of full participation of the congregation in the sacred action of the mass, reversing a long historical process that located all action in the priest. The decree on religious liberty was the fruit of philosophical reflection on the changed political and social conditions that began to prevail after the French Revolution. It validated forms of separation of church and state, which overturned previous papal condemnations of the idea. The decrees on ecumenism and non-Christian religions (especially Judaism) resulted from research into the historical origins of religious divisions and diversities, from philosophical and theological reflection on them, and from a more acute realization of the cost in human life and suffering those divisions and differences had caused. They seemed to take a polar-opposite position from Pius XI's encyclical *Mortalium Animos*, which forbade Catholic participation in ecumenical endeavors.

The final decree of the council "On the Church in the Modern World" attempted to reverse the papacy's utter rejection of that world proclaimed in the nineteenth century and reiterated in more muted terms in the twentieth. The document made clear that the church is not against the modern world, nor is it for the modern world. It is *in* the world as a privileged partner in dialogue with it and hence takes its share of responsibility for the well-being of the world. Although Leo XIII's *Rerum Novarum* first notably moved the church in this direction, the decree took it incomparably farther.

Immediately after the council Paul entered into the great task of promoting better relationships among the churches. He made the Secretariat for Christian Unity a permanent body in the curia, met in Rome with the new Archbishop of Canterbury, Michael Ramsey, traveled to Istanbul to meet with Athenagoras and later received him in the Vatican. Even while the council was in session he set about a vigorous implementation of the decree on the liturgy and began celebrating mass on Sundays in Roman churches according to the new rite. In the decade after the council the Holy See issued a number of directives further implementing the decree.

Following in the footsteps of his predecessors, he in 1967 issued the encyclical *Populorum Progressio*, a plea for social justice. That same year he issued *Sacerdotalis Coelibatus*, a firm reassertion of the traditional discipline that he made clear was his position when the matter threatened to come to the floor during the council. Just as the council was ending he began making changes in the functioning of the curia.

By 1968 five years had passed since John XXIII established the commission on birth control. The very fact of the commission's existence indicated a reconsideration of Pius XI's prohibition in *Casti Connubii*, and the passing of the years without a definitive statement on the matter from the Holy See seemed to suggest that a change was in the wind. For most Catholics, including probably a majority of bishops, the silence indicated consent. On July 25, 1968, however, Paul issued *Humanae Vitae*, his most famous and controversial encyclical, in which he renewed the prohibition.

Paul seems to be the first pope to write his own encyclicals, and his personal touch is evident in *Humanae Vitae*. The encyclical, more often criticized than studied, is a rich meditation on married love. What the world seized upon, however, was the reiteration of Pius XI's strictures. The reaction was fierce. Theologians denounced it. Bishops publicly distanced themselves from it. In France fifty percent of Catholics interviewed in a survey said they would ignore it. When word eventually leaked that Paul had overruled the majority opinion of the commission, to which he had added members of his own choosing, the reaction turned bitter.

The encyclical could not have come at a worse time for society at large. A rebellion against authority burst upon the world in 1968. The members of the generation born after World War II chafed under the buttoned-down culture that prevailed and that was at odds with their needs and aspirations—rock and roll, the Beatles, the Kinsey Reports, which purported to reveal more active and varied sexual practices among respectable people than anybody wanted to admit. Then "the pill."

But the context was broader than the exploding sexual revolution. In France the prolonged crisis over Algeria had already for several years generated violence in the streets. In the United States the brutal assassinations of Martin Luther King, Jr., and of Robert Kennedy, following on that of President Kennedy, reverberated around the world. Resistance to the draft that obliged young men to fight and die in a war in Vietnam they detested sparked riots on campuses across the country, and hatred of American foreign policy ignited student riots in countries far distant from the United States. In Italy Communist-inspired demonstrations and strikes paralyzed cities, interrupted travel, hurt the economy, and projected an image of a country in disarray. Into this matrix Paul's encyclical fell. He would be pope for ten more years, but he never wrote another encyclical.

Paul was surprised, shocked, and profoundly saddened at the reaction to *Humanae Vitae*. Beginning in 1970, moreover, he had to deal with Archbishop Marcel Lefebvre, who made public his severe criticisms of Vatican II, which he summed up in the cynical question, "To be Catholic must one become Protestant?" From 1972 onward the relationship of the archbishop to the church continued to deteriorate, despite Paul's patience with him and efforts to prevent a schism. Finally in 1976 Paul suspended Lefebvre *a divinis* which meant the archbishop was forbidden to perform any priestly acts. The schism that during the council the pope worked so hard to forestall had begun to unfold before his eyes. It remained small but was notorious.

On March 16, 1978, the Red Brigade, the extremist Communist terrorist group in Italy, kidnapped Aldo Moro, leader of the Christian Democratic party, the longest serving prime minister in post-war Italy up to that time and a personal friend of Paul VI. The condition the

Brigade demanded for Moro's release was the release from prison of terrorists from the Brigade. The government refused to negotiate, and the nation held its breath for fifty-five days. Paul, in anguish, offered his life in exchange for Moro's, to no avail. On May 9 Moro's mutilated body was discovered in the trunk of a car parked in the center of Rome midway between the national headquarters of the Christian Democratic and the Communist parties. Paul's last public appearance was to preside at Moro's funeral in Saint John Lateran. Three months later he himself died of a heart attack suffered during mass at Castel Gandolfo.

Sad though the last years of Paul's life were in many respects, he did not curtail his activities. In 1970 he declared Saint Teresa of Avila and Saint Catherine of Siena doctors of the church, the first women so honored. That same year he set a mandatory retirement age for bishops at seventy-five and decreed that cardinals over eighty would not participate in future conclaves. By 1976 he had raised the total number of cardinals to 138, of which the Italians were now a small minority. He declared 1975 a Holy Year and was gratified at the large number of Catholics who flocked to Rome for it. He continued his travels, which included a trip in 1969 to Uganda to honor its martyrs. On a trip to the Far East in 1970 he narrowly escaped assassination in Manila.

Papa Montini is in danger of becoming like Benedict XV a "forgotten pope." His pontificate fell between two superstars, John XXIII and John Paul II. He deserves better. In his appreciative biography Peter Hebblethwaite described Paul as "the first modern pope." Paul grew up in a family engaged with the political situation of the "new Italy." As a young priest he helped prepare the politicians who led Italy into its post-war prosperity. He read widely in modern literature, philosophy, and theology. Among his close friends were the philosopher Jacques Maritain and the lay theologian Jean Guitton. He traveled widely and well. With the Second Vatican Council he tried to adjust the church to the exigencies of the modern world and presided over the often painful process that adjustment entailed.

John Paul II:
The World Is My Parish

P aul VI's funeral took place outdoors, in Saint Peter's square. His coffin was covered by a simple white pall with a Bible resting on it. The gospel passage read at mass was from the twenty-first chapter of John's gospel where Jesus gives Peter his commission: feed my lambs, feed my sheep. It was a glorious summer day, a fittingly bright ending to an important but troubled pontificate.

The cardinals in conclave, enclosed in the stifling heat of the Sistine Chapel, were in no mood to dawdle. They veered away from the two "favorites," Cardinal Siri of Genoa because he was too outspokenly negative on the council and Cardinal Benelli of Florence because, as substitute secretary of state for Paul VI, he was too closely identified with the previous pontificate. On the fourth ballot, they elected Albino Luciani, patriarch of Venice, the third pope elected from that see in the twentieth century. He surprised everybody by taking a double-name, John Paul, the first pope to do so, in honor of his two predecessors.

Luciani was little known outside Italy but respected and even loved inside it. He, like John XXIII, came from humble origins. His father had been a migrant worker until he found a permanent job in Murano, an island just off Venice. Father Luciani began his priestly ministry as pastor in his native village, but his talent caused him to rise rapidly. He loved literature (Dickens was a favorite), held conservative theological views, was easy to meet and converse with, hated ecclesiastical pomp. He dispensed with the coronation ceremony with which popes had been installed in office since the Middle Ages. The papal tiara, or crown, became an historical artifact.

Although the world at large was unaware of it, the new pope was not well. One day Cardinal Jean-Marie Villot, his secretary of state, remarked to him on his seeming fatigue and swollen legs, to which he replied that when a pope dies, they get another one. In the early morning of September 29, just a month after his election, Father John Magee, the Irish priest who was his personal secretary, found the pope dead in bed, presumably from a heart attack. Rumors spread that he was poisoned. Although without the slightest foundation in fact, the rumors made a lot of money for authors of scurrilous articles and books.

When the cardinals gathered for a second time in less than two months, they knew one another better than the first time, but that did not make the conclave easier. Siri and Benelli, it seems, got a respectable number of votes in the early balloting, until it became clear neither could carry the day. Numerically speaking, non-Italians dominated the conclave, so it was not surprising that when no strong Italian candidate emerged those cardinals turned to one of their own. Cardinal Franz König of Vienna early proposed Karol Wojtyła, the young (age 58) archbishop of Craców, and persuaded others, including the fervidly anti-Communist cardinals of North America, of his suitability. On the eighth ballot Wojtyła was elected by an overwhelming majority, the first non-Italian pope since Hadrian VI in the early sixteenth century. Television commentators, completely unprepared for him, stuttered over the pronunciation of his name.

A more striking contrast with Paul VI is hardly imaginable. Paul, shy, frail, sensitive, introspective, given to self-doubt. John Paul II, athletic, assertive, robustly self-confident, was born for the spotlight. More is known about him and more has been written about him than any other pope. Everything about his long pontificate of nearly twenty-seven years, the second longest in history, seems oversized.

In 104 pastoral visits outside Italy he traveled to every corner of the globe, logging up over 750,000 miles—no prisoner of the Vatican, he! As bishop of Rome he visited 317 of the city's 333 churches, and he made 146 pastoral visits to other cities and towns within Italy. In his public audiences every Wednesday in the Vatican he spoke to a total of well over seventeen million pilgrims and addressed many more millions during his travels. More than eight million pilgrims came to Rome during the Holy Year, 2000. He held 738 meetings or audiences with heads of state around the world. He created 231 cardinals, and by the time he died there were very few bishops in the church that he had not named. He canonized 482 saints, far more than all his predecessors put together, and declared 1,338 individuals blessed. While he was pope he published in his own name (therefore not officially as pope) five books, the last of which appeared the year he died. He had hardly been laid to rest when his successor initiated the process for his canonization. He in many people's minds was the Man of the Century.

People reacted to John XXIII with affection and the feeling that he was almost a member of their family. They reacted to Paul VI with a certain bewilderment, not quite sure what his next step might be but, more deeply, with sympathy for a man caught amidst powerful and conflicting forces in both the church and society at large. They reacted to John Paul II with admiration, sometimes bordering on awe, and often with a partisan loyalty. By his very person the new pope commanded attention and provoked strong reactions.

Born in 1920 in an industrial town about thirty miles southwest of Craców, he as a boy was not only exceptionally bright but also a superb athlete, excelling in soccer, swimming, and canoeing. In 1938 the family moved to Craców, and Karol entered the university there to study literature and dramatics. The next year World War II broke out with the German invasion of Poland, and the miseries of Karol's homeland began. For the next several years he worked as a day laborer but was able in some fashion to continue his studies. During the German occupation he helped found in Craców the Rhapsodic Theater made up of underground anti-Nazi comedians. In 1946 he published his first collection of poems, *Song of the Hidden God*.

Meanwhile he felt a call to the priesthood, which he later described: "I worked in the factory, devoting myself, as much as the terror of the occupation allowed, to my love of literature and drama. My vocation took shape in the midst of all that, as an inner truth of absolute and indisputable clarity." He was ordained the same year his poems were published and, despite the restrictions on the church imposed by the Russians who now occupied the country, was in 1946 sent to Rome for a doctorate in theology. His dissertation was on faith in Saint John of the Cross, the sixteenth century poet-mystic, an unusual person to focus on for a degree in theology but the choice was consonant with Wojtyła's literary and mystical bent. He later, 1954, completed another doctorate, this time in philosophy, on the German phenomenologist and ethicist, Max Scheler, a Jew converted to Catholicism. About the same time he was named professor of ethics at the Catholic University of Lublin.

Pius XII in 1958, the year he died, named Wojtyła auxiliary bishop of Craców, which entitled him to participate in the Second Vatican Council when it opened in October 1962. Paul VI named him archbishop of Craców the next year. At forty-two Wojtyła was one of the youngest bishops at the council but, always deferential to the austere and revered primate, Cardinal Stefan Wyszyński, archbishop of Warsaw, he emerged as a leader of the Polish bishops and caught the favorable attention of others. Two years after the council ended Paul VI, with whom he was becoming increasingly close, created him a cardinal. It is now known that Paul made use of Wojtyła's book, *Love and Responsibility*, in drafting the encyclical *Humanae Vitae*.

From that point forward he both in Poland and on the world stage emerged as a person to reckon with. When with Russian insistence the Communist government in Poland began taking a harder line with the church, his experience growing up under the regime gave him the skills to counter it or skirt around it. He was often in Rome and traveled widely outside Europe—Africa, Asia, Australia, the Middle East, and North America. It would be difficult to imagine any candidate for the papacy with a more varied cultural and political background. A gifted linguist, he felt ready to deal with the multicultural and postcolonial church that had developed since World War II and especially since Vatican II.

As pope he seems never to have been more at home than when he was away from home. Seemingly bursting with energy, he came even more to life at rallies and gatherings of huge crowds, whose adulation he clearly enjoyed. His gratification was obvious when the crowds chanted, "John Paul II, we love you!" He had a gift for the dramatic gesture, the most familiar of which was falling to his knees and kissing the tarmac the first moment he arrived in a new country. His face was the most familiar worldwide of any world leader over a longer period of time since photography was invented. Although sometimes a stickler for protocol, he had no qualms being photographed in a Mexican sombrero or a Native American headdress. His pontificate cut across the presidencies of Jimmy Carter, Ronald Reagan, George H. W. Bush, Bill Clinton, and George W. Bush.

He was the first Slav pope in the history of the church, an inheritance of which he was proud. He believed, correctly, that the focal

31.1: John Paul II with Mother Teresa
Pope John Paul II and Macedonian-born Mother Teresa, whose real name was Agnes Gonxha Bojaxhiu, during the Pope's visit to India.
© Gianni Giansanti/Sygma/Corbis

center of the Catholic Church had always been the European West—primarily Italy and France, followed by Spain and Portugal—but with Central Europe, "Germany," also pivotal. Eastern Europe in this scenario seemed almost an afterthought, a slight John Paul intended to set right. In 1980, just two years after his election he declared Saints Cyril and Methodius, the ninth-century "Apostles to the Slavs," co-patrons of Europe along with Saint Benedict.

The apple of his eye was his beloved Poland, which he was determined to help throw off the Communist yoke. Poland was so staunchly Catholic that even the Communists had been forced to make concessions to the church that other Communist regimes behind the Iron Curtain never made. In 1962, for instance, the Polish government, reluctantly but without too much red-tape, allowed the whole Polish hierarchy to travel to Rome for the Second Vatican Council. It rightly feared what the election of a Polish pope might mean.

With severe and well-founded misgivings the Polish government allowed the new pope to return to his native land for an "Apostolic visit" just six months after his election. Moscow had sternly warned against it, but the government really had no choice. For the Communists the visit turned into an unmitigated disaster. For the pope it was an unmitigated triumph. Rapturous, deliriously cheering crowds turned out in massive numbers every place he went—an estimated one third of the population of the entire country saw and heard him.

The visit was one of the most political nonpolitical events in world history. It delivered a hard punch to the solar plexus of an already shaky regime and led to the emergence of an independent labor union, "Solidarity," following the visit—something until then that was unheard of behind the Iron Curtain and ominous for the regime. By the time John Paul departed for Rome, the end was nigh for Communism in Poland.

The pope certainly did not bring down the Berlin Wall, nor did he bring about the collapse of the Communist regimes in Eastern Europe. The system, as we now know, was disintegrating from the inside. Nonetheless, in the great drama of the twilight years of the Cold War, he was a major player, and he strengthened the resistance to the regime of great numbers behind the Iron Curtain who were not Roman Catholics.

The pope's fierce anti-Communism meant he could not abide any suggestion of Marxist analysis in addressing society's ills. He therefore did his best to suppress Liberation Theology as advocated by the Peruvian priest, Gustavo Gutierrez, the Brazilian Leonardo Boff, and others like them in Latin America. He was displeased with the stance against the violation of human rights taken by Oscar Romero, Archbishop of San Salvador. Even after Romero's assassination by government thugs in 1980 while he was celebrating mass, the pope maintained a decidedly reserved attitude toward his memory. In 1997, however, he permitted the cause for his beatification and canonization to move ahead.

The fact that John Paul II was so deeply opposed to Communism does not mean that he took a favorable attitude toward the capitalist West. In two social encyclicals, *Dives in Misericordia* ("Rich in Mercy"), 1980, and *Sollicitudo Rei Socialis* ("Concern for Social Issues"), 1988, he denounced both "liberal capitalism" and "Marxist collectivism" as defective systems. Capitalism as currently practiced fostered the growing gap between rich and poor, and it steamed ahead with money-making schemes oblivious to the common good. It promoted an outlook as materialistic as its Marxist counterpart. This message did not sit well with many conservative American theologians and politicians, who thought popes should side with them, the heralds of the good news of capitalism.

Once the Communist regime fell in Poland, the pope was dismayed to see his country surrender so quickly to the tawdry enticements of Western materialism and consumerism. His visit there in 1991, though it still held crowds enthralled, was less rapturous, more confrontational than his earlier ones. He was shocked to find in Poland agitation for a liberalized law on abortion. Not surprisingly under the circumstances, he took the Ten Commandments as the theme for his public addresses. He wept and shook his fist at a flock he found increasingly wayward and untrue to its heritage.

Vatican Council II had tried in a qualified way to reverse the centralizing process in internal church governance that had been growing for centuries but especially since the Ultramontanist movement in the nineteenth century. Its signature decision in that regard was ratification of the principle of episcopal collegiality, which among other things implied a responsibility of the bishops for the central governance of the church. The council, more generally, tried to strengthen decision-making on the local level, of course under the ultimate supervision of the Vatican but with more autonomy than common since the days of Pius X and the implementation of the Code of Canon Law, 1917.

Papa Wojtyła convoked in the Vatican a number of Bishops' Synods dealing with different aspects of church life, but it soon became clear that his mind was made up on most of the questions before the bishops had a chance to speak. National episcopal conferences gradually lost what little margin they had for independent decision-making. This was the dark side of his self-assurance. Almost every decision he took reasserted the authority of the papacy over that of other entities in the church, including the bishops. The new Code of Canon Law that he promulgated in 1983 bore the imprint of that reassertion.

He in that regard sometimes displayed a willfulness that startled even his most fervent admirers. The tornado that swirled around Wolfgang Haas, bishop of the Swiss diocese of Chur, is a case in point. Haas, radically reactionary in his theological views and in-your-face confrontational in his administrative style, almost immediately upon his appointment in 1988 alienated his whole diocese, clergy and laity alike. Public demonstrations erupted against him. Only two years later the other Swiss bishops went to see the pope to get Haas removed. The pope refused to take action. Finally, after seven more years had passed and the situation deteriorated even further, the Holy See divided the diocese and transferred Haas to the new (admittedly tiny) see of Vaduz cut out of it, but only after creating him an archbishop. Such petty obstinacy was unworthy of John Paul II but indicative of his determination to demand unquestioned acceptance of papal decisions, cost what it may.

Karol Wojtyła had come out of a siege situation in Poland, where loyalty, a united front, and the ability to resist pressures from outside were the indispensable prerequisites for effective action against the enemy. These qualities remained for him the qualities he sought in all those who were engaged with him in ministry in the church, especially theologians and bishops. In regard to the former he discouraged any speculation that might suggest qualification of an official position. In regard to the latter, he insisted that the prime consideration in the appointment of new bishops was the candidates' willingness to stand unconditionally with him on a number of potentially explosive issues. That consideration overrode virtually all others.

Those issues revolved most prominently around sex and gender. After the negative reaction to *Humanae Vitae* in 1968, the birth-control issue seemed to be dying a natural death as more and more Catholics made up their own minds. Paul VI had had his say but then, for whatever reasons, did not press the point for the last ten years of his pontificate. John Paul II changed all that, campaigning in season and out against all "artificial" forms of birth control. Condoms became the focus of the campaign after the outbreak of the HIV-AIDS epidemic when health workers and others began advocating their use to help prevent and contain the disease. The pope held his ground: there is never a justifiable reason for using condoms. At one point rumors spread that he was about to declare *Humanae Vitae* infallible.

He fought his campaign against abortion even more fiercely. In the encyclical *Evangelium Vitae* ("The Gospel of Life") he denounced "the culture of death" that he found endemic to materialistic societies and saw its ugliest form in abortion. He called for a new culture of life and love in its stead, which was a culture that, besides eschewing abortion also eschewed capital punishment and did all in its power to forestall war. Under him the Congregation for the Doctrine of the Faith issued several documents dealing with homosexuality, a condition it described as "intrinsically disordered." He declared in 1995 that since Christ had chosen only men as apostles, the church had "no authority whatsoever to confer priestly ordination on women and that this judgment is to be definitively held by all the faithful of the church." In his encyclical *Veritatis Splendor* ("The Splendor of Truth"), 1993, he reaffirmed the unchangeable and objective nature of moral truths.

The pope wanted to unite Catholics behind unambiguous choices and in obedience to clear teaching. Thus the church would stand united for all the world to see. One flock, one shepherd, speaking with one voice. In many of its decisions, however, the Holy See under John Paul seemed to have surrendered its traditional role as arbiter of disputes among Catholics. It seemed all too often prematurely to have taken sides. The result of this strategy was counterproductive. Rather than ensure unity, it sharpened differences within Catholicism and engendered rancor and suspicion. "Real Catholics" accused those with whom they disagreed of disloyalty and even heresy, and they felt they had backup in the highest quarters.

On May 13, 1981, the world reacted with shock when it learned that a Turkish gunman, Mehmet Ali Agca, had shot and seriously wounded the pope as he entered Saint Peter's Square to address a large crowd of pilgrims. The pope lost three-quarters of his blood and underwent a five-hour operation. After weeks in the hospital, John Paul returned to the Vatican and eventually seemed to be as good as new, but the trauma to his system probably contributed to his decline in health that began about a decade later when he was only seventy.

He felt that the assassin's bullet was miraculously deflected from his vital organs by the Blessed Virgin of Fatima, Portugal. He later recalled that the incident took place "on the [anniversary] day and at the hour when the first appearance of the Mother of Christ to the poor little peasants" occurred. Mary's care for him, he said, was "stronger than the deadly bullet." His survival strengthened his mystical sense of the special mission God had for him as pontiff, which in turn strengthened the authoritarian strains in his personality.

That sense of his special destiny accounts for his later determination to soldier on even as he grew weaker, as his speech became slurred to the point of being incomprehensible, and as his face became as immobile as a mask of stone. For years he provided for the world a model of sickness borne with dignity and with devotion to duty that knew no surcease. He never seems to have entertained the thought of resigning because of incapacity. The end, so long in the making, finally came swiftly, on April 2, 2005. His last words, spoken in Polish, were, "Let me go to the house of my Father."

His body lay in state in Saint Peter's basilica from April 4 to April 7 and drew over four million people, the likes of which had never been seen before. Each successive papacy seemed to outdo its predecessor in the sheer magnitude of response to its important moments. John Paul's funeral set world records for the number of dignitaries present for the equivalent of a state funeral. His successor referred to him as John Paul "the great" in his first address from the balcony of Saint Peter's. In death as in life everything about *Papa Wojtyła* was oversized.

Of the 115 cardinals who assembled for the conclave John Paul had named all but two. In the group there were few obvious giants. By 2005 the highly esteemed former archbishop of Milan, Cardinal Carlo Maria Martini, had already retired and was suffering from the early stages of Parkinson's disease, which put him out of the running. Cardinal Joseph Ratzinger, head of the Congregation for the Doctrine of the Faith since 1981, was at this point also dean of the College of Cardinals. He presided and preached at the funeral of John Paul II and presided at the General Congregations of the cardinals that administered the church between the death of the pope and the beginning of the conclave. He had, therefore, an extraordinarily high profile.

Before the conclave the Italian newspapers predicted his election, but many people doubted the cardinals would elect such a controversial figure. As head of the Congregation for the Doctrine of the Faith he had imposed measures and issued statements that were severely criticized and resented especially in the theological establishment. In his favor as a candidate, however, was his close association with John Paul, which commended him to all those cardinals who owed their position to John Paul and whose legacy they wanted to continue. His age, seventy-eight, was against him, yet it was also a point in his favor because it seemed to promise a short pontificate after an extremely long one.

The cardinals elected him on the fourth ballot. He chose to be called Benedict, which distanced him from his four immediate predecessors and suggested a somewhat new trajectory. Did it suggest a trajectory away from the Second Vatican Council, in which he participated as a young but important theologian? Since his election he has tried to reassure his critics on that score, but the reservations on the council he expressed as cardinal stick in people's memories. The favor he has shown toward the so-called Tridentine mass, which the council displaced, led to much puzzlement. His lifting in January 2009, of the excommunication of four schismatic bishops who were ordained by Archbishop Marcel Lefebvre and who still refused to accept Vatican II has only deepened the puzzlement.

One thing is certain. Although Pope Benedict worked closely with John Paul II, he has an entirely different personality and style. A former university professor, he is more at home with books than with large crowds. He is reluctant to undertake long journeys, though it is already clear that he can handle himself well on the occasions when he does so. His visit to the United States in the spring of 2008 was on all counts a resounding success. Especially appreciated was the sensitivity he showed to the victims of sexual abuse by clergy.

Benedict heads a church of some one billion members worldwide. It is a church beset with problems but that, as this book has amply shown, is nothing new. The central institution of the church is the papacy, embodied today in Benedict. The papacy remains the oldest, still functioning institution in the Western world, and it is arguably as strong and vital today as it has ever been. With Benedict XVI, as with every pope, it moves into another moment of its long history. We wait to see what he will make of it.

EPILOGUE

The history of the papacy, let it be said again, is not the history of Catholicism. Constantine dominated the history of the church in the early fourth century, alongside whom Pope Silvester was no more than a shadow in the wings. From the tenth to the twelfth century, while the popes were trapped as pawns in the often sordid intrigues of their families, the astute and saintly abbots of Cluny strode across the stage of Western Europe and called its leaders to religious commitment. Saint Bernard of Clairvaux did the same in the early twelfth century, and he remains to this day far better known and far more important than any of his papal contemporaries. Pope Paul III successfully convoked the Council of Trent, crucial for the subsequent history of Catholicism, but in that very epoch missionaries to Latin America and Asia like Bartolomé de las Casas and Saint Francis Xavier laid the foundations for a truly world church. Who is more expressive of core Christian values—Francis of Assisi or his patron, Innocent III?

Nonetheless, there is no denying the popes their place in the history of the church and in the history of the West for the past two millennia. Among them were a few like Gregory the Great and Gregory VII who get star billing on the playbill of their own times and of all times. The vast majority of the popes, however, were men of lesser stature, usually no match for the political and intellectual leaders of their age. For that reason the history of the papacy as an ongoing institution is more important than the history of the popes considered as individuals. Yet, without popes, no papacy! It was those 265 (more or less) individuals who gave the institution its shape and substance.

As I hope the book makes clear, the shape and substance look different at different epochs. The papal job description shifted as over time the popes took on new responsibilities and sloughed off old ones, only to repeat the process a little later and repeat it again later still. Nonetheless, the institution has a strong identity, easily recognizable in every century. That identity is owed to the simple and unshakable conviction of every bishop of Rome that he was the successor of Saint Peter and that he therefore possessed an authority in the church altogether preeminent.

In the sphere of practical politics popes sometimes had to make concessions regarding their Petrine prerogatives and bow to pressure. Over the course of the centuries they exercised their leadership prerogatives in different styles and defined them in different ways. In principle, however, they clung to those prerogatives with unyielding tenacity. In so far as popes admitted change in their leadership role, it was change by way of increment. They glided easily from being vicars of Peter to being vicars of Christ. The sweep of the authority-claims of the popes of recent centuries dwarfs those of the popes of earlier times. No third-century pope ever entertained the idea that he was infallible or thought he had the right to appoint other bishops to their see. Yet, despite such diversity, the same principle has prevailed from the time for which we have reliable records up to the present: the other churches and their bishops owe special deference to the see of Blessed Peter and must heed the word that comes from it.

Just as interesting as charting how through the ages the popes never wavered in proclaiming the principle and seizing opportunities to make it prevail is charting the shifts in agenda the principle has admitted over the course of time. From the eleventh until the seventeenth century, for instance, popes assumed that a major responsibility was to rally European leaders to holy wars against the infidel. For five centuries they thought they had the duty of deposing erring monarchs and had the right to do so. From the eighth until the nineteenth century, popes not only assumed that governing the Papal States and preserving them intact was a sacred duty, but they devoted probably more time, energy, and resources to that task than to any other.

The loss of Rome and the Papal States was a precondition for the emergence of new job descriptions. The popes after 1870 had more time for the church. It is no coincidence that as the political fortunes of the papacy foundered, popes assumed more and more responsibilities for the well-being of their flock worldwide. For the past hundred and fifty years, writing encyclicals has surfaced as among the popes' most characteristic undertakings. With the encyclicals the popes claimed teaching as a primary function, which enriched and expanded their more traditional function as judges in contested cases, and it gave them a new, not always happy, relationship to professional theologians. "The Magisterium," by which today is almost inevitably meant the *papal* magisterium or teaching authority, now dominates the Catholic theological enterprise in ways and to a degree unknown in earlier centuries. In his *Summa Theologiae*, for example, Aquinas hardly mentions it.

Air, train, and auto travel have made the popes into leaders of great rallies. Every Wednesday the pope, amid shouts and cheers, addresses thousands upon thousands of pilgrims either in the great audience hall of the Vatican or in the piazza outside it. Since 1964 popes have traveled the globe to preside over even larger rallies and to inflame enthusiasm and support for the office they bear. Thanks to photography and television few indeed are the Catholics throughout the world today who do not recognize the visage of the reigning pontiff, and virtually every one of them knows his name. Fostering "loyalty to the pope" is now one of the popes' principal responsibilities, just as taking such loyalty to heart now sometimes seems to be almost the core of Catholic self-definition.

Contemporary means of travel and communication have speeded up a process of centralization of decision-making in the papacy that had been under way for centuries. By far the most important development in the past century has been the total control the papacy has gained over the appointment of bishops. Although the "free election" of bishops, which was for centuries the ideal, never quite worked as envisaged, the selection process almost always entailed involving in it more than one person or entity—local clergy, local notables, kings and emperors, and even the popes. Now, for the first time in history the popes have not only gained control, but they exercise it through a process of their own devising that gives them untrammeled freedom in establishing criteria for the appointments.

Modern medicine, nutrition, and sanitation have also had an effect on the papacy. In times gone by a ten-year papacy was a long papacy. In the past hundred and fifty years the papacies have, despite a few notably short ones, been notably long—anywhere from fifteen to thirty-two years. Longer papacies give popes opportunities to influence the church's course with a new consistency and allow them to leave an imprint on it stronger and deeper than was possible in the past.

Developments and changes in culture at large have thus had as much or even more impact on the papacy than initiatives taken by the popes themselves. This phenomenon is perhaps most discernible in political developments—the emergence of the Frankish monarchy in the eighth century, for instance, soon turned the popes into emperor-makers. But nonpolitical developments outside the strictly ecclesiastical sphere were just as important, as with the invention of printing, the airplane, and penicillin. The history of the papacy is incomprehensible apart from general history.

Nor is it a history without its ironies, as seeming catastrophes have in the long run made the institution stronger. Pius IX viewed with horror the unification of Italy in the mid-nineteenth century since it necessarily meant the end of the Papal States. However, as that unification brought an end also to the other political units in Italy, it delivered into the hands of the pope the appointment of bishops that previously had been in the hands of the rulers of those units. This was a great boon. Not so momentous but just as ironical has been the popes' relationship to the city of Rome. Although they in 1870 lost the city and formally ratified the loss in 1929 with the Lateran Agreements, they today are still the biggest figures on the Roman landscape and can in a different key still call the city their own. "Rome" is today as much the center of Catholicism as it has ever been.

The popes, as well as most devout Catholics, viewed the French Revolution as a disaster for the church without parallel, yet by an ironical twist of fate it eliminated Gallicanism in France and its counterparts in other places. In so doing it provided impetus for the powerful Ultramontanist movement that exalted papal authority and prepared the way for the definitions of papal primacy and infallibility at Vatican Council I later in the century. Catholics today live in an essentially Ultramontanist church.

Explain it as you will, the papacy has proved to be a remarkably resilient institution. Often seemingly at death's door, it has invariably risen again to striking vitality. One thing surely has helped keep it going: the unshakable conviction of the popes that it will keep going. "The gates of hell will not prevail against it." Those words of Jesus apply to the church, not to the successors of Peter. But popes have a penchant for forgetting the distinction and identifying the two as one.

LIST OF POPES

roviding a list of the popes is not the simple matter it might seem. The difficulty begins at the beginning: who was the first pope? As I mentioned in chapter 1, the earliest lists begin not with Peter but with Linus because Peter was an apostle, which was a much higher status than bishop (pope). Some historians today, for example the much respected Eamon Duffy, follow that tradition and number Linus as the first pope. Yet, as I argued in chapter 1, it is possible to consider Peter a bishop because in the Church of Rome he presumably exercised a special leadership role in the community, which is what we mean by a bishop. I therefore follow the practice of the *Annuario Pontificio*, the annual and official "catalog" of the Holy See, which characteristically names Peter the first pope.

How to list the popes when two or three men simultaneously claim the office? In most instances, contemporaries or subsequent tradition clearly distinguished between the validly chosen pope and his rival(s), the anti-pope(s). But that is not always the case. The popes at the time of the Great Western Schism pose a special problem because even today some reputable historians of the era hesitate to pronounce on the matter. As mentioned above in chapter 15, until 1947, the *Annuario* listed the two claimants of the Pisan line (Alexander V and John

XXIII) as legitimate. Only beginning in 1947 has it listed them, along with the two Avignonese popes (Clement VII and Benedict XIII), as anti-popes.

Another problem is the use of ordinal numbers to tell one pope from another. By the sixth century it became necessary to distinguish popes of the same name by assigning them a number, but this was not done in a systematic way. In some cases considerable confusion ensued, which was especially marked for popes named Martin, Felix, and Stephen. The issue is thoroughly discussed in the entry "Onomastics, Pontifical," in *The Papacy: An Encyclopedia* (Routledge, 2002), especially pp. 1065–1066.

Below I follow the list of popes and anti-popes as given in the current *Annuario*, but I feel justified in doing so only after having called attention to the problem of providing a list of the "true" popes. I also follow the practice in that listing of indenting the names of the anti-popes. Except for Peter and Clement, no certain dates can be assigned the first six popes, and the dates assigned to others beginning with Sixtus I are approximate into the third century.

Peter	c. 64	Urban I	c. 222–230
Linus		Pontian	230–235
Anacletus		Anterus	235–236
Clement	c. 96	Fabian	236–250
Evaristus		Cornelius	251–253
Alexander I		Novatian	251–258
Sixtus I	c.117–c.127	Lucius I	253–254
Telephorus	c. 127–c.136	Stephen I	254–257
Hyginus	c. 138–c. 142	Sixtus II	257–258
Pius I	c. 142–c. 155	Dionysius	260–268
Anicetus	c. 155–c. 166	Felix I	269–274
Soter	c. 166–c. 174	Eutychian	275–283
Eleutherius	c. 174–c. 189	Gaius (Caius)	283–296
Victor	c. 189–c. 199	Marcellinus	296–?
Zepherinus	c. 199–c. 217	Marcellus	c. 306–c. 309
Callixtus I	c. 217–222	Eusebius	310
Hippolytus	217–c. 235	Miltiades	311–314

Sylvester	314–335	Pelagius II	579–590
Mark	336	Gregory I	590–604
Julius I	337–352	Sabinian	604–606
Liberius	352–366	Boniface III	607
Felix II	355–365	Boniface IV	608–615
Damasus	366–384	Adeodatus I	615–618
Ursinus	366–367	Boniface V	619–625
Siricius	384–399	Honorius I	625–638
Anastasius I	399–401	Severinus	c. 638–640
Innocent I	401–417	John IV	640–642
Zosimus	417–418	Theodore	642–649
Eulalius	418	Martin I	649–653
Boniface	418–422	Eugene I	654–657
Celestine I	422–432	Vitalian	657–672
Sixtus III	432–440	Adeodatus II	672–676
Leo I	440–461	Donus	676–678
Hilarus (Hilary)	461–468	Agatho	678–681
Simplicius	468–483	Leo II	682–683
Felix III (II)	483–492	Benedict II	684–685
Gelasius I	492–496	John V	685–686
Anastasius II	496–498	Conon	686–687
Symmachus	498–514	Theodore	687
Lawrence	498–499, 502–506	Paschal	687
		Sergius I	687–701
Hormisdas	514–523	John VI	701–705
John I	523–526	John VII	705–707
Felix IV (III)	526–530	Sisinnius	708
Dioscorus	530	Constantine I	708–715
Boniface II	530–532	Gregory II	715–731
John II (Mercury)	533–535	Gregory III	731–741
Agapitus I	535–536	Zacharias	741–752
Silverius	536–537	Stephen II (III)	752–757
Vigilius	537–555	Paul I	757–767
Pelagius I	556–561	Constantine	767–768
John III	561–574	Philip	768
Benedict I	575–579	Stephen III (IV)	768–772

Hadrian I	772–795	Stephen VIII (IX)	939–942
Leo III	795–816	Marinus II (Martin III)	942–946
Stephen IV (V)	816–817	Agapitus II	946–955
Paschal I	817–824	John XII	955–964
Eugene II	824–827	Leo VIII	963–965 [sic]
Valentine	827	Benedict V	964 [sic]
Gregory IV	827–844	John XIII	965–972
John	844	Benedict VI	973–974
Sergius II	844–847	Boniface VII	974, 984–985
Leo IV	847–855	Benedict VII	974–983
Benedict III	855–858	John XIV	983–984
Anastasius	855	John XV	985–996
Bibliothecarius		Gregory V	996–999
Nicholas I	858–867	John XVI	997–998
Hadrian II	867–872	Sylvester II	999–1003
John VIII	872–882	John XVII	1003
Marinus I (Martin I)	882–884	John XVIII	1003–1009
Hadrian III	884–885	Sergius IV	1009–1012
Stephen V (VI)	885–891	Gregory VI	1012
Formosus	891–896	Benedict VIII	1012–1024
Boniface VI	896	John XIX	1024–1032
Stephen VI (VII)	896–897	Benedict IX	1032–1044, 1045
Romanus	897	Sylvester III	1045
Theodore II	897	Gregory VI	1045–1046
John IX	898–900	Clement II	1046–1047
Benedict IV	900–903	Damasus II	1048
Leo V	903	Leo IX	1049–1054
Christopher	903–904	Victor II	1055–1057
Sergius III	904–911	Stephen IX (X)	1057–1058
Anastasius III	911–913	Benedict X	1058–1059
Lando	913–914	Nicholas II	1059–1061
John X	914–928	Alexander II	1061–1073
Leo IV	928	Honorius II	1061–1064
Stephen VII (VIII)	928–931	Gregory VII	1073–1085
John XI	931–935	Clement III	1080, 1084–1100
Leo VII	936–939	Victor III	1086–1087

Urban II	1088–1099	Gregory X	1271–1276
Paschal II	1099–1118	Innocent V	1276
Theoderic	1100–1101	Hadrian V	1276
Albert	1101	John XXI	1276–1277
Sylvester IV	1105–1111	Nicholas III	1277–1280
Gelasius II	1118–1119	Martin IV	1281–1285
Gregory VIII	1118–1121	Honorius IV	1285–1287
Callixtus II	1119–1124	Nicholas IV	1288–1292
Honorius II	1124–1130	Celestine V	1294
Celestine II	1124	Boniface VIII	1294–1303
Innocent II	1130–1143	Benedict XI	1303–1304
Anacletus II	1130–1138	Clement V	1305–1314
Victor IV	1138	John XXII	1316–1334
Celestine II	1143–1144	Nicholas V	1328–1330
Lucius II	1144–1145	Benedict XII	1334–1342
Eugene III	1145–1153	Clement VI	1342–1352
Anastasius IV	1153–1154	Innocent VI	1352–1362
Hadrian IV	1154–1159	Urban V	1362–1370
Alexander III	1159–1181	Gregory XI	1370–1378
Victor IV	1159–1164	Urban VI	1378–1389
Paschal III	1164–1168	Clement VII	1378–1394
Callixtus III	1168–1178	Boniface IX	1389–1404
Innocent III	1179–1180	Benedict XIII	1394–1417
Lucius III	1181–1185	Innocent VII	1404–1406
Urban III	1185–1187	Gregory XII	1406–1415
Gregory VIII	1187	Alexander V	1409–1410
Clement III	1187–1191	John XXIII	1410–1415
Celestine III	1191–1198	Martin V	1417–1431
Innocent III	1198–1216	Eugene IV	1431–1447
Honorius III	1216–1227	Felix V	1439–1449
Gregory IX	1227–1241	Nicholas V	1447–1455
Celestine IV	1241	Callixtus III	1455–1458
Innocent IV	1243–1254	Pius II	1458–1464
Alexander IV	1254–1261	Paul II	1464–1471
Urban IV	1261–1264	Sixtus IV	1471–1484
Clement IV	1265–1268	Innocent VIII	1484–1492

Alexander VI	1492–1503	Alexander VIII	1689–1691
Pius III	1503	Innocent XII	1691–1700
Julius II	1503–1513	Clement XI	1700–1721
Leo X	1513–1521	Innocent XIII	1721–1724
Hadrian VI	1522–1523	Benedict XIII	1724–1730
Clement VII	1523–1534	Clement XII	1730–1740
Paul III	1534–1549	Benedict XIV	1740–1758
Julius III	1550–1555	Clement XIII	1758–1769
Paul IV	1555–1559	Clement XIV	1769–1774
Pius IV	1559–1565	Pius VI	1775–1799
Pius V	1566–1572	Pius VII	1800–1823
Gregory XIII	1572–1585	Leo XII	1823–1829
Sixtus V	1585–1590	Pius VIII	1829–1830
Urban VII	1590	Gregory XVI	1831–1846
Gregory XIV	1590–1591	Pius IX	1846–1878
Innocent IX	1591	Leo XIII	1878–1903
Clement VIII	1592–1605	Pius X	1903–1914
Leo XI	1605	Benedict XV	1914–1922
Paul V	1605–1621	Pius XI	1922–1939
Gregory XV	1621–1623	Pius XII	1939–1958
Urban VIII	1623–1644	John XXIII	1958–1963
Innocent X	1644–1655	Paul VI	1963–1978
Alexander VII	1655–1667	John Paul I	1978
Clement IX	1667–1669	John Paul II	1978–2005
Clement X	1670–1676	Benedict XVI	2005–
Innocent XI	1676–1689		

NOTES

CHAPTER 4

page

39   Sermon 5.4, quoted in Robert B. Eno, *The Rise of the Papacy* (Wilmington, DE: Glazier, 1990), p. 108.

40   Letter 127:12, quoted in "St. Jerome and the Barbarians," in *A Monument to Saint Jerome: Essays on some Aspects of His Life, Works, and Influence*, ed. Francis X. Murphy (New York: Sheed and Ward, 1952), p. 192.

CHAPTER 5

45   Preface, *Dialogues*, quoted in Jeffrey Richards, *Consul of God: The Life and Times of Gregory the Great* (London: Routledge and Kegan Paul, 1980), p. 36.

47   Letter to Princess Theoctista, quoted in Richards, *Consul*, p. 42.

48   See the bull, *Industriae Tuae*, 880, addressed to Svatopluk, king of Greater Moravia, in Franttišek Grivec, et al., ed., *Fontes* (Zagreb, 1960), pp. 72–73.

CHAPTER 9

89   "Decrees of the Council of Rheims," in Brian Tierney, *The Crisis of Church and State 1050–1300* (Englewood Cliffs, NJ: Prentice-Hall, 1964), p. 31.

CHAPTER 10

98   Letter of Pope Gregory VII to Desiderius, Abbot of Monte Cassino, April 23, 1073, in *The Correspondence of Pope Gregory VII*, ed., Ephraim Emerson (New York: Columbia University Press, 1932), p. 2.
100   "The *Dictatus Papae*," in Tierney, *Church and State*, pp. 49–50.
101   Letter of Emperor-elect Henry IV to Pope Gregory VII, 1076, in Tierney, *Church and State*, pp. 59–60.
104   Second Deposition of Henry VI, March 1080, in Tierney, *Church and State*, p. 64.

CHAPTER 12

126   *Patrologia Latina, 214: 292*, quoted in R. W. Southern, *Western Society and the Church* (Grand Rapids, MI: Eerdmans, 1970), p. 105.

CHAPTER 13

137   Charges against Boniface presented before a royal council in Paris, June, 1303, in Tierney, *Church and State*, p. 190.

CHAPTER 15

155   Norman P. Tanner, ed., *Decrees of the Ecumenical Councils*, 2 vols. (Washington, DC: Georgetown University Press, 1990), 1:408.

CHAPTER 18

183   Martin Luther, *Selections from His Writings*, ed. John Dillenberger (Garden City, NY: Doubleday, 1961), pp. 419–43, passim.

CHAPTER 19

191   "The Consilium de Emendanda Ecclesia," in *The Catholic Reformation: Savonarola to Ignatius Loyola, Reform in the Church, 1495–1540*, ed. John C. Olin (New York: Harper and Row, 1969), pp. 186–87.

CHAPTER 23

236 Quoted in Adrien Dansette, *Religious History of Modern France*, 2 vols. (New York: Herder and Herder, 1961), p. 152.

CHAPTER 24

248 *"Constitutio Dogmatica Prima de Ecclesia Christi,"* in Tanner, *Decrees*, 2:814–15.

CHAPTER 25

256 *"Aeterni Patris,"* in Claudia Carlen, ed., *The Papal Encyclicals*, 5 vols. (Wilmington, NC: McGrath, 1981), 2:17–27, at 24.

CHAPTER 26

263 Quoted in Igino Giordani, *Pius X: A Country Priest*, trans. Thomas J. Tobin (Milwaukee, WI: Bruce, 1954), p. 47.

CHAPTER 28

285 *Acta Apostolicae Sedis* 17 (1945), pp. 10–22, my translation.

CHAPTER 29

294 Quoted in Peter Hebblethwaite, *John XXIII: Shepherd of the Modern World* (Garden City, NY: Doubleday, 1985), p. 269.
295 Quoted in Hebblethwaite, *John XXIII*, p. 360.

CHAPTER 30

304 Quoted in Peter Hebblethwaite, *Paul VI: The First Modern Pope* (New York: Paulist Press, 1993), p. 329.
307 *Acta Synodalia Sacrosancti Concilii Vaticani II*, 35 vols. (Vatican City: Typis Poliglottis Vaticanis, 1970–99), 4/1, 28–36. For an English translation, see Henri Fesquet, *The Drama of Vatican II: The Ecumenical Council, June 1962–December 1965*, trans. Bernard Murchland (New York: Random House, 1967), pp. 662–70.

INDEX

ABOUT THE AUTHOR

John W. O'Malley, currently university professor in the theology department of Georgetown University, is a church historian whose specialty is sixteenth and seventeenth century Europe. Among his best known books are *The First Jesuits, Trent and All That, Four Cultures of the West*, and *What Happened at Vatican II*, all published by Harvard University Press. *The First Jesuits*, translated into ten languages, won both the Jacques Barzun Prize for cultural history and the Philip Schaff Prize for church history. John O'Malley was elected to the American Academy of Arts and Sciences in 1995 and to the American Philosophical Society in 1997. He is past president of the American Catholic Historical Association and the Renaissance Society of America. A Catholic priest and member of the Society of Jesus, Father O'Malley has received lifetime achievement awards from both the Renaissance Society of America and the Society for Italian Historical Studies.